The Detonators

Also by Chad Millman

Pickup Artists: Street Basketball in America

The Odds: One Season, Three Gamblers, and the Death of Their Las Vegas

The Detonators

The Secret Plot to Destroy America and an Epic Hunt for Justice

Chad Millman

LITTLE, BROWN AND COMPANY
New York Boston

Little, Brown and Company
Hachette Book Group USA
1271 Avenue of the Americas, New York, NY 10020

Map by Jeffrey L. Ward

First Edition: July 2006

Library of Congress Cataloging-in-Publication Data

Millman, Chad.
    The detonators : the secret plot to destroy America and an epic hunt for justice /
Chad Millman.—1st ed.
        p. cm.
    Includes bibliographical references and index.
    ISBN-10: 0-316-73496-9 (hardcover)
    ISBN-13: 978-0-316-73496-7 (hardcover)
    1. World War, 1914–1918—New Jersey—Black Tom Island. 2. World War,
1914–1918—United States. 3. World War, 1914–1918—Secret service—Germany.
4. World War, 1914–1918—Secret service—United States. 5. Espionage—United
States—History—20th century. 6. Sabotage—United States—History—20th
century. 7. Sabotage—New Jersey—Black Tom Island—History—20th century.
8. United States—Claims vs. Germany. 9. Germany—Claims vs. United States.
10. Mixed Claims Commission, United States and Germany. I. Title.

D570.85.N31B63 2006
940.4'87430973—dc22   2005024401

10   9   8   7   6   5   4   3   2   1

Q-FF

Book design by Renato Stanisic

Printed in the United States of America

FOR STACY AND ZAC

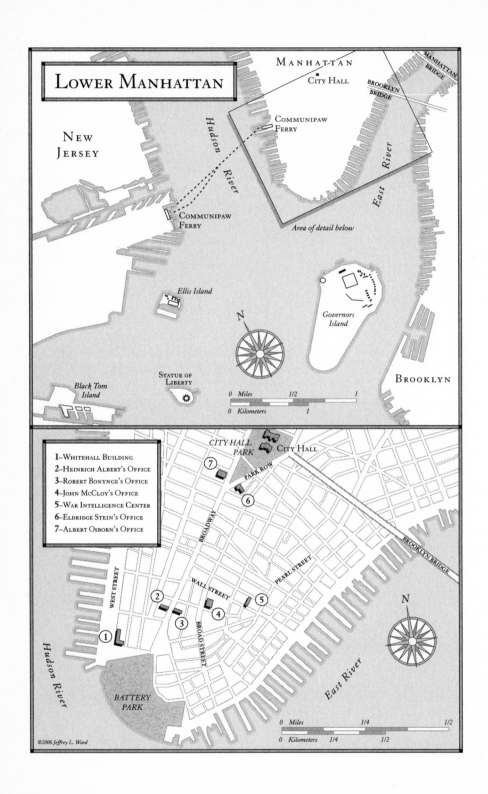

LOWER MANHATTAN

MANHATTAN
■ CITY HALL

MANHATTAN BRIDGE

BROOKLYN BRIDGE

NEW JERSEY

Hudson River

COMMUNIPAW FERRY

East River

COMMUNIPAW FERRY

Area of detail below

Ellis Island

N

Governors Island

BROOKLYN

Black Tom Island

STATUE OF LIBERTY

0 Miles   1/2   1
0 Kilometers   1

CITY HALL PARK

■ CITY HALL

1–WHITEHALL BUILDING
2–HEINRICH ALBERT'S OFFICE
3–ROBERT BONYNGE'S OFFICE
4–JOHN McCLOY'S OFFICE
5–WAR INTELLIGENCE CENTER
6–ELDRIDGE STEIN'S OFFICE
7–ALBERT OSBORN'S OFFICE

⑦

PARK ROW

⑥

BROADWAY

BROOKLYN BRIDGE

PEARL STREET

WEST STREET

WALL STREET

② ⑤

④

③

⑤

N

BROAD STREET

Hudson River

① L

BATTERY PARK

East River

0 Miles   1/4   1/2
0 Kilometers   1/4   1/2

©2006 Jeffrey L. Ward

He was thinking of many things — of his superiors, of his reputation, of the law courts, of his salary, of newspapers — of a hundred things. But I was thinking of my perfect detonator only.
—THE SECRET AGENT, *Joseph Conrad*

GERMAN ESPIONAGE OPERATION, 1914–1916

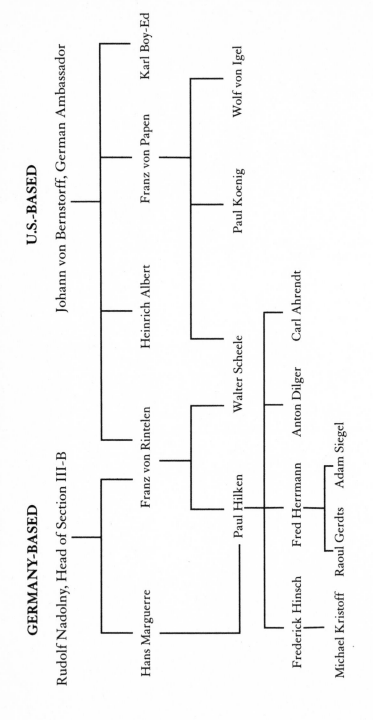

U.S.-BASED

Johann von Bernstorff, German Ambassador

Karl Boy-Ed

Franz von Papen

Wolf von Igel

Paul Koenig

Heinrich Albert

Walter Scheele

Carl Ahrendt

Anton Dilger

GERMANY-BASED

Rudolf Nadolny, Head of Section III-B

Franz von Rintelen

Paul Hilken

Fred Herrmann

Adam Siegel

Raoul Gerdts

Hans Marguerre

Frederick Hinsch

Michael Kristoff

Contents

Contents

Preface

FOR NEARLY TWO miles Liberty State Park in New Jersey stretches along the western edge of New York Harbor. From this side of the Hudson River, the shimmering towers of downtown Manhattan are framed by blue sky and green water — with tour boats and tugboats gliding along the bottom of the scene and traffic and police helicopters whirring through the top. Visitors can buy ferry tickets to the Statue of Liberty inside a restored, steeple-topped railroad terminal; they can stroll along a brick path on the water's edge called Liberty Walk; or they can take a meandering drive through the grounds on a road named Freedom Way.

At the southernmost tip of the park — sandwiched between the end points of Freedom Way and Liberty Walk — is a small picnic area. Shrouded by sycamore trees it is an unlikely destination for tourists, and therefore a haven for locals. On breezy, late-summer days, contented retirees cast fishing lines into the harbor as small waves splash lazily against the stones. The wind, perfect for flying a kite, carries the scent of lit charcoal from one side of the park to the other. Kids laugh as they race around a playground toward the Statue of Liberty, whose back is turned to them. Seemingly within reach, she's never closer to land than here.

A yellowed sign encased in glass and planted at the entrance to the picnic area is largely ignored. From a distance it looks no different than one of several park maps telling visitors where they are, but up close it screams for attention. EXPLOSION AT LIBERTY! a headline blares across the top of the sign, alongside a picture of bombed-out buildings. "On July 30, 1916, the Black Tom munitions depot exploded, rocking New York Harbor and sending sleeping residents tumbling from their beds," it continues. "The noise of the explosion was heard as far away as Maryland. Shrapnel pierced the Statue of Liberty. It is not known how many died. According to historians, the Germans sabotaged the depot.

"You are walking on a site which saw one of the worst acts of terrorism in American history."

Black Tom, a piece of land in New York Harbor named for the way it resembled a black tomcat with its back up, housed the largest munitions depot in the country. It was here where railroad shipping ended and harbor shipping began. Between 1914 and 1917, during World War I, millions of tons of American-made munitions bought by the British and French militaries were sent from Black Tom to the front. And when it detonated—with shells and bullets flying—the impact was fierce. Nearly sixty years later geologists sampling rock from the area determined that the explosion would have registered as a 5.5 earthquake on the Richter scale.

In 1916, the United States was at the precipice of war with the kaiser's army; German submarines had sunk the cruise liner *Lusitania*, killing 128 innocent Americans; German saboteurs were suspected of several bombings on ships headed overseas and munitions factories nationwide. Public figures attacked any group of citizens who called themselves both German and American. Amid the soot and noise of rising American cities, and in the quiet and sweat of a nation still deeply rural in its focus, there was a palpable fear of terrible things to come.

Still, even those at the highest levels of government thought espionage was strictly a phenomenon of European mistrust. It certainly wasn't something the United States—still an ocean away from its greatest threats—need engage in. Insulated and absent-minded, America relaxed. It would be a costly disposition.

History is full of small sparks that become huge fires. Twenty-three years would pass before a group of American lawyers—chasing down spies, piecing together clues, and overcoming conspiracies as they investigated Black Tom—showed how vulnerable, and naïve, the United States had been. Their struggles with the case mirrored the growth of the nation, through a world war, a Great Depression, and to the brink of another, more deadly, fight overseas. Together they became wiser, and more wary, of the world abroad. Whatever horrors had seemed impossible in 1916 were all too plausible in 1939.

Shortly after 9/11, Liberty State Park historian Mike Timpanaro received a call from an FBI agent who said he was looking for information to fill out his Black Tom file. That was followed by another call, this one from someone working on an article for the CIA publication *Studies in Intelligence*. That story would begin, "Intelligence officers responding to the attacks on 11 September 2001 perhaps had little inkling that they were following in paths trod long ago by their forebears."

Black Tom may be gone, but history has stirred its ghosts. This is their story.

Cast of Characters

The American Lawyers

Robert Bonynge: Lead lawyer representing the U.S. government and American claimants before the Mixed Claims Commission.

Harold Martin: State Department lawyer and U.S. representative to the Mixed Claims Commission; top aide to Robert Bonynge.

John McCloy: Lawyer for claimants in the sabotage cases; partner at Cravath, Henderson & de Gersdorff.

Amos Peaslee: Lawyer for claimants in the sabotage cases; partner at Peaslee & Brigham.

Henry Arnold: Lawyer for claimants in sabotage cases; partner at Rumsey & Morgan.

The German Lawyers

Karl von Lewinski: German agent to the Mixed Claims Commission, August 1922–January 1931.

Wilhelm Tannenberg: Von Lewinski's assistant before taking over in January 1931.

Richard Paulig: German agent to the Mixed Claims Commission, May 1934–October 1939.

The Mixed Claims Commission
William H. Day: Umpire, August 1922–May 1923.

Edwin H. Parker: Umpire, May 1923–October 1929.

Roland Boyden: Umpire, January 1930–October 1931.

Owen J. Roberts: Umpire, March 1932–October 1939.

Chandler Anderson: American commissioner, May 1923–August 1936.

Christopher Garnett: American commissioner, September 1936–October 1939.

Wilhelm Kiesselbach: German commissioner, August 1922–May 1934.

Victor Huecking: German commissioner, June 1934–March 1939.

The Detonators
Heinrich Albert: German commercial attaché to the United States prior to World War I.

Karl Boy-Ed: German naval attaché to the United States prior to World War I.

Anton Dilger: American doctor trained in Germany; ran anthrax lab in Chevy Chase, Maryland, prior to World War I.

Raoul Gerdts: Assistant to Fred Herrmann.

Martha Held: German madam whose New York brownstone doubled as headquarters for German spies.

Fred Herrmann: American citizen turned German spy.

Paul Hilken: Baltimore-based paymaster for German spies in the United States prior to World War I.

Frederick Hinsch/Francis Graentnor: German merchant marine interned in Baltimore before World War I; Hilken's top enforcer and agent.

Wolf von Igel: Top aide to Franz von Papen; would take over as German military attaché in 1916.

Kurt Jahnke: German spy based in San Francisco.

Paul Koenig: Aide to Franz von Papen; head of Germany's War Intelligence Center in New York.

Michael Kristoff: Austrian immigrant; U.S.-based German spy.

Hans Marguerre: Staff member of Section III-B in German Foreign Office.

Rudolf Nadolny: Head of Section III-B in German Foreign Office.

Franz von Papen: German military attaché to the United States prior to World War I.

Franz von Rintelen: German navy captain sent to the United States to stop American shipments of munitions to the Allies.

Walter Scheele: German chemist living in New Jersey; creator of "cigar" bombs.

Adam Siegel: German spy who befriended Fred Herrmann.

Lothar Witzke: German spy based in San Francisco; protégé of Kurt Jahnke.

The Handwriting Experts

Albert Osborn: Hired by the Germans to authenticate the Herrmann message.

Eldridge Stein: Hired by the Americans to authenticate the Herrmann message.

The Investigators

Thomas Tunney: Head of the New York City Police Department's bomb squad.

Reginald "Blinker" Hall: Head of Room 40, the British government's secret group of code breakers.

Leonard Peto: Vice president of the Canadian Car & Foundry, which suffered damages in the Kingsland explosion.

The Witnesses

Carl Ahrendt: American aide to Paul Hilken and Frederick Hinsch.

James Larkin: German labor leader recruited by the Germans to plant bombs in the United States prior to World War I.

Part One

Chapter One

HEINRICH ALBERT WAS forty years old, carried a briefcase, and worked in an office high above Broadway in one of downtown Manhattan's brand-new skyscrapers. From his window he could see West Street, crowded with merchants leading horse-drawn carts of fruit, dockworkers pulling on pieces of bread while on their way to the piers, and policemen walking their beats. He watched as cargo ships hauling grain and coal were emptied onto the covered piers stretching out into New York Harbor—ninety-nine of them on the west side of Manhattan, ranging from six hundred to one thousand feet long. Originally built to accommodate ocean liners such as the *Lusitania* and the *Olympic,* the piers were too important to use just for luxury travelers. By 1914, more material moved in and out of New York Harbor than anywhere else in the world. The mayor at the time, John Mitchel, worried aloud about the economic consequences worldwide if someone demolished his harbor, and not a soul considered his fears without justification.

The scene was always so hurried, so full of purpose, so earnest. So typically American, Albert thought.

How he hated the view.

Past the piers, the Statue of Liberty glistened in the late-afternoon sun. Every day, immigrants from Europe, refugees from the war, arrived at nearby Ellis Island. Albert himself was a stranger here, having moved to New York shortly after the conflict in Europe had begun in August 1914. He had come alone, leaving his wife, Ida, and their three young children in Germany.

On a clear day, if he squinted, Albert could see beyond the Statue of Liberty to Black Tom Island, a mile-long spit jutting into the harbor from Jersey City, New Jersey. Black Tom was laid with dozens of intricately woven rails and long piers extending like spokes from one side of the thin finger of land. From sunrise to sunset, workers unloaded trains that brought dangerous cargo from all over the country, transferring the goods to the ships waiting in the piers. The largest munitions depot in the country, Black Tom was the last stop for American-made shells, dynamite, and bullets before they were sent to the front. The British and French were buying them by the ton, as fast as the American companies could make them, and then using them to beat back the Germans in the countryside of France and off the coasts of Europe.

Albert watched the business of Black Tom with dismay. He was not alone. President Woodrow Wilson had declared the United States neutral when war broke out in 1914, and the harbors in port cities up and down the East Coast were veritable parking lots filled with German merchant ships, battleships, and U-boats, all of them interned for the duration of the war. Wilson's neutrality policy not only meant that he would not take sides or commit his military. It also meant that he would not allow any ships docked in the United States at the outbreak of World War I to join the fight. As a result, along the Hudson River there were nearly eighty German vessels interned, tied together in groups by thick ropes and watched at all times by patrolling U.S. Navy ships. With the British navy controlling the seas, wayward German vessels looking for safe haven often docked in the United States when their supplies ran low. They, too, were interned and forbidden to leave. Eventually, the harbor became so crowded with cargo ships, luxury liners, and idle warships that the German boats were towed across the water to New Jersey. By the fall of 1914, it was common for German naval officers and merchant marines setting sail from Germany to shout, "I'm going to heaven, hell, or Hoboken."

As busy as the harbor was during working hours, it was mostly desolate at night. The piers, hoisted twenty feet above the water, had small rowboats tethered to their wooden pinnings so workers had access to the lower reaches of the ships. After sunset, given the dense cover of the piers' roofs, it was common for crooks to borrow those rowboats and be quietly ferried from one unmanned ship to the next.

Directly in front of the piers, running parallel to the river, was West Street. So hurried in the light of day, it lay still after dark, littered with grain and loose pieces of coal that had fallen from carts; water pooled in the crevices between the cobblestones. There were no lights along the docks, and the only sounds came from small waves on the Hudson River slapping against the hulls of ships. In the night shadows, resentful, interned German seamen—loud, bored, and frustrated—stumbled along West Street, tripping on the uneven lane, drawing rebukes from the cops walking the beat. The Germans spent their days maintaining their ships, scraping down the sides, and watching big steamers leave wispy trails as they chugged away from Black Tom, headed for the war. They spent their nights wandering and drinking. They weren't prisoners, but they weren't free. No matter where they went, they were viewed with suspicion—although all who found themselves dockside at midnight were to be doubted. "In districts where you find few people, you will rarely find lights, and where there are no lights you may well expect crime," opined Thomas Tunney, then the head of the New York Police Department's bomb squad. "On the waterfront, for every thoroughfare which can pass as a street there are a dozen or two alleys, footpaths, shadowy recesses and blind holes . . . and, as Shakespeare said, there are land rats and there are water rats."

●   ●   ●

The British blockade not only neutered the German navy, but it also made it nearly impossible for the Central powers—Germany, Austria-Hungary, Bulgaria, and the Ottoman Empire—to import food and material. From 1914 through 1916, American exports to Britain and France combined rose from $750 million per year to $2.5 billion. Meanwhile, exports to Germany shrank from $345 million to just $2 million a year.

Albert, sent to America as Germany's commercial attaché, needed to find ways to change that. The U.S. government may have been neutral, but American companies were open for business. Nothing, he knew, was as seductive to an American as money.

On the surface, Albert was an unlikely seducer. He wore stiff-collared white shirts and black pin-striped suits. He parted his light brown hair closer to the side, forgoing the greased, split-down-the-middle style so many of his countrymen preferred. Exceedingly polite and unnecessarily formal, he hid his contempt for America underneath his businessman's uniform. The only visible evidence of his undying commitment to the kaiser was the shallow red battle scars on both cheeks, saber cuts earned as an infantryman in the German army. They looked chronically inflamed against his fair skin and soft blue eyes.

German-American banks had granted Albert millions in loans, motivated as much by events abroad as by Albert's personal appeal. The country was bitterly divided over the war, with most Americans believing that Germany was responsible for starting it. But pockets of the nation were sympathetic, and during the first days and weeks of the war, German-Americans around the country demonstrated in support of their native land. Wealthy second-generation German-Americans wrote Albert checks. In Chicago, a parade of reservists carried the German colors. Inspirational speeches meant to spur volunteers to the front were given at every rally. German fight songs were sung, and telegrams were sent to Kaiser Wilhelm praising his decision to fight. German reservists from every state, as well as from South and Central America, came to New York, lined up outside the German Embassy, and demanded to be shipped to the front.

Most Americans saw these acts of German patriotism as uncharacteristic and even unsettling. Nativism was rampant in the United States, as millions of European immigrants were increasingly blamed for poverty, disease, and crime. Fears that new-world values would erode beneath the increasing waves of old-world cultures prompted "Americanization" programs in public schools. Classes that taught immigrant children about the importance of punctuality, hard work, and the superiority of the "American way" became required parts of the curriculum.

Germans, however, remained largely untouched by prejudice in the years leading up to the war. Among the earliest settlers of New Amsterdam, they came to the United States by the millions during the mid-1800s. The Irish (who immigrated in equal numbers during the same time) left a homeland that could not feed, house, or employ them. They arrived poor and, in New York, largely took jobs as unskilled laborers, often working on the docks. Meanwhile, hundreds of thousands of middle-class, liberal-minded Germans left their country in 1848, following a failed revolution to create a unified, democratic German government. Millions more fled over the next three decades as several religious groups—Quakers, Lutherans, and Jews among them—were persecuted. In New York, they settled along the East River on the city's Lower East Side, a part of town that quickly became known as Kleindeutschland. By 1900, Germans accounted for the largest immigrant group in the city. They hadn't come empty-handed, and they used their capital to open small businesses as cabinetmakers, tailors, bakers, cigarmakers, and brewers. They also became leaders in creating trade unions. Ten years later, with growing German populations in Chicago, Milwaukee, St. Louis, and Cincinnati, first- and second-generation settlers accounted for 10 percent of the entire U.S. population.

As eastern European Jews and Italians became the dominant immigrant groups, settling in Lower East Side tenements, Germans left Kleindeutschland for more well-to-do parts of Man-

hattan. A new subway built in 1904 encouraged development uptown. German immigrants bought homes in the Yorkville section
of the Upper East Side and, crossing the Hudson, in the suburbs
of New Jersey. While they were proud of their heritage, keeping it
alive through hundreds of German social clubs, beer halls, and
German-language newspapers, they wanted to be citizens of the
United States first. No immigrant group seemed to assimilate as
quickly or as easily. Seven out of ten Germans became naturalized
citizens, proudly referring to themselves as German-Americans.
One study done during the early 1900s and published in the *American Journal of Sociology* asked sociologists, journalists, psycholo-
gists, and social workers to rate ethnic groups based on various
personal traits. Germans ranked first, ahead of Americans, in self-
control, moral integrity, and perseverance. The image most Americans held of Germans reflected what they thought of themselves:
they were hardworking and aspired to be upwardly mobile.

All that would change in the summer of 1914. As the war
raged overseas, the United States was forced to examine how it
wanted to interact with the world. For the first time, it was a
country strong enough, economically and politically, to shape
events in Europe by choice. And while Americans may have been
separated from battle by an ocean, it was impossible for them not
to feel the war's tension. Often their new neighbors from Italy,
Russia, England, and Germany had family living along the front
lines. These newcomers were vocal about their reactions to the
war and their allegiance to the countries they had left behind. This
behavior raised questions of divided loyalties among other Americans. The rampant nativism was ratcheted up, as were fears and
prejudices toward immigrants. This was especially true regarding
German-Americans. The goodwill heaped on them by their
adopted countrymen disappeared in a flash of gunpowder as soon
as the kaiser's army crossed the Belgian border, signaling the start
of World War I. In several books that were rushed into print that
summer, the kaiser was depicted as intelligent, imaginative, cruel,
and bent on world domination. A typical political cartoon in an
American magazine depicted a German soldier marching through

Belgium with women and babies hanging from his bayonet. Many in the United States believed that the kaiser's plan included mobilizing millions of German-Americans—beginning with those who were begging the German ambassador in Washington, D.C., Johann von Bernstorff, to draft them into the war.

As much as he may have wanted to, von Bernstorff couldn't harness the energy of his countrymen. Getting them to the front lines in Europe was impossible. In the unlikely event that the ships hauling them across the Atlantic passed the U.S. Navy on patrol, they'd be sunk by the British once out in the open sea. But providing Germany with manpower wasn't really von Bernstorff's concern. His mission was to keep the United States out of the war.

Von Bernstorff had been raised for this job. The son of the former German ambassador to England, he had spent the first decade of his life in England. He spoke English without a German accent and had married an American. When he was named ambassador to the United States in 1908, one German paper declared that with von Bernstorff in place, a German-American partnership on balance with the British-French-Russian alliance was possible. As he said, his "main instructions from the emperor and the chancellor were to inform the American public about the peaceful and friendly intentions of German foreign policy."

With his piercing blue eyes and handlebar mustache, the ambassador quickly became a popular guest at dinner parties in Washington and New York. He summered in New England and was so skilled at befriending influential Americans that he was awarded honorary degrees from ten different universities, including Columbia, Brown, the University of Chicago, Princeton, and the University of Pennsylvania.

Once the war broke out, he needed every bit of that charm. The ambassador's budget had always included several thousand dollars that went toward paying reporters for writing positively about German policies, but with battles raging overseas, he increased his propaganda efforts. When the German-American newspaper *Staats-Zeitung* nearly went bankrupt, von Bernstorff persuaded the German Foreign Office to invest $200,000 to keep it afloat. He then paid $625,000 for an interest in the *New York Evening Mail*. He knew that the daily dispatches from the front were the only ways Americans learned about what was happening in Europe. Those stories, and the debates in local pubs, on elevated trains, and around dinner tables, shaped American opinions about the war—and Germany's role in causing it. The more it appeared that Germany was fighting for a righteous cause, the more support von Bernstorff would get, and maybe— just maybe—the United States would change its mind about who was in the right.

It was Albert's job to make von Bernstorff's ideas happen. Early in 1915, he raised millions from American investors by selling short-term German notes. One bank showed that he made deposits of nearly $13 million between September 1914 and November 1915; another recorded $11 million between 1915 and 1917. His success did nothing to change his opinion of America. Actually, it did quite the opposite. "I find myself like a healthy man who sees a great strong lout suffering from shriveling of the brain," he wrote to his wife. "Germany ought to treat the United States like a great big child."

One. Two. Three. When Martha Held went looking for a house to rent, she wanted an address that would be easy for her countrymen to remember: 123 West 15th Street was perfect, a three-story brownstone fronted by a stoop in the middle of a tree-lined block on the west side of Manhattan. At street level, underneath the stoop, was a door that led to a basement big enough for a wine cellar, a full-service kitchen, and a bathroom. A large dining room, with a formal dining table, and a parlor were located on the first floor. Bars covered the windows in the front of the house, and the shades were almost always drawn.

Held claimed to be a German baroness by marriage, although no one ever saw her with a husband. Before moving to the United States from Germany in 1912, she had been an opera star, and she decorated the house with pictures of herself dressed in elaborate costumes from her days on the stage. Held was middle-aged when World War I began, but she still carried herself like a diva. Buxom and handsome, her dark blue eyes and glossy black hair were usually set off by sparkling earrings. She wore heavy, Victorian-style dresses that covered her greatly expanding girth, and she belted out arias late into the night.

During the summer, when windows stayed open and neighbors gathered on their stoops to escape the heat, they gossiped about what was going on inside Held's house. Her singing carried down the block, rising above the din that lingered in the air whenever her door opened and closed. The neighbors noticed that beautiful women would arrive early in the evening and then disappear through the door leading into Held's basement. Hours later, men speaking German, often dressed in German military uniforms, would follow. Interned German merchant marines were regulars at Held's house, as were the kaiser's diplomats.

Occasionally, that included von Bernstorff himself, and when he'd walk in the door and shed his coat, there'd be an ovation. Germany's military attaché, Franz von Papen, and its naval attaché, Karl Boy-Ed, visited often as well. When von Bernstorff was there, the two attachés often acted imperiously, as if they had earned posts of distinction. In fact, before World War I, it was considered an insult to be assigned to the United States; the greatest militaries in the world were in Europe. The Germans thought the military attaché to the United States was such a minor position that they made it a dual post, adding Mexico to the light workload. The thirty-four-year-old von Papen, a cavalry officer, had been given the assignment because his wealthy and influential father-in-law had pushed for it, not because he had shown any potential.

But the German Foreign Office had misjudged him. Lazy and undisciplined before the war, he was emboldened by the conflict. Still, on West 15th Street, he often revealed his wild side. He lorded over the crowd at Held's house, demanding that he be catered to. Held introduced him to women he could take to Delmonico's, near Wall Street, or on carriage rides through Central Park. They listened as he boasted about his close relationship with the German ambassador, then they'd take him back to Held's, where he'd drink wine until he fell asleep.

When the war began, von Papen was in Mexico City. He took the train back to Washington, where von Bernstorff instructed him to open a New York branch of the embassy at 60 Wall Street, just a five-minute walk from Albert's office at 45 Broadway. Officially, the office was named the Bureau of the Military Attaché, but von Papen would refer to it as the War Intelligence Center. His objective was simple and brutal: find ways for Germany to advance against the Allies, even if it meant waging a war against the United States.

Von Bernstorff considered von Papen unrefined as a diplomat, someone who openly drank to excess, womanized, and never hid his beliefs that the German way was the only way. All these traits, in the ambassador's eyes, made von Papen a liability. They also made him expendable.

With the Allies boarding merchant vessels that sailed from America for Europe and demanding that every traveler show identification, von Papen's main focus was on getting interned sailors fake passports. Bankrolled by Albert, von Papen's men approached visiting sailors from neutral countries such as Spain and Denmark, offering each ten dollars for his passport. Even better were U.S. passports, which at the time were easy to come by. Von Papen's men paid twenty-five dollars each to sympathetic German-Americans, as well as to bums and petty thieves, who were willing to fill out a passport application (including the requisite signatures of two American citizens confirming the applicant's nationality) and then hand it over to von Papen.

In December 1914, the U.S. State Department made photographs a passport requirement, complicating von Papen's operation. He hired a German-American attorney, Hans von Wedell, who earlier in his life had been a newspaper crime reporter. Some of von Wedell's old contacts and current clients were expert forgers who could duplicate the new U.S. passports. Von Wedell hired an assistant, and together they opened an office on Bridge Street, a few blocks south of von Papen's War Intelligence Center. There they provided papers to anyone carrying a letter of reference from von Papen. For twenty dollars, a German could become a "native-born" American.

As von Bernstorff suspected, von Papen went about his business carelessly. He handed out letters of reference to nearly anyone who walked into his office, making no effort to check the person's background. It didn't take long for von Wedell to hear from his old newspaper sources that beat cops had been tipped off to his operation. Just weeks after he began working with von Papen, on December 25, 1914, von Wedell disappeared, leaving only a letter to von Bernstorff explaining his absence:

> I know that the State Department had withheld a passport application forged by me. Also, ten days before my departure I learnt from a telegram sent by von Papen that one of our clients had fallen into the hands of the English. That gentleman's forged papers were liable to come back any day and could, owing chiefly to his lack of caution, easily be traced back to me. . . . I now travel to Germany with the consciousness of having done my duty as well as I understood it, and of having accomplished my task.

Several days later, on January 2, 1915, the U.S. Justice Department raided the Bridge Street office. Among the evidence gathered were the letters of recommendation written by von Papen. When the German Foreign Office heard of the raid and asked for an update, von Bernstorff casually replied, "Details have unfortunately become known to public opinion and the American Government started an investigation. There is no reason to fear that the Embassy will be compromised. State Department informed me definitely that the U.S. government attached no importance to the rumors that the Embassy had been concerned." While von Papen landed on the U.S. government's watch list, von Bernstorff and the embassy were still trusted.

• • •

Perhaps one reason the Germans showed little concern was that they had already shifted priorities. Sneaking Germans out of America to fight on the front was an inefficient and costly exercise. For every man who made it through the blockade, there was a boatload of American-made bullets being distributed to the Allies. In November 1914, while working hard on his passport operation, von Papen received a cable from the Foreign Office, which read, "It is indispensable to recruit agents to organize explosions on ships sailing to enemy countries, in order to cause delays in the loading, the departure and the unloading of these ships." Two months later, on January 26, 1915, von Papen received another cable, this one more pointed and more urgent: "In United States sabotage can reach to all kinds of factories for war deliveries. . . . Under no circumstances compromise Embassy."

Von Papen knew just where to go. Day after day, interned sailors and merchants stood around the docks, tending to their ships, watching other boats leave the harbor. They were bored, frustrated, and angry at the United States. Eager to get on von Papen's good side, they volunteered information about movements in the harbor, new cargo that had come in from all over the United States, and especially movement to and from Black Tom Island. With three-quarters of the ammunition being sent to the front leaving from Black Tom, its daily activities became an obsession for von Papen and the interned Germans, and what they observed was invaluable. They knew that arriving train cars loaded with flammable materials were always parked at the north end of the yard and were all clearly marked. They knew that that end of Black Tom was remote and unlit. They knew that, despite a rule prohibiting loaded barges from being docked overnight, the workload was so backed up that many ships packed with ammo sat tied to the piers for days at a time. There were no gates separating the street from the piers, and when the shift ended on Saturday night, the yard was dead until Monday. All of this information was passed along, from one German to another, at Martha Held's brownstone. Her bordello was a house of spies.

The Germans cursing the Americans and the munitions shipments that steamed in and out of the harbor shared a bond with the hundreds of thousands of Irish immigrants in America: their mutual hatred of England.

James Larkin was an Englishman who had earned his reputation as a firebrand by organizing labor unions in Belfast and Liverpool and all along the coast of Scotland. He had grown up on the docks, working in Liverpool from the time he was eleven years old. Larkin had no formal education, but he had street smarts learned by observing life in Liverpool's seedy districts. He saw men of industry abusing hookers on the streets. He saw how those who were supposed to be providing a living wage and food for the poor enriched themselves and paid almost nothing to their workers. As an adult, he spent every Sunday morning on a soapbox, preaching to his fellow workers about the value of banding together and fighting their bosses for better wages and working hours — in short, to be treated like human beings.

Larkin never drank, and he demanded that his men live as temperately as he did. He always wore a black suit and a broad-brimmed hat, and he usually had a pipe dangling from his mouth. Unlike many other union leaders, he never took money out of his workers' paychecks. He once refused to speak at a union rally because the organizer had beaten his wife and treated her in a "most shameful fashion." Larkin made just a little more than two pounds a week and spent much of that giving handouts to the families whose fathers had drunk away their earnings. He had a habit of beating the husbands until they sobered up, went home, and promised to do better by their families. He was the boss not just of the union but also of the community.

In 1914, just six years after settling in Dublin, Larkin was named the chairman of the Irish Trade Unions Congress. Now the most powerful man in the Irish labor movement, he used his pulpit to preach not just about the labor movement but also about socialism—about the ills of capitalism and how it was the root of all corruption—and not just in Ireland but also in the United States, where masses of Irish immigrants were working on the docks for low wages and long hours. In November 1914, Larkin set sail for America to raise money for the union. He was already a minor celebrity in the United States, his union fights having been chronicled by revolutionary rags such as the *International Socialist Review* as well as by mainstream papers such as the *New York Times.* His fiery oration and labor-first philosophy had inspired so many union members that the *New York Sun,* hearing American union members invoking his name and spouting the tenets he believed in, branded this philosophy Larkinism.

But Larkin's speeches in the United States garnered attention for a different reason. Beyond trying to incite labor and tweak big business, Larkin assaulted the war now under way in Europe. He denounced it as a capitalist sham and implored America to stay out. He urged both Irish-Americans and German-Americans to rally, insisting that whatever difficulties they created for Britain were in Ireland's best interests as well. In one of Larkin's first interviews upon his arrival in America, with the socialist *New York Call,* he said, "The war is only the outcome of capitalist aggression and the desire to capture home and foreign markets." Days later, speaking in front of fifteen thousand people at Madison Square Garden, Larkin was even more incendiary, saying, "We are against war on a field of battle. But we are against a more brutal war, the war of capital against the men who are oppressed and who have only their labor power to sell. . . . We want more than a dollar increase for the workers. We want the earth." In Philadelphia, he was even more direct: "Why should Ireland fight for Britain in this war? What has Britain ever done for our people? Whatever we got from her we wrested with struggle and sacrifice. We shall not fight for England. We shall fight for the destruction of the British Empire and the construction of the Irish Empire. . . . We will fight to free Ireland from the grasp of that vile carcase [*sic*] called England."

When Larkin returned to New York, von Papen and Boy-Ed called on him. Meeting at 60 Wall Street, they flattered him, praised him, complimented his speeches, and talked about their shared interests. Neither of them wanted the United States to join the war. Boy-Ed told Larkin that an alliance already existed between Irish-Americans and German-Americans and described the political pressure both groups were putting on Washington to remain neutral, no matter what the costs or how provoked.

Then Boy-Ed explained to Larkin that Germany had created a "secret department charged with hindering or interfering with the transportation of supplies." He wanted Larkin to organize the Irish arm of Germany's sabotage unit. No one had more clout in the immigrant community. No one else could rally the dockworkers by sheer force of personality. Larkin seemed to be in a perpetual state of calling for revolution, and Boy-Ed wanted to tap into that energy. He told Larkin this was his chance to strike back at England, not just with words but with actions. Germany's military victory would help bring about Irish independence. He offered Larkin $200 a week to work for Germany.

Despite his hatred for England, Larkin declined. "I am," he said, "not for the Kaiser any more than I am for England." Larkin excused himself and hoped that he was done dealing with Boy-Ed. He would soon be disappointed.

Chapter TWO

THE DISTANCE SEPARATING one immigrant community from another in New York was often nothing more than a narrow cobblestone street, but the disparities between the communities were vast. The boundaries were the Bowery, running north to south through lower Manhattan, and Houston Street, running east to west. Along the East River, south of Houston and east of the Bowery, Russian and Polish Jews lived in the Lower East Side settlements abandoned by the Germans. They read Yiddish newspapers, spoke Yiddish at the kosher butcher, and followed street signs that were, of course, written in Yiddish. On the west side of the Bowery, Italian men pushed carts of fruits and vegetables up Mulberry Street and down Elizabeth Street, shouting out prices in their native tongue. Syrians, Turks, and Greeks created a small enclave at the southwestern tip of Manhattan, shadowed by the burgeoning skyscrapers in the financial district. The Irish moved north along the Hudson River, on the western edge of the city, creating some separation from the docks on the Lower West Side where so many of them worked.

In one New York City school district that served twenty thousand children, three-quarters of the students were foreign-born, representing twenty-six countries. Under the roof of the Washington Market, just off West Street, hundreds of butchers, fish-mongers, and farmers set up stalls to sell their goods to immigrant women looking to give their families a taste of home. As shoppers moved along, the smell of dried mushrooms, whole milk, and spices gave way to that of freshly slaughtered grouse, boars, and elk, all hung from the stalls by metal hooks. The market, the largest in the world of its kind, covered twelve square blocks.

The great equalizer among immigrant men was the harbor. While the Irish dominated the ranks of the longshoremen, the docks offered a never-ending supply of death-defying work to anyone willing to do it, whether they be Irish or Italian, black or white. This was a place where greed trumped prejudice, with the only requirement for employment being a tacit understanding that your wages would be shared with job captains and the local saloon keepers (who charged for the privilege of using their bath-rooms, the only ones on the waterfront). Workers sometimes spent thirty straight hours loading and unloading three thousand pounds per hour, breathing in buckets of coal dust and coming perilously close to being separated from their heads by airborne cargo and swinging cables. Hernias were common, as was heat ex-haustion in the summer and pneumonia in the winter. Men died when accidentally hung by low-hanging ropes, when runaway cargo knocked them overboard, or when logs came loose and flat-tened them. They were also killed when drums of chemicals and boxes of ammunition headed for the European front unexpectedly exploded.

Still, plenty of ammunition made its way safely to Europe, and by 1915 the Germans were desperate to stem that flow any way they could. During three months at the First Battle of Champagne in northern France, 90,000 German troops were killed. In just a single day of fighting at the Battle of the Falkland Islands in De-cember 1914, 2,200 German sailors died. The munitions factories in Germany had such a hard time keeping up with the troops' de-mand that special permission was needed for German soldiers to perform target practice. One German-American newspaper quoted an American CEO as saying, "Give us an order and we'd be happy to sell to the Germans also." But it wasn't that simple. Getting past the blockade was impossible.

Franz von Rintelen, a captain in the German navy, was rattled by the dispatches coming from America soon after the war began. The news seemed worse when he read urgent cables from von Papen describing the scene in American ports: U.S. merchant ships were loading up cases of ammunition, then sailing toward Europe with a British escort. "Something must be done to stop it," one of von Papen's cables concluded. In an autobiography written years later, von Rintelen described the shipments of American munitions as "the ghosts which haunted the corridors of German Army Command."

Von Rintelen was the scion of a prominent banking family in Germany. His father had served as the imperial minister of finance and the managing director of the Discento Bank of Berlin. Family dinners included visits from Walter Rathenau, who would go on to become Germany's foreign minister after the war. In the early 1900s, while in his midtwenties, von Rintelen worked in the London and New York offices of the Kuhn, Loeb & Co. bank. He took pride in the fact that he was one of only three Germans with a membership to the New York Yacht Club, the other two being the kaiser and Prince Henry of Prussia. Always impeccably dressed, he carried himself like an heir to wealth and importance. He had a smooth oval face, a high forehead, light blue eyes, and light blond hair. His five-foot eight-inch, 155-pound frame was ramrod straight.

Before the war, von Rintelen, though a member of the military reserves, planned to follow in his father's footsteps. Once called to active duty during the war, he pleaded with the War Ministry, Foreign Office, and Finance Ministry to send him abroad. He ended each speech with the same phrase: "I'll buy up what I can and blow up what I can't." His superiors bought into his rhetoric, and in March 1915 he was ordered to sail for New York on a Norwegian steamer. He was given a Swiss passport with the name Emile V. Gache and a new family history to memorize. Among his various belongings were pictures of his fictitious parents' house in

Switzerland and of his family's mountain cottage in the Swiss Alps. His new initials were sewn into his clothes, which were then laundered several times to look worn; $500,000 was cabled in Gache's name to a bank in New York. Von Rintelen called the cash a "starter."

Von Rintelen arrived in New York in early April and booked a room as Emile Gache at the Great Northern Hotel on West 57th Street. Soon thereafter, he opened an office on Cedar Street in lower Manhattan, just a few blocks north of von Papen's War Intelligence Center. Von Rintelen appeared to be a legitimate businessman. The sign outside his two-room office read, E. V. GIBBONS, INCORPORATED. He had two assistants working in the outer office, assigned to him from von Papen's group of ambitious interned Germans. During his first few days in New York, he wandered the nearby docks and visited explosives dealers, asking them what they could supply and how much it would cost. He could be flattering and charming and knew how to make these men feel important. He pressed them for details about who was buying their explosives, where they were being shipped from, and which boats were carrying them across the ocean. Some dealers were more forthcoming than others. One even showed him a bill for explosives paid by the Italians five weeks before Italy officially joined the war.

Almost instantly, von Rintelen realized that his $500,000 wouldn't buy very much. He also realized that munitions were being produced so quickly that whatever he could buy would be easily replaced. He remembered the promise he had made to the German ministers: "I'll buy up what I can and blow up what I can't."

There was nothing to buy.

Shortly after arriving in New York, von Rintelen was visited by a New Jersey chemist named Walter Scheele, who had been sent to him by von Papen. Scheele had been an artillery lieutenant in the German army until 1893, when he was assigned to the United

States to study chemistry for two years and report new advances to his superiors. Scheele's reports proved so valuable that he was told to stay in the United States, keep studying, and continue reporting via the German military attaché in Washington. For this, he was paid $1,500 a year. Scheele married an American woman, opened a pharmacy in Brooklyn, and for twenty years lived a peaceful life as a neighborhood pharmacist.

Once the war began, Scheele's knowledge became even more valuable to the Germans. In August 1914, von Papen gave him $10,000 and instructed him to sell his pharmacy and devote himself full-time to the kaiser. His job: to manufacture chemical bombs. Scheele moved to Hoboken, New Jersey, and opened an office under the name New Jersey Agricultural Chemical Company. In a room filled with test tubes and jars of potent chemicals, he put into practice the lessons he had been learning during the previous two decades.

Scheele met with von Rintelen in mid-April 1915. Nervous, he kept one hand shoved into his pants pocket even after he sat down. He was separated from von Rintelen by a desk, so von Rintelen pulled his chair around to make the meeting more intimate. Von Rintelen assured his guest that there was nothing to be scared of, that he could be trusted, that he was "the most discreet man in all of New York."

Scheele then pulled from his pants pocket a four-inch-long piece of lead pipe, the same length and width as a cigar. A slim copper disk had been placed upright in the middle, dividing the pipe into two equal halves. Scheele explained that he poured sulfuric acid into one end of the pipe and chlorate of potash, picric acid, or some other flammable chemical into the other end. Both ends were then sealed with wax or tin. The sulfuric acid would eat through the copper, and once it mixed with the other chemical, the pipe would burst into flames at both ends. The heat would be sufficient to destroy the pipe itself, and if anything flammable was nearby, an inferno was possible.

It was a powerful weapon, easily hidden and untraceable, and it piqued von Rintelen's curiosity. Musing about undetectable time-release bombs—some that would go off as soon as four hours after they had been planted, and others that wouldn't explode for five days, when a ship full of munitions would be in the middle of the ocean—he wrote, "I had hit upon a plan in which this 'cigar' should play the chief part."

Scheele said that he needed $2,500 for supplies, an isolated space to manufacture and test the bombs, and a few days to perfect the timing mechanism. Von Rintelen kept that kind of cash in his desk, and he knew the perfect place for Scheele's lab. Laughing, he suggested that Scheele take advantage of a diplomatic loophole in their own backyard. The interned German ships in New York Harbor were technically German territory. They were also floating manufacturing plants, with machine shops for repairs to be made during long trips between ports. And while the local police on the docks kept a watchful eye on the crews and U.S. ships patrolled the harbor, no one was allowed to board the ships for inspection. In particular, the *Frederick the Great,* a German battleship, was docked in the harbor, just waiting to be used.

Scheele had the German sailors build the bomb casings on board the *Frederick the Great.* Back in his lab, he cut copper disks of varying widths: the thicker the disk, the longer it would take for the flames to ignite. One afternoon, von Rintelen went to visit Scheele in Hoboken and asked for a demonstration of the product. Scheele chose one of the thin copper disks, fixed it in place, and put two small bottles of chemicals—one of sulfuric acid and one of chlorate of potash—in opposite pants pockets. The two walked into some nearby woods. Scheele poured the chemicals into the pipe, laid it next to a tree, and walked a safe distance away. Within seconds, a blinding, white-hot flame was shooting from both ends of the "cigar." When the fire burned out, no signs of the pipe remained.

On May 3, 1915, there was an explosion at the Anderson Chemical Plant in Wallington, New Jersey, just a few miles from Scheele's Hoboken office. Three people were killed. On May

8, two pipe bombs were discovered in the cargo of the SS *Bankdale*. On May 10, another explosion occurred, this one at the DuPont munitions plant in Carneys Point, New Jersey, near Wilmington, Delaware. On May 13, the SS *Samland* caught fire at sea. On May 25, there was another explosion at the DuPont factory in Carneys Point. And on it went. From early 1915 until the United States joined the war in April 1917, there were nearly one hundred fires or explosions on merchant ships leaving New York Harbor and at chemical and munitions factories from New Jersey to California. "There was a maddening certainty about it all," wrote New York Police Department bomb squad captain Thomas Tunney.

The use of high explosives as weapons was a relatively new phenomenon. The Swedish chemist Alfred Nobel had first tamed nitroglycerin in 1867, thereby making it portable and packable. He had then traveled throughout Europe selling his new product—named dynamite after the Greek word for power—to miners, proving before their eyes how much more efficient it was than a pickax. Nobel would become so rich selling dynamite to both sides during the Franco-Prussian War of 1870–1871, as well as to mining companies all over the world, that he inspired a revolution in studying chemistry as a weapon. In the early 1870s, a German chemist discovered that potassium chlorate, manganese dioxide, and nitric acid could all act as explosive catalysts when mixed with such harmless substances as paraffin or sugar, as well as more volatile chemicals such as picric or sulfuric acid. Over the next thirty years, as political revolt became commonplace in Italy, Germany, France, and Austria-Hungary, these explosives became more refined and sophisticated. By the end of the century, their use was no longer confined to Europe.

In 1903, a wave of bombings disrupted life on Manhattan's Lower East Side. Businesses, mostly Italian-owned, were being mysteriously and, at first glance, randomly targeted. The fear in the neighborhood's tenements was that this was the work of the Black Hand, or Mafia, which was punishing merchants who wouldn't pay them for protection. That year, the New York Police

Department formed its first bomb unit, originally dubbed the Italian squad, but it never made any arrests.

Over the next decade, as New York became a safe haven for anarchists from Italy, Spain, Russia, Ireland, and Austria-Hungary, bombings became less about business and more about political statements. On July 4, 1914, three members of an Italian anarchist group called the Brescia Circle blew themselves up while building a bomb in their apartment at the corner of 104th Street and Lexington Avenue on Manhattan's Upper East Side. The bomb was supposed to be planted on the suburban New York estate of John D. Rockefeller. On October 12, to honor one of their fallen leaders, the Brescia Circle detonated a bomb on the steps of St. Patrick's Cathedral. The next day, another bomb blew up on the steps of St. Alphonsus Catholic Church in Brooklyn.

Tunney had just taken over the bomb squad before the Brescia Circle bombings. In his early forties, he had been a cop for eighteen years. He kept his hair trimmed short and had a salt-and-pepper mustache. His jowls were just beginning to protrude from the confines of his high-buttoned dress uniform. He had spent the last five years of his career on the bomb squad, studying explosives and the motives of the people who planted them. Almost always, he felt, the bombers were politically motivated. But Tunney was always careful not to let rumor, prejudices, and conjecture mislead him. He never assumed, never tried to guess who had done what, until he had a piece of evidence off of which he could investigate. This was especially true of the harbor bombings that began in 1915. Interned German sailors were already viewed with suspicion by local police. That suspicion increased after von Papen's passport operation was uncovered. But Tunney, despite rumors along the docks, had scant evidence to connect them to any of the explosions. Only once had he seen one of the recent bombs, in the cargo of the steamship *Kirkoswald,* which had been laden with sugar and grain and headed for France. He had never encountered anything like it: a slim metal tube divided into two compartments by a small disk; one side held potassium chlorate, the other sulfuric acid. The bombs he had dealt with from the Black Hand were crude and obviously homemade, done cheaply and thoughtlessly. But this was different; the craftsmanship was professional, purposeful. And it was costly. There weren't any anarchists in the city with the money to build something like this.

Even so, Tunney had no names, no proof of who had bought the chemicals, no clue as to where the bomb had been made. Shipping companies didn't keep records of the cargo loaders they employed. There were so many able-bodied men looking for work that it was unnecessary to keep track of them. In several cases, cargo loaders had spotted the bombs, thrown them overboard, and not bothered to report what they'd seen until the end of the day, after they had been paid.

After every incident, whether it was an undetonated bomb or a mysterious fire, Tunney started a file. But even he admitted that "the sum total of these reports was . . . nothing."

President Woodrow Wilson's files, however, were beginning to bulge with evidence of German misdeeds in the United States. Wilson had not planned on making foreign policy a focal point of his administration. "It would be the irony of fate if my administration had to deal chiefly with foreign affairs," he said before his inauguration in 1913. But within eighteen months, the war in Europe would consume his attention. The idea of joining the fight sickened Wilson. "Americans must have a consciousness that is different than the consciousness of every other nation in the world," he said during a speech in 1915. "The example of America must be a special example. The example of America must be the example, not merely of peace because it will not fight but of peace because peace is the healing and elevating influence of the world, and strife is not."

But Wilson often allowed his hopes and ideals, and occasionally his political instincts, to cloud his judgment, especially with regard to U.S. intelligence. While England, France, and Germany cultivated advanced secret service operations, America's spy agencies — the Office of Naval Intelligence (ONI), the Military Intelligence Division (MID), and the Secret Service—were still in their early stages. The ONI, established in 1882 to keep the U.S. Navy abreast of developing warship technology in Europe, was the most reliable of the three. A dozen junior officers analyzed foreign technical journals, and the captain of every navy ship included an intelligence officer on his crew. These officers carried cameras and made it part of their routine in foreign ports to chart local waterways, tour seaside forts, and get as close to shipbuilding yards as possible. The ONI's role quickly focused almost entirely on future threats to the United States. As early as 1900, the officer in charge of the ONI was so unsettled by the buildup of the German navy and the politics of the kaiser that he determined a conflict would be inevitable. To ensure security within the ranks, he demanded that every U.S. sailor with a German surname be strip-searched for pro-German tattoos. Over the next decade, the ONI assiduously planned for war with Germany.

Meanwhile, the MID, created just three years after the ONI, was a tangled and misdirected bureaucracy. Initially, it had so little support within the army that it was given just one office and one clerk. Only after Congress approved funding for an attaché program in 1888 did it have the resources to hunt for information abroad. As opposed to the well-integrated ONI, however, the more the MID grew, the more inefficient it became. By 1903, it was so large that it had to be broken up into three divisions: administrative, intelligence gathering, and war planning. The general in charge of the MID refused to let the three groups share information with one another, instead demanding that all material be funneled through him.

In 1912, President William Howard Taft assigned a joint army-navy board to prepare a war plan against Germany. The ONI and MID provided vital strategic information. Shortly before Wilson's inauguration in March 1913, the board's purpose was leaked to the press, stoking fears that a war was imminent. Wilson immediately ordered that it be disbanded. Soon afterward, the intelligence budgets of both the army and the navy were slashed. By the end of 1913, the ONI could do no more than it had done in 1882, and the MID, despite a worldwide attaché network that was second only to Russia's, no longer had the analysts to sift through the hundreds of reports sent to its headquarters. Early in 1915, when an army captain was asked to evaluate the state of German forces should the United States join the war, his only references were a 1914 almanac of world armies and a shipping register from the same year. One high-ranking intelligence officer warned the army chief of staff, "We are no better prepared, so far as intelligence duties are concerned, than the day the staff was created. . . . Information on hand is now so old as to be practically worthless."

Wilson seemed unwilling to believe that there was a shadow war already under way. After he left office, he made a speech poking fun at how ill informed he had been when it came to espionage: "I not only did not know it until we got into this war, but I did not believe it when I was told that it was true, that Germany was not the only country that maintained a secret service. Every country in Europe maintained it."

Of course, America did, too. But in 1915, compared to its European counterparts, the U.S. Secret Service appeared to be no more sophisticated than a small-town sheriff's office. Formed in 1865 to pursue rampant counterfeiting after the Civil War, the Secret Service was the country's sole national police force, and the only agency with a congressional mandate to investigate fraud against the government. During the early 1870s, it trailed members of the Ku Klux Klan in the Carolinas, Georgia, Alabama, Florida, and Tennessee, which led to more than a thousand arrests. While skimpy budgets limited it to eleven bureaus throughout the country and a force that didn't exceed forty-seven agents until after 1910, the Secret Service's scope increased again in 1898, this time to include counterintelligence during the Spanish-American War. It tracked down Spanish agents from Louisiana to New York and from Washington, D.C., to Washington State. It uncovered a plot that implicated a Spanish Embassy attaché as the leader of a vast network of Spanish spies living within the United States. The Secret Service played such an important role in President William McKinley's war strategy that its director, John Wilkie, became one of his regular wartime advisers.

After America's victory over Spain, McKinley received death threats from European anarchists, and Wilkie assigned Secret Service agents to protect the president at the White House and while traveling. (An agent was standing next to McKinley on September 6, 1901, when McKinley was shot and fatally wounded by an assassin.) Shortly after McKinley's death, presidential protection, which had begun sporadically with Grover Cleveland in the mid-1890s and wouldn't be made law until 1951, became one of the Secret Service's top, unofficial priorities. Yet for all its success in disrupting espionage and its increased responsibilities, the Secret Service's budget and membership increased only slightly over the next several years. Spies, Americans believed, were a European invention, the product of too many borders and long-standing animus between countries. The security of peacetime—a feeling that the United States was in danger only when at war—ran deep. The Secret Service was caught unaware when World War I began. In early 1915, the agency's best sources—especially concerning German espionage inside America—were the eighty U.S.-based British spies.

Because the United States was neutral, Wilson believed that Germany wouldn't infiltrate his country with secret agents. After he found out that the German Embassy and von Bernstorff were loosely tied to the passport forgery business being run by von Papen, he wrote to his attorney general, "I hope that you will have the matter looked into thoroughly, but that, at the same time, you will have all possible precautions taken that no hint of it may become public until it materializes into something upon which we have no choice but to act." Close, more skeptical, advisers took comfort in small victories, such as getting the president to allow the German Embassy's phones to be tapped and diplomats such as Albert, Boy-Ed, and von Papen to be followed. But when his staff pushed him to have von Bernstorff removed from the country, Wilson and his top counsel, Colonel Edward House, refused.

House was a wealthy Texas cotton farmer turned political

junkie who had been instrumental in managing Wilson's campaign. He didn't hold an official position in Wilson's government, but there was no one the president trusted more. House had built a close relationship with von Bernstorff and believed, despite any of the German ambassador's transgressions, that having him in the United States made staying neutral easier. Expelling him, House claimed, was tantamount to declaring war. He and Wilson also hoped a good relationship with von Bernstorff would one day be vital during peace talks.

American newspapers advocating war ridiculed Wilson's neutrality policies, and people at pro-German rallies booed him. Meanwhile, the prejudice toward German-Americans and immigrants from other countries became worse. Former president Theodore Roosevelt made speeches across the country denouncing those who identified themselves as German-American, Irish-American, or Italian-American—anyone whose loyalties appeared divided between the New World and the Old. "Those hyphenated Americans," Roosevelt said, "terrorize American politicians."

Several newspaper reports speculated that the hundreds of thousands of German-Americans living in New York had instructions to mobilize and take over the city. Other stories theorized that German-Americans were building concrete artillery installations along the East Coast to prepare for a German invasion. Fears intensified on May 7, 1915, when a German U-boat submerged off the coast of Ireland torpedoed the British luxury liner *Lusitania,* which was en route to Liverpool from New York. The ship sank in eighteen minutes. Nearly 1,200 passengers, including 128 American tourists, were killed.

Still, Wilson resisted declaring war, even as the *New York Times* called on him and his administration to make sure "the Germans shall no longer make war like savages drunk with blood." Wilson also resisted cutting off diplomatic ties when he received a letter in July 1915 from Anne Seward, the niece of William Seward, Abraham Lincoln's secretary of state, warning him of von Rintelen's antics. She had met von Rintelen in Germany before the war and was stunned when she saw him in the United States, introducing himself under a false name. "His utterances are distinctly offensive and his threats alarming," Seward wrote. "His national prominence in Germany and his high military rank coupled with his various aliases and his frequent change of address give rise to uncomfortable suspicions." When Wilson had a member of the secretary of state's office interview Seward personally, she claimed that von Rintelen had admitted being a secret agent. Despite this harrowing story, her testimony was ignored.

Wilson refused to expel von Bernstorff, von Papen, Boy-Ed, and Albert even after more substantial evidence of German sabotage was uncovered. On July 23, 1915, Albert was riding uptown on the Sixth Avenue elevated train. The temperature hovered near seventy degrees, but a light wind from the east made it feel cooler. Albert, juggling his legitimate efforts to get food through the blockade to Germany and his illegitimate efforts to fund von Papen and von Rintelen's operations, was exhausted. The rumbling of the train and the summer sun, shining through the train's windows, lulled him to sleep. He woke up at the 50th Street station, his stop, and slipped through the doors just as they closed. But in his haste to get off the train, he left his briefcase behind. He turned back toward the train and saw a man sprinting away, clutching the case. Albert assumed he was a petty thief and ran after him. As another train passed, the man with the briefcase hopped on, told the conductor he was being chased, and begged him to speed away. The conductor looked out the window, saw Albert running full speed toward the train, and sent the train onward, leaving Albert behind.

In fact, the man with the briefcase was not a petty thief, but the U.S. Secret Service agent assigned to follow Albert. (In the agent's report of the incident, he wrote, "The wild-eyed appearance of [Albert] corroborated my statement and the conductor called to the motorman to pass the next corner without stopping so the nut could not get on.") In the briefcase were papers recapping the pro-German stories that von Bernstorff had planted in the

American press. There were logs of payoffs to German-American and Irish-American organizations to influence public opinion. There was proof that Albert had used the money he raised to purchase a munitions plant in Bridgeport, Connecticut. Wilson brushed these documents aside, leaving it up to House to decide how the material should be dealt with.

House's faith in von Bernstorff was shaken by what he saw. Feeling angry and betrayed, he gave Albert's papers to the *New York World* for publication, as long as the editors agreed not to reveal their source. On August 15, 1915, the *World* published its scoop under the headline HOW GERMANY HAS WORKED IN U.S. TO SHAPE OPINION, BLOCK THE ALLIES AND GET MUNITIONS FOR HERSELF, TOLD IN SECRET AGENTS' LETTERS.

By now, the belief that Germany was actively working to undermine America was widespread in the United States. One political cartoon in the *Chicago Daily News* pictured a man peeking out from a tent made of the American flag. The word SPY was written on his back, and he was surrounded by boxes of dynamite. The California Board of Education banned the teaching of German in public schools because it was a language that disseminated "ideals of autocracy, brutality and hatred." Local libraries threw out German books, and the Metropolitan Opera stopped performing German works. Restaurants renamed sauerkraut "liberty cabbage" and hamburgers "liberty sandwiches." A Minnesota minister was tarred and feathered after he was heard praying with a dying woman in German. Because of rumors that German-Americans intended to put ground glass in bandages being sent to the front, people with German names were banned from working for the Red Cross.

Amid this wave of report and rumor, Wilson could no longer blindly preach peace. He wrote to House, "I am sure that the country is honeycombed with German intrigue and infested with German spies. The evidences of these things are multiplying every day."

•   •   •

Paul Hilken lived with his wife and young daughter in a big house in Roland Park, a posh, wooded and secluded section of Baltimore, where the houses were built on narrow, winding roads. They had a front room with a grand piano, a large formal dining room, and an attic quickly filling with cobwebs and must.

Hilken was a boyish-looking man in his midthirties, with a mustache covering his lip and hair that was swept back dramatically from his forehead. He had much in common with Franz von Rintelen. Both had benefited from having powerful fathers, were well schooled and well traveled, and showed off their pedigrees. Hilken's father was the honorary German consul in Baltimore and the local head of the North German Lloyd, Germany's largest shipping fleet. Hilken was the old man's heir apparent, also working at the German Lloyd.

When Hilken had work to do, he retreated to his basement, where it was quiet and he could focus. His life was large and full, and he was respected—so much so that after the war broke out, his employees at the German Lloyd nicknamed him the "von Hindenburg of Roland Park," after Germany's most brilliant and respected general.

Hilken had been raised in the United States, studied engineering at Lehigh University, and settled near where he had grown up in Baltimore. But he was loyal to Germany. "Our home was German," Hilken once said in the *Baltimore Post*.

> We were not allowed to speak English at home. It was always German. We were sent to school in Germany for two years and when I was eight years old and returned to the United States, I could not speak English and had to learn again. When I went to Lehigh University, I still spoke with a German accent and was made fun of. I was called Prince, Dutch, Duke, Bismarck—always some connection with German. And as my initials were Paul G. L. Hilken, I was called Paul German Lloyd Hilken. From Lehigh I went to the Massachusetts Institute of Technology, and when I grad-

uated from there I had the belief that Germany was the place to continue to study after graduation. . . . My whole upbringing was with the thought of superiority of Germany in the arts and engineering and so forth.

In December 1913, Hilken moved to Germany to work in the German Lloyd's Bremen office. He received five months of training, then returned to Baltimore to train his successor. He was scheduled to move to New York in January 1915 to become the German Lloyd's managing director. "But then the war broke out," Hilken said.

Internment put a halt to all of the German Lloyd's business. The ships were idle, gathering barnacles in Baltimore Harbor. Suddenly, Hilken was a captain with no command. His comfort and his wife and children's security depended on his proving his loyalty to the kaiser. "I felt that my entire future was with the German Lloyd, a German company," Hilken told the *Baltimore Post*. "Naturally when war came I did all in my power to assist Germany." When Franz von Rintelen summoned him to the Ritz in Philadelphia for a meeting in April 1915, Hilken could think of no reason to say no.

Von Rintelen was waiting when Hilken walked through the ornately carved doors of the Ritz's writing room. The two had never met, and von Rintelen watched Hilken for several minutes before he approached and asked him his name. Von Rintelen could tell that Hilken was anxious. Clandestine meetings with members of the German navy were uncommon for businessmen from Baltimore.

Quickly, von Rintelen steered the conversation toward topics that would put Hilken at ease. They talked about their legitimate work, their loyalty to Germany, and how angry they were about the American-made munitions being sent to the front. The two privileged children of mighty men soon felt a kinship, and von Rintelen felt comfortable enough to tell Hilken about his mission.

Von Rintelen told Hilken that he was in the United States to interfere with the manufacture of munitions and their transportation to the Allies. "That was his main job, irrespective of how he did it," Hilken recalled. Von Rintelen said that he was instigating strikes on the docks to keep supply ships from being loaded. He described his relationship with Irish labor leaders and told Hilken about his cigar bombs.

The more von Rintelen shared, the more excited Hilken became, and the more he admired this mysterious man. Von Rintelen was brave, committed, willing to sacrifice his comfort for the German cause. Hilken wanted to contribute; he needed only for von Rintelen to ask.

Von Rintelen told Hilken that he needed to expand his operations south. After New York, Baltimore was one of the busiest harbors on the East Coast. There were already dozens of German merchant ships interned there and a built-in network of potential saboteurs. Von Rintelen could tell that Hilken didn't have the constitution to handle lethal situations; he was a manager, more comfortable with payoffs than real dirty work. But Hilken could be the Baltimore operation's moneyman. He'd funnel cash through legitimate businesses, then distribute it to German operatives. He had the respect of the business community in Baltimore, and he could open multiple accounts at several banks and make large deposits without drawing any suspicion.

He'd need someone to assist him, von Rintelen said—someone to do his recruiting, to approach potential agents, organize them, and give them assignments. It had to be a German, someone who could speak the language of the interned, literally and in spirit, and also could intimidate, cajole, and threaten with physical harm if secrets were spilled. Hilken would have to be able to distance himself from this person if plans went awry. Hilken knew just the man.

Chapter Three

BY 1914, THEODORE Roosevelt had been out of office for
five years, but he had never left the public's consciousness.
He was still a heroic figure with strong opinions about America's
place in a world that was increasingly dangerous. He constantly
gossiped with U.S. diplomats about foreign policy and then used
the frightening stories he heard about what was happening abroad
to publicly criticize Wilson, casting the current president as a cow-
ard unfit to protect America's best interests.

Roosevelt often stumped for American military preparedness,
if only because a formidable, trained military would intimidate
potential enemies. It was a policy Wilson deplored, believing the
very notion undermined America's neutrality. But Roosevelt was
still a galvanizing speaker, and slowly, especially on college cam-
puses, the preparedness movement took hold.

Students were on summer break when European hostilities
broke out during the first week of August 1914. As they returned
to campus that fall, the debate over the war was spirited. Germany
had marched into Belgium, a neutral country, on its way to invad-
ing France. Americans were appalled at the reports of German
atrocities in Belgium. Some college newspapers printed editorials
warning that one day soon, America would have to join the fight.

Students and influential alumni urged their administrators to offer military training classes.

John McCloy was a junior at Amherst College, in Massachusetts, when World War I started. The more he read about Germany's advances in Europe, the more he opposed Wilson and believed Roosevelt. When the dean at Amherst refused to add military training to the curriculum, McCloy looked for alternatives. "I was a supporter of Roosevelt who was bitter about Wilson's neutralist policy," McCloy once wrote. "I was worked up about the rape of Belgium and I was caught up in the need for our participation."

Small military training camps were popping up all over the country, offering one- or two-month courses during the summer of 1915. Some college students chose to attend these camps and receive training in shooting a rifle, marching, and riding a horse as part of the cavalry. The camp in Plattsburgh, New York, was particularly popular among students from the best schools. Nestled on Lake Champlain, with views of both the Green and Adirondack mountains, the camp trained 613 students in the summer of 1915, at a charge of $27.50 per student. Thirty percent of those students were attending Harvard, Yale, or Princeton. One of the campers was Archie Roosevelt, Theodore's son. Another was John McCloy.

McCloy had been born in 1895 on the wrong side of Philadelphia's Main Line, the area west of the city where the elite had settled. At the time, Philadelphia, more than any other American city, still reflected the old-world English values that had existed before the American Revolution: privilege and status were birthrights. The Main Line epitomized high society; where McCloy was from did not. That made him acutely aware of how much social status played a part in career advancement.

McCloy's father, John McCloy Sr., was a high school dropout who spent his free time studying pocket editions of the writings of Shakespeare and Dickens and learning foreign languages. John Sr. knew that he wasn't the smartest man, but he was curious and interested—the type of person who, once he realized how much he didn't know, wanted to know it all. He worked his way up from clerk at the Penn Mutual insurance company to the head of applications and death certificates. He and his wife, Anna, believed that struggle led to self-improvement, that morality was bound with effort, and that the city's upper class embodied these traits. They longed for their son, John Jr., to join the ranks of the elite.

In 1900, the McCloys lived in a clean, well-appointed row house in North Philadelphia. John Sr. had taught himself Latin and was now studying Greek. On Saturday afternoons, he'd read to his son in those languages. Both he and his wife thought that the classics were a vital part of a legal education, which they expected John Jr. to get. The men they admired most in Philadelphia were lawyers.

One day in January 1901, after a heavy snowfall, John Sr. had to walk two miles from his office in the center of Philadelphia to his home. He had a bad heart, and while trudging through the snow, he began to feel weak. When he arrived home, Anna put him to bed. He wouldn't make it through the night. From his deathbed, he told Anna "to be sure and have John study Greek." At the time, John Jr. was six years old; Anna was thirty-three.

Years later, it was his father's books that John Jr. remembered most. "I'd read them on my way to work as he did," McCloy wrote. "Pocket-sized copies of authors such as Shakespeare, Dickens, Thackeray, the early American poets and essayists. They were my only recollections of him. Those little books still had his firm and well-written signature."

Despite being a respected manager at Penn Mutual when he died, John Sr. didn't have any life insurance. Because of a heart murmur, his own company had refused his application for insurance. Penn Mutual did give Anna a one-time payment equal to her late husband's $3,000-a-year salary, which she decided to use for her son's education. She dreamed of sending him to private school, not just because she despised the public schools in Philadelphia but also because she knew that the people John would meet at private school were the gatekeepers to the other side of the tracks.

But $3,000 was not enough to make Anna's dreams come true.

So she woke up every morning at six and made her way to the fancy town houses on Rittenhouse Square in the center of the city or to the elegant homes on the Main Line. She supported herself and her son as a hairdresser — "doing heads," McCloy called it — charging fifty cents per client. At first, she used her contacts at Penn Mutual to build her client base. But she also spent many hours knocking on doors and offering her services. She styled the hair of department store mogul John Wanamaker's wife, who gave John toys her children no longer played with. Another client, the wife of the Shakespearean scholar H. H. Furness, offered her the complete works of Shakespeare. During the summer, Anna and John moved to the Adirondacks so that Anna could dress her clients' hair at their mountain retreats. John worked at the local resorts, carrying water, wood, ice, and milk to campsites. During his downtime, Anna encouraged him to take up hunting, trout fishing, and especially tennis, a sport enjoyed by the upper classes.

When John was twelve, one of Anna's clients helped him get admitted to Peddie, a private school in Hightstown, New Jersey, only ten miles from Princeton. The school was just a one-room building surrounded by farmland. It wasn't as prestigious as Andover or Exeter, but it was private, and it had the same goal as New England's more elite schools: to groom its students to assume the responsibilities of wealth and power.

John had always been aware that this was what his mother expected of him, and Anna had never hesitated to remind him how hard she had worked for him. But once he was at Peddie, she made it clear that he had to want success for himself as much as she wanted it for him. His destiny was now his responsibility. "You've got one semester to prove yourself and get a scholarship," Anna said. "Because that's all I can afford." After dropping him off at Peddie, Anna went straight to New York, signed up to work as a waitress on a cruise ship, and began to travel around the world. She sent her son postcards from wherever she docked, but John was on his own.

At Peddie, John fulfilled his father's wishes: he studied the classics in their original Greek. He recited the *Odyssey* and the *Iliad* hundreds of lines at a time. "I could almost see the sand along the shore at Troy, with the heroes exercising in their armor," he later recalled. He even won his class's Greek Prize, a check for five dollars. But he rarely dazzled his classmates or his teachers with his brilliance. In most things, he was a notch below the best students, who seemed naturally smarter and more talented.

By the time he was in his final years at Peddie, McCloy was a wiry five foot seven. His mentor was his tennis coach, who encouraged him to "get in there and run with the swift." The more he played against or studied with "the swift," the more he realized that what he lacked in talent, he made up for in endurance. No one worked harder or longer than he did.

After Peddie, McCloy entered Amherst, where he met Lew Douglas, the son of a copper-mining magnate from Arizona and one of the wealthiest students at the school. Whereas Douglas was brash, vocal, and willing to speak his mind on any subject, McCloy kept to himself. Douglas loved to chase girls; McCloy spent most of his time alone in his room holding what he called "reading debates." He would often read three or four books on one topic, all with different views, so that he could see all sides of an issue. From Douglas's perspective, McCloy spent too much time working and not enough time enjoying himself. McCloy simultaneously envied Douglas for his confidence and carefree attitude and loathed him for how little he took advantage of his opportunities. While McCloy was waiting tables or tutoring students to earn money for tuition, he would think of the rakish Douglas and work even harder.

McCloy attended the Plattsburgh military training camp in the summer of 1915. He returned the next year, after he graduated from Amherst. This time, Douglas accompanied him. The experience at Plattsburgh went beyond military training. It also reawakened the patriotic spirit of the country's upper-crust college students. This was where the men who thirty years later would reshape America's post–World War II foreign and domestic policy first formed their opinions.

At night, after the day's training was over, the campers and officers sat around the campfire and talked about how vulnerable the nation was to an attack. There were also reporters at the camp, writing about the preparedness movement and these sons of the wealthy and influential who were growing in opposition to Wilson's neutrality policy.

Early on the morning of August 25, 1915, Theodore Roosevelt himself appeared, dressed in full Rough Rider regalia: broad-brimmed hat, suspenders, blue shirt, brown pants, and a gun holstered at his side. All day, he observed as the twelve hundred future warriors practiced maneuvers against members of the U.S. Army. That night, standing by the campfire, Roosevelt addressed his subjects. The sun was setting against the Green Mountains, and as the sky grew darker, the flames of the fire cast shadows on his familiar face. They were "fulfilling the prime duty of free men," Roosevelt said, unlike those "professional pacifists, poltroons, and college sissies who organize peace-at-any-price societies." The next morning, his comments were front-page news.

When McCloy returned to school that fall, he could not be dissuaded from his stance that America needed to intervene in Europe. "Justice never was and never will be provided by the weak," he wrote in the school newspaper. "Crime and intrigue among nations will stop only when nations take a stand against them."

He didn't know how prophetic this would be.

By the middle of 1915, despite his moral objections, Wilson had seen too much evidence that German spies were active in the United States not to act. Albert was being followed. Von Papen, because of his passport business, was also under observation. The German Embassy, though assured by the State Department that von Papen's passport scam didn't put it on a government watch list, was indeed being watched. Wilson was so wary that he assigned eleven additional Secret Service agents to New York. The information the federal government gathered trickled down to the local police, including bomb squad captain Thomas Tunney.

A tip put Tunney on the trail of a German named Paul

Koenig, a former security chief for the Hamburg-American passenger line. Tunney wrote in his autobiography, "In spite of the dull times thrust upon the German businesses, Koenig was curiously busy, and we became curiously busy to find out why." Koenig was massive around the belly and had a long, oval face. He combed his long black hair back and kept it matted down with palmfuls of grease. Before the war, he and his men had often done the legwork for the police department when Hamburg-American ships had been robbed. They'd investigate, chase down leads, coerce a witness, and then hand the case over to the police to make it official. The cops would get their man, and Koenig's company would get its merchandise back. Koenig knew every dockworker, sailor, and tug captain working on the piers. He knew the rhythms of the harbor, and he knew where men hid when they didn't want to be found. Koenig didn't sweet-talk people when he wanted something done; he intimidated them. And because of his status with the German passenger company, he was well known by Albert, von Papen, and Boy-Ed. Once the war began, von Papen could think of no one more suited to manage the day-to-day operations of his secret service.

Koenig recruited his wartime force from among the interned merchant marines who loitered around the docks and from the stateside German employees of Hamburg-American. He also culled recruits from the lists of German reservists anxious to contribute. One of his key sources was Frederick Scheindl, a reservist who also worked as a clerk at the National City Bank of New York. Scheindl handled telegrams from the Allies transmitting money for the purchase of war materials. Often these telegrams listed the vessels carrying the cargo into New York Harbor and the ships that would be carrying it out.

Koenig nicknamed Scheindl "B-1," paid the bank clerk twenty-five dollars per report, and considered him an important contact. In a small black notebook, Koenig reminded himself:

> In order to accomplish better results and to shorten the stay
> of the informing agent at the place of meeting it has been de-

cided to discontinue the former practice of dining with this agent prior to receiving his report. It will also be made a rule to refrain from working on other matters until the informant in this case has been fully heard, and all the data taken down in shorthand. . . . Also, I will refrain from drinking beer or liquor with my supper prior to receiving agent B-1 for the reason that I wish to be perfectly fresh and well prepared when he reports.

The operation Koenig ran was broken down into three parts: the Pier Division, the Division for Special Detail, and the Secret Service Division, which Koenig called his "S.S. Division." The agents for the first two units met and did their business with Koenig in his office at 45 Broadway, the same building where Heinrich Albert worked. The S.S. intentionally lacked a permanent home. A street number for a meeting in Manhattan meant that the meeting would take place five blocks farther uptown than the street mentioned. Two weeks later, the code would be reversed, and the meeting place would be five blocks downtown. A message to meet at Penn Station really meant to meet at Grand Central; the Hotel Belmont meant the bar in Pabst's Hotel at Columbus Circle. These rules would last a week, maybe two, before Koenig would change them again. Only Koenig, who scratched out new codes, rules, and meeting places in a notebook he carried with him at all times, knew exactly where he was going next. No one else was allowed to write anything down. And none of the thirty-four agents working on what he called the "D" cases knew who else was working for Koenig.

Two of the names on Koenig's list of "D" case agents were Barton Scott and Jesse Burns. Koenig met them during the summer of 1915 at Jersey City's Communipaw Avenue ferry station. He had gone there several times after eluding the tail by Tunney's bomb squad. It was a convenient place to hide and wait late at night, long after the regular commuters had come and gone. Koenig saw the same faces at this time of night, stragglers going to or coming from their jobs at nearby factories, loaders getting off from a long day, guards walking toward their jobs at the end of the piers. It was the last group that interested him most, the people headed toward the Jersey City Terminal, as Black Tom Island was officially known. He focused on their eyes. Could he trust them? Could he entice them?

Scott and Burns, dressed in uniform, always commuted together, arriving at dusk. Koenig, wearing his usual long black raincoat and black fedora, followed them to their jobs at the end of the Jersey side of the harbor. He discovered that they were guards at Black Tom.

One night, before the two left the station, Koenig approached them. He asked them if they were guards on the piers. When Burns said yes, Koenig slipped some money into his hand. There was more, Koenig said, as long as he didn't watch too carefully down by the docks. "I didn't see no particular harm in taking some money that was being handed out," Burns would say years later. "I think I would have been a fool if I hadn't. It wasn't much of anything, only small pieces of change from time to time."

Burns spent most of the money on booze. He'd give Scott a couple of bucks and send him to the Whitehouse Saloon on Communipaw Avenue, right by the ferry station, to buy some whiskey. They'd have a couple of nips, settle in for the night, and do as Koenig asked.

At dusk one early summer evening in 1915, von Rintelen hopped into a car waiting for him along the shore in Jersey City. He drove past marshes, fields, and meadows until he reached the Communipaw Avenue station. As he drove, the landscape became increasingly industrial, and crisscrossing railroad lines caused the car to shake and rattle, sounding as though it might jump off its axles. The late light of summer had yet to fade, and he could see rags and debris scattered on the ground, remains from boxcars and barges. To his left, piers stretched into the harbor. In the distance, he could still make out the shadows of the growing New York City skyline. At the end of the road, along the harbor side of the street, was a shed, protected by a small gate. Beyond it, a few lamps lit the piers. Von Rintelen could see Black Tom Island stretching into the harbor, as though it were reaching out to touch the base of the Statue of Liberty.

There was a guard at the gate, but von Rintelen was not alarmed. One night at Martha Held's, he had heard Paul Koenig brag about his Black Tom connections. Von Rintelen confidently handed the guard a wad of cash and passed easily through the gate.

He had Black Tom to himself. Carefully, he paced off distances and diagrammed the best locations for small craft to land and relaunch. His notes included details about which barges carried what, how far it was from the shack to the nearest pier, how many lights lit the docks, and how well guarded Black Tom was—or wasn't. As he toured the empty yard, von Rintelen "could not help urging upon myself the advisability of giving Black Tom a sound knock on the head—its mere name sounded so good to me."

James Larkin continued to agitate into 1915. Although his harsh rhetoric for the war and widespread support among Irish workers won him praise and publicity, it did not pay the bills.

Larkin lived in a one-room apartment in Greenwich Village. The entrance to the apartment lay at the end of an alley called Milligan Place. Surrounded by the working poor and their problems, Larkin continued to preach. His apartment was his stage, albeit a small one, but in such a confined space, his audience was all the more captive. Dockworkers came by, as did cargo loaders and immigrants just off the boat. Larkin brewed a black tea as dark as night and drank it constantly to keep his senses sharp. Sometimes he could be found at the harbor, under the green banner of the Irish Socialist Foundation, trying to organize the longshoremen.

Larkin had few paid speaking engagements these days. An ad for a free lecture in Pittsburgh in February 1915 included a notice that Larkin would be in town all week and available to speak for a nominal fee. He had no takers. By April, he was so broke that when he sent for his wife to come to America, she had to ask the head of the Dublin Transport Union for money to cover her travel expenses.

Larkin's shame at his inability to provide overwhelmed him. A fellow Irishman named John Devoy put him in touch with the Germans. Larkin knew that they would push him to commit to sabotage, as Boy-Ed and von Papen had tried to do in late 1914, but he didn't want that job. Instead, he would offer to organize workers and plan strikes along the East Coast. He'd cause the industrial machine to stall, but he wouldn't plant bombs—and Devoy would be his witness in this refusal. "Jim was asked by one of the Germans how much he thought the work would cost," Devoy wrote to a friend years later. "He answered ten or twelve thousand dollars."

In July alone, Larkin organized a strike of 5,000 men at Standard Oil's Bayonne, New Jersey, plant; a strike of 1,200 machinists at a munitions factory in Bridgeport, Connecticut; and a work stoppage by 1,500 longshoremen in New York Harbor. But the Germans wanted more; the strikes were merely stopgaps. Far better for the Germans was destroying deadly cargo, not just delaying it from being loaded.

In the fall of 1915, Wolf von Igel, von Papen's assistant, met with Larkin and pressed him to take over the sabotage operations on the docks. Larkin refused, but he accepted von Igel's offer to see how the bombs were made. From Manhattan, the two boarded a Hoboken-bound ferry. As they crossed to New Jersey, they could see the harbor's shipping lane filled with cargo-laden steamers that would fortify the Allies on the front.

Von Igel took Larkin to Walter Scheele's bomb-making plant. There von Igel explained how German chemists worked with various forms of phosphorus and other chemicals to create explosives. They called the potion "liquid fire" and packed it in small metal tubes they called cigar bombs. Von Igel showed Larkin a small bomb created to disable the propellers of a ship heading out to sea. Larkin was intrigued, impressed, and a little desperate. He still would not agree to perpetrate sabotage, but he did agree to keep in touch with von Igel.

The two men met often throughout the fall, becoming friendly and learning to trust each other. Then, one day in November, after Larkin returned to his downtown office from a meeting with von Igel, he noticed police officers camped out in the lobby and official-looking men loitering in front of his door. Larkin thought they looked like secret service agents. Were they British? American? He didn't stay to find out. He walked past the building and, without going home to pack, took the next train to Chicago. When he arrived, he sent for his wife; they were through living in New York.

I n May 1915, von Rintelen took the train to Baltimore to visit Paul Hilken. They met at Hilken's home in Roland Park. Upon entering, von Rintelen admired the piano in the front room and complimented Hilken on his wonderful life and beautiful home. His subtext was clear: "Look at all that Germany has provided you."

The two men walked into Hilken's basement office. There to greet them was Captain Frederick Hinsch. For six months, Hinsch had been interned in the United States along with the crew of his steamship, *Neckar*. He was bored, tired of having his men repeatedly repaint the ship and scrape off barnacles.

Before docking in Baltimore, Hinsch had earned the respect and admiration of his men for his daring. The *Neckar* had cruised the South Atlantic for weeks after the war had begun, dodging the British fleet while giving Germans access to his boat, which was loaded with grain, oil cake, cotton, and cottonseed meal, as a supply base. Once on dry land, the rotund Hinsch commanded respect by intimidation and force. His crew—still dependent on him for food, shelter, and work while they were locked down in the United States—feared him. He was in his early forties, nearly twice the age of most of his merchant marines. He was quick to raise his voice and use his fists. Hilken, who had been so taken with von Rintelen's courage after their meeting at the Ritz, knew that Hinsch was the type of man von Rintelen wanted. No one would cross him. No one would refuse him. And best of all, he would stop at nothing to get back to Germany.

The three men spoke briefly. Von Rintelen reiterated what he had told Hilken in Philadelphia. He didn't wait for Hinsch to accept the offer.

Chapter Four

V ON RINTELEN HAD always enjoyed the New York social
scene. At night, dressed in a formal suit and white tie, he'd
attend concerts, the opera, or lectures on American politics. In
these settings, he was loose with his name and his views. Emile
Gache, the Swiss president of E. V. Gibbons, often vanished. Mingling with the high-society people he considered his peers, he
sometimes introduced himself as Captain Franz von Rintelen of
the German navy. If he used his own name, he reasoned, no one
would suspect him of being anything other than a diplomat trying
to keep the peace between the United States and Germany. Only if
he tried to conceal his identity and was somehow discovered would
it be assumed that he had "something nefarious up my sleeve."

But Anne Seward's warnings and the work of American
agents had prompted a belated investigation, and word of its
progress had reached von Bernstorff. The German government
knew that von Rintelen's cover had been blown, and in early
July 1915 he received a cable recalling him to Germany immediately. He closed up the E. V. Gibbons office on Cedar Street,
checked out of the Great Northern Hotel, and reacquainted
himself with his Swiss identity, boarding the SS *Noordam,* of the
Holland America Line, bound for Rotterdam, on August 3.

For ten days, von Rintelen steamed across the Atlantic without incident.

On the morning of August 12, the *Noordam* slowed down as it approached the white cliffs of Dover, England. It would take a day to pass them, as the British navy would have to board the ship, check everyone's passport, and inspect the cargo. Von Rintelen steeled himself in the bar. "Nobody who had done what I considered it my duty to do in America, and was in possession of a forged passport, would have been anxious to converse with British officers opposite the white cliffs of England," he later wrote.

The first day passed peacefully, and von Rintelen began the next morning relaxing in a bath. Suddenly, he heard a knock on his door. Without waiting for von Rintelen to answer, the ship's steward called, "Some British officers wish to have a word with you." He sounded scared.

Before World War I, British kings and queens had relied on well-placed lookout ships to patrol enemy waters and warn them if an attack was imminent. But by 1914, German submarines and underwater mines had made such patrols dangerous and unproductive. "The risk to ships is not justified by any services they can render," Winston Churchill, lord of the Admiralty, said in September 1914 when proposing that all lookout ships be recalled. Four days after he made his case, three British vessels on patrol in the North Sea were sunk by a German U-boat. Fourteen hundred men were killed.

Churchill favored more modern spy games. In early August 1914, just as Britain joined the war, a British cable-cutting ship began slicing the German telegraph cables embedded in the ocean. The Germans then had only two options for overseas communications: unreliable, easily intercepted wireless messages or via cables that ran through ostensibly neutral countries such as Sweden. British cable companies were dominant throughout Europe, and it became common for the British military to simply ask the companies for copies of German cables. As a consequence, almost as soon as Britain entered the war, Churchill's staff in the Admiralty began seeing German messages.

At first, lacking able cryptographers, the British were ill equipped to break the German code. Alfred Ewing, an engineering professor by trade who was then in charge of the British navy's educational programs for cadets, spent days reading old German codebooks stored at the British Museum. Then he picked five linguists from the different naval colleges around England to work as his code breakers. Every day, they crammed into Ewing's office, studying intercepted messages. Only three could fit in the room at a time, so they worked in shifts. If Ewing had company in his office, the cryptographers had to gather their notes and leave.

As an academic exercise, Ewing's efforts were useful. But without up-to-date codebooks, trying to decipher German messages was futile. Then the British got lucky. An Australian crew boarded a German steamship just a week after Britain entered the war and managed to grab a current codebook. In early October 1914, the Russians found another book amid the wreckage of a German cruiser in the Baltic. In late November, a British trawler fishing near Texel, an island just off the northern coast of the Netherlands, felt a tugging in its net. When the crew hauled in its catch, it found a lead-lined chest filled with German documents. Among the papers yanked from what turned out to be the wreck of a sunken German ship was a third codebook. With it and his team of code breakers, Churchill was ready to act.

In November 1914, a few weeks before the British found the third German codebook, Churchill appointed a new director of naval intelligence, Admiral Reginald Hall. Known to most by his nickname, "Blinker" Hall was forty-four years old and unhappy to be on dry land. Back in August, he had been the captain of the battle cruiser *Queen Mary,* a position he loved. But three months into his tour, he became ill and had to be reassigned. Churchill handed him Ewing and the intelligence unit and expected him to coax results out of the cryptographers.

Hall was bald, with cottony white hair clinging to the sides and back of his head. He had a hawkish nose that nearly resembled a beak. His thin upper lip jutted out so far that it hid his bottom lip and seemed to rest on his dimpled chin. But his most distinctive trait was his eyes: because of a facial tic, they rarely stopped blinking, thus his nickname. When he was excited, his eyes would blink even faster. When his blinking was under control, however, his gaze was paralyzing. "I felt like a nut about to be cracked by a toucan when Hall fixed me a horn-rimmed, horny eye," said one of his agents. Like the sea he loved, Hall's surface could be kinetic, but underneath all was cold and still.

Before pushing his staff to decipher the stacks of German messages, Hall worked on acquiring more office space. He moved the cryptographers out of Ewing's office and into Room 40 of the Old Admiralty Building, a heavy brick building tucked inside the massive British civil service complex known as Whitehall. From their windows, Hall's decoders had a view of St. James's Park across the road. They formed a perfect team, each man's skills complementing the others': one broke the code, another analyzed the messages, and three men worked as what they called "watch-keepers," logging the intercepts as they came in and doing the initial translations. At first, intercepted messages were carried from the telegraph office in the basement of the building to Hall's men by couriers making their regular rounds. But in the spring of 1915, a pneumatic tube was constructed between the two offices. Messages were then shoved into a metal cylinder and shot toward the cryptographers' office. The sound of the cylinder, rattling and hissing through the tube as it was pushed along by a jet of compressed air, echoed through the building. Collectively, Hall's cryptographers became known around Whitehall as "Room 40." But few people actually knew what they were doing.

Within a month of Hall's arrival, Room 40 started producing good information. In December 1914, a last-minute intercept helped the British navy successfully defend against a German raid in the North Sea. A month later, Room 40 predicted a North Sea attack early enough that the British were able to go on the offensive. A likely massacre at the hands of the Germans ended with 951 German sailors killed, against just 10 British deaths. The few people who knew what Room 40 was up to regarded the information that Hall's cryptographers provided with awe. The U.S. ambassador in England once wrote of Hall to President Wilson, "Neither in fiction nor in fact can you find any such man to match him. Of the wonderful things that I know he has done there are several that it would take an exciting volume to tell. The man is a genius, a clear case of genius. All other secret service men are amateurs by comparison. I shall never meet another man like him."

Despite the fact that Britain and Germany had fully developed secret service networks, signal intelligence was a relatively new, and scandalous, spy game. It wasn't until 1925, when Ewing gave a speech at the University of Edinburgh, that the full details of Britain's cryptography program were revealed. Even then, the morality of using such deception, albeit during wartime, was publicly debated.

Hall wasn't satisfied with breaking German naval codes. The more he worked at decoding signal intelligence, the stronger he felt that diplomatic messages should be intercepted as well. These communications, he argued, contained military instructions, diplomatic tactics, and strategy concerning espionage. The Germans used Swedish transatlantic cables to send messages to their diplomats in the United States. Those cable lines ran underneath the North Sea toward the eastern coast of England, and messages sent along them were easily intercepted by Hall's men.

In the spring of 1915, Hall established a branch of Room 40 whose cryptographers reported directly to him, bypassing Ewing. Hall insisted on decoding these intercepts himself, deciding what was important to share with his colleagues and what was not. "He had unbounded confidence in his ability to decide how much of the information should be sent on to other government departments," one of his cryptographers said. Hall had even more material to work with beginning in 1916, when von Bernstorff convinced President Wilson to allow Germany to use America's transatlantic cables, which also passed close to England. After the war, Hall would have the nearly ten thousand messages his men had intercepted and decoded packed in boxes and carted to the basement of his London home. Among those he saved was a cable from the German Foreign Office to Franz von Rintelen telling the captain to return to Berlin.

Von Rintelen slowly lifted himself from his tub and put on his bathrobe. When he opened the door, the steward was no longer there. Instead, von Rintelen was staring at ten sailors and two officers, all with bayonets fixed on his belly.

"You are Mr. Gache?" one of them asked.

"Yes. What can I do for you?"

"We have orders to take you with us."

"I have no intention of disembarking here," von Rintelen snapped. "I am going to Rotterdam."

"I am sorry. If you refuse, we have orders to take you by force."

Three days later, von Rintelen was in Scotland Yard, a prisoner of war. The first person to interrogate him was Blinker Hall.

American policy and public opinion were constantly at odds those first twelve months of World War I. To some extent, this was due to von Bernstorff, who skillfully walked the line between diplomacy and subterfuge, placating House and Wilson with promises that Germany wanted a quick peace, while giving his tacit approval for attacks on American-made munitions and supplies. He understood how desperately Wilson clung to his neutrality policy, even as American newspapers were reporting suspected German acts of sabotage.

Von Bernstorff's greatest asset against the press was his own stable of American journalists, whom he paid to push the German agenda. There was no one he trusted more than James Archibald, a reporter who had been covering Germany for several years when the war broke out. Von Bernstorff put him on the embassy's payroll. Archibald placed pro-German articles in legitimate newspapers and also acted as a courier, using his U.S. passport to pass through the blockade and carry important documents to Europe.

On September 1, 1915, British sailors boarded a ship docked at Falmouth, in southwestern England, on the English Channel. Because of Hall's decoded messages, they knew that Archibald was a passenger, and in his briefcase they found messages from the Austro-Hungarian ambassador to the United States, Constantin Dumba, approving the financial support of striking workers at a munitions plant in the United States. There were also notes mocking Wilson and his foreign policy. The British wasted no time in sending copies of these missives to Wilson, who expelled the ambassador. It was the first time he had acted openly against one of the warring countries and an indication that he was losing patience with Germany.

Von Papen had used Archibald as a courier as well, and mixed in with the pile of Dumba documents were letters to von Papen's wife. In one, he responded to good news from the European battlefields: "How splendid on the eastern front! I always say to these idiotic Yankees that they should shut their mouths and better still be full of admiration for all that heroism."

Again hoping to incite American entry into the war, the British leaked the letters to the press. The *Washington Post, Chicago Tribune,* and *New York World* reprinted von Papen's insults on page one. The public outcry that followed was too much for Wilson to ignore. The president demanded that the military attaché be expelled, even at the expense of neutrality and a quick peace. Wilson, who for so long had held back the State Department's investigation of von Papen and German sabotage, now ordered officials to find the truth. It wouldn't take long for him to get it.

Thomas Tunney had never stopped pursuing Paul Koenig. While U.S. Secret Service agents fed Tunney tips, his beat cops tailed Koenig incessantly. When one tail lost him, a new one would start over. Slowly, Tunney and his men built a case, eventually gathering enough proof that Koenig was breaking the law that they were allowed to tap his phones.

In the fall of 1915, agents heard a call that piqued their interest: a man was yelling at Koenig, saying that Koenig owed him money and that he had been lied to. Tunney's men traced the call back to a pay phone outside a bar. The bartender identified the man as George Fuchs, a loner and distant relative of Koenig's who had moved to New York from Niagara Falls. Koenig paid Fuchs eighteen dollars a week to work as a spy, gathering information about the docks and munitions shipments and, at some point, to row a boatload of dynamite into Canada and deliver it to German agents there. But Fuchs spent as much time in bars as he did on the docks. Eventually, Koenig decided to let him go. Fuchs was fired on a Saturday, and Koenig refused to pay him $2.57, one-seventh of his weekly pay. When Tunney confronted Fuchs, he didn't need much encouragement to tell his story.

Shortly thereafter, the bomb squad raided Koenig's office and home. The officers found his black loose-leaf notebook, which contained typed notes including the names of Koenig's agents, how to contact them, what their aliases were, what cases they were working on, and the keys to his myriad codes for where to meet. Also, under the heading "Secret Service Division Key to Bureau's Connections," Koenig listed the code names of the people on his payroll, including Jesse Burns and Barton Scott, as well as the man he worked for: von Papen.

After von Papen's letters to his wife had been found and printed, he headed west, with Boy-Ed by his side. Stupidly—or arrogantly—they used their full names and titles when registering at hotels. Reporters had been following them from New York, filing daily updates of their travels, and their utter lack of disguise allowed newspapermen from the West to easily pick up their trail. After a stop at Mammoth Hot Springs in Yellowstone National Park, the Germans went to Denver, where they were besieged by photographers and reporters, who wouldn't leave until von Papen had explained his "idiotic Yankees" letter. When faced with hostile questions from reporters in San Francisco, the men replied, "We have nothing to say," and used newspapers to cover their faces when photographed. All over the West, pictures of the two men, their faces hidden behind newspapers, were printed on front pages underneath the headline WE HAVE NOTHING TO SAY.

Returning from their trip in October, von Papen and Boy-Ed realized that their recall to Germany was inevitable. In late November, U.S. attorney general Thomas Gregory denounced what he suggested were German-led "attacks upon lawful American industries and commerce through incendiary fires and explosions in factories, threats to intimidate employees and other acts of violence." On November 29, Secretary of State Robert Lansing encouraged Wilson to have von Papen and Boy-Ed expelled. He wrote, "I feel that we cannot wait much longer to act. . . . The increasing public indignation in regard to these men and the general criticism of the government for allowing them to remain are not the chief reasons for suggesting action in these cases, although I do not think that such reasons should be ignored. We have been over patient with these people."

On December 3, Wilson gave Lansing permission to request that the German government recall von Papen and Boy-Ed. Four days later, Wilson addressed Congress:

"There are citizens of the United States, I blush to admit, born under other flags but welcomed under our generous naturalization laws to the full freedom and opportunity of America, who have poured the poison of disloyalty into the very arteries of our national life; who have sought to bring the authority and good name of our Government into contempt, to destroy our industries wherever they thought it effective for their vindictive purposes to strike at them, and to debase our politics to the uses of foreign intrigue. . . . A little while ago such a thing would have seemed incredible. Because it was incredible we made no preparation for it. We would have been almost ashamed to prepare for it, as if we were suspicious of ourselves, our own comrades and neighbors!

But the ugly and incredible thing has actually come about and we are without adequate federal laws to deal with it. . . . They have formed plots to destroy property, they have entered into conspiracies against the neutrality of the Government, they have sought to pry into every confidential transaction of the government in order to serve interests alien to our own. . . . I urge you to enact such laws at the earliest possible moment and feel that in doing so I am urging you to do nothing less than save the honor and self-respect of the nation. Such creatures of passion, disloyalty, and anarchy must be crushed out."

The day after Wilson's speech, Secretary of State Lansing sent von Bernstorff a letter demanding the men's recall. He wrote, "The relations of the two attachés with individuals who participated in illegal and questionable activities are established." Two days later, on December 10, von Bernstorff told Lansing that von Papen and Boy-Ed had been recalled.

December 13 broke cold, gray, and snowy in New York, effects from a blizzard that had raced east from the Midwest. In ten days, von Papen would be leaving the city with a diplomatic guarantee of safe passage granted by the United States. Before departing, he sent a note to Heinrich Albert, referring to the remaining funds in his account: "I humbly beg you to be good enough to place the sum of $75,337.80 with the Chase National Bank in the name of Wolf von Igel, my assistant." He also bid good-bye to his chief of intelligence, Paul Koenig. The two met at 6:30 p.m. at the German Club on Central Park South. The departing attaché thanked Koenig for running "the bureau," as Koenig called it, and then wished him good luck.

Five days after their meeting, as von Papen prepared to sail safely to Berlin, Koenig was arrested for conducting sabotage. Bail was set at $50,000.

•   •   •

Von Papen was looking forward to the promotion that awaited him upon his return to Berlin. He considered himself innocent, claiming, in a public statement before he left, that he had a "clean record" and denying all "misrepresentations and calumnies." His confidence was bolstered by an authorized statement from the Foreign Office sent to the *New York Times* denying that anyone in the German government "accepted the support of any person seeking to promote the cause of Germany by contravention of law or by any means whatever that could offend the American people."

As his ship sailed into Falmouth, England, members of the British navy came aboard. Although von Papen had been granted safe passage, they said, his luggage had not. Inside his suitcase they found several incriminating documents. One of them was a checkbook showing deposits of more than $3 million from Heinrich Albert. They also found check stubs with the names of suspected German saboteurs listed as the payees. Von Papen was allowed to continue on to Germany, but within months the United States would indict him in absentia for conducting sabotage. He'd never return to face the charges.

In any case, it did not matter that he had been recalled, that von Rintelen was being interrogated by Scotland Yard, or that Koenig had been arrested by the bomb squad. The sabotage network didn't need them anymore. It had moved deeper within the German-American community and farther away from New York, where it would be much harder to find.

Chapter Five

TWENTY-SEVEN-YEAR-OLD German-American Carl Ahrendt had been working with Paul Hilken or his father at the North German Lloyd since he was seventeen. In those ten years, Ahrendt, born in Baltimore to German parents, had risen from lowly clerk to the most trusted confidant of the heir to the shipping line. Ahrendt adored his boss. He had been the first to nickname him the "von Hindenburg of Roland Park" and spent many nights sharing a meal with Hilken's family. Ahrendt never questioned Hilken's orders, always assuming they were in the best interests of the company. The German Lloyd, and by extension Germany, were the only two things that Ahrendt loved as much as he did Hilken, his loyalties to them impossible to separate.

Hilken and Ahrendt were American in citizenship only. They pledged allegiance to Germany first and trusted only those who did the same. As a result, Hilken gave Ahrendt access to his von Rintelen–funded accounts, and he briefed him on every aspect of the operation. He also introduced Ahrendt to Captain Frederick Hinsch, the *Neckar*'s barrel-bellied, ill-tempered skipper, who was busy building a network of spies and saboteurs. Almost instantly, Ahrendt and Hinsch became nearly inseparable. The impressionable Ahrendt sought to emulate Hinsch, a fierce German committed to helping the kaiser through intimidation, force, and secrecy. In the bookish and obsequious Ahrendt, Hinsch saw someone he could easily manipulate. Hilken assigned the two to share an office, with desks facing each other. Eventually, Ahrendt would move into Hinsch's house along the Maryland shore outside Baltimore.

In early January 1916 the German government sent Albert Heinrich $3.2 million, under the pretense that, as commercial attaché, he would use the money to buy food, rubber, and other supplies his country desperately needed. Meanwhile, with some of the money von Papen had left him, Wolf von Igel, the interim military attaché, renewed the lease on his office at 60 Wall Street, home of the War Intelligence Center. The transfer of power was seamless. Between January 10 and 15, three DuPont plants that manufactured explosive powder suffered heavy damage from serious fires. Later that month, the British ships the SS *Sygna* and SS *Ryndam* exploded at sea, and two undetonated bombs were found on the SS *Rosebank*.

But von Igel had less impact as a spymaster than his predecessor. Although he had Albert's cash to work with, the agents developed by Koenig and von Papen were difficult to find. The network they had built partially disbanded when the duo's work became public. Von Igel, under constant surveillance by Secret Service agents and the New York bomb squad, could not rebuild without making himself a target.

Thus the Germans needed Hilken and Hinsch badly. The two men from Baltimore were unknown to Tunney and his officers and to anyone trolling the docks. The Germans moved their base of operations from von Igel's War Intelligence Center at 60 Wall Street to the Whitehall Building, farther downtown and farther west, where the German Lloyd had a New York office. Twenty stories high, located where West Street met Battery Park at the southernmost tip of Manhattan, the sixteen-year-old Whitehall was among the largest office buildings in New York. Facing south toward the Statue of Liberty, it had clear, unobstructed views of the harbor. Even the offices nearly at the top of the building could hear the bustle of West Street fifteen stories below.

The German Lloyd's New York office was run by a German named Paul Hoppenburg. He weighed three hundred pounds, had hands as big as bear paws, and had a jovial laugh that came from deep in his gut. He liked to joke with Hilken and Hinsch when they visited him at his Whitehall office, teasing them in German. They would share a drink, gaze out at the harbor, talk about their allegiance to Germany, and formulate plans of attack. Unlike von Igel, Hinsch had no trouble finding volunteers for his missions.

While interned German sailors, German diplomats, and their privileged sympathizers spent their evenings enjoying the party at Martha Held's, working-class, first- and second-generation German-Americans gathered in Yorkville. Snug along the river, Yorkville felt like Berlin or Munich. German sausage shops lined the streets; German newspapers were sold at newsstands. At the Café Bismarck on 86th Street, the locals celebrated German victories on the European front with Rhine wine. The pubs served large steins of cheap brew, and the more men drank, the rowdier they became about the war. Few debated the issues; instead they railed against their sworn enemies, the British and the French. They hated America, too, for being too frightened to join the fray. They wished they could go and fight themselves.

There were little pockets of protest like this all over the city. Another was located at Penn Station, on 33rd Street and Seventh Avenue. Modeled on the ancient Roman baths, the elegant granite and marble station stretched over nine acres, from just west of midtown Manhattan toward the piers along the Hudson. The entrance to the station was protected by fifty-three-foot-tall, pink Doric columns, and because the building was so big, the three-ton stone eagles at the top looked as small as pigeons perched on a windowsill. Light poured into the station through glass-topped vaulted ceilings. For many immigrants, this was their last view of

New York before leaving for points west in search of work or family. In 1916, Penn Station was just six years old, but it had become the busiest train depot in the world.

The blocks surrounding Penn Station were crowded with merchants selling liquor, newspapers, soap, and just about anything else someone in a hurry to get out of town or overwhelmed upon his arrival would need. The air smelled of fresh sausages, beef, and chickens being cooked over hot coals and roaring flames, and the ground was cluttered with waste. The whole of Europe was represented on these blocks, where newly minted Americans congregated to share a taste of their homeland.

At a line of German carts, over bratwursts and schnitzel, German-Americans and German immigrants loudly and angrily protested American neutrality and bashed President Wilson. This was a popular spot for dockhands who worked at the nearby piers to gather. Older men, past their working days, and unemployed day laborers, desperate for work, came here looking for companionship as well. Frederick Hinsch came often, listening for the angriest voices. Among them was Michael Kristoff, a twenty-three-year-old Austrian immigrant who often found himself out of work, drifting from a boardinghouse to an aunt's home near Jersey City to the street. The threadbare clothes he usually wore hung on his gaunt six-foot three-inch, 147-pound frame. A long-billed beret covered his flaming red hair and pale blue eyes, and on sunny days, it cast a shadow over his perpetually ruddy cheeks and reddish brown mustache. His soft chin sloped toward his neck, seeming to pull his whole head down when he spoke. Slow-witted and gullible, Kristoff habitually repeated other people's arguments as his own. When Hinsch first saw Kristoff hanging around Penn Station, he felt that the man was malleable, eager, and, perhaps most important, needy.

In January 1916, Kristoff packed a bag and made his way to Penn Station, where he would catch a train to Columbus, Ohio, to stay with his sister. He hadn't worked in weeks and had been kicked out of his boardinghouse for not paying the rent. With no job prospects, he had nowhere else to go.

As always, the station was bustling, with new arrivals to New York coming within steps of those who had had enough of it. Sometimes they collided, as people absentmindedly checked for their trains, were blinded by the sunlight streaming through the ceiling, or were just too tired to get out of the way. While waiting for his train, Kristoff noticed a tall man, carrying a lot of weight in his middle, walking briskly toward him. Up until the moment the man stopped, his pinhole blue eyes focused on Kristoff's face, Kristoff thought that the man would walk right through him.

Frederick Hinsch asked Kristoff, "Do you know what time it is?" He knew that Kristoff wouldn't be able to answer—he had observed that Kristoff did not have a watch.

"No," Kristoff answered, disarmed by Hinsch's thick German accent. He asked Hinsch where he was from, and then the two began discussing the war—how frustrated they were to be stuck in America, how much they detested Wilson, and how they wished there was something they could do to contribute. After a few minutes, Hinsch asked Kristoff where he was headed. He listened as Kristoff explained that he was broke, had no job, had no place to live, and was going to visit his sister. Then Hinsch offered Kristoff an alternative. He introduced himself as Francis Graentnor, a businessman and engineer who was going on an extended trip. He needed someone to carry his bags, watch his possessions when he was staying in strange hotels, and be a companion to him. Hinsch told Kristoff that he would pay him twenty dollars a week and that he could help Kristoff get a factory job when they returned from the trip. Kristoff didn't hesitate to accept.

The men began their trip in Philadelphia in early February. Hinsch would leave the hotel early each morning with one of his briefcases. Inside were blueprints of munitions factories and wads of cash. Kristoff would rarely leave the hotel, preferring to stay and mind the rest of Hinsch's belongings. Hinsch had warned him against looking inside the briefcases, fixing upon the feeble Kristoff his most menacing gaze. Kristoff did as he was told.

While they were in Philadelphia, Hinsch disappeared for several days in a row. During that time, the Bethlehem Projectile plant, about seventy miles from the city, was destroyed. Then they moved on to Bridgeport, Connecticut, where the routine was the same: Kristoff waited in the hotel, Hinsch disappeared with one of the briefcases, and there was an explosion at the Bridgeport plant of the Union Metallic Cartridge Company. They went to St. Louis and Detroit, where again Hinsch disappeared for a few days. While he was gone, a large chemical plant in Cadillac, Michigan, less than two hundred miles northwest of Detroit, was destroyed. And then it was on to Chicago and Cleveland and Akron, as they traveled by train through the heart of the Midwest.

One night in Columbus, Ohio, Kristoff could no longer resist looking in one of the briefcases. Inside he saw the blueprints of factories, sketches of bridges, and cash. As he began to search another briefcase, Hinsch walked into the room. He was furious. He wanted to hit Kristoff, but he refrained, perhaps chastened by the way Kristoff recoiled in the face of the threat. Whatever Kristoff knew, he'd be too scared to repeat. The trip ended soon after that.

When the men returned to New York in March, Kristoff paid his aunt, Anne Rushnak, three months rent in advance for a room in her Bayonne, New Jersey, home. Hinsch, with the help of a bribe, found him a job at the Eagle Iron Works forging metal. The factory was in Jersey City, which bordered Bayonne. When he reported for work, Kristoff had no idea that his new employer was on the same stretch of road as New York Harbor's largest munitions depot, Black Tom Island.

The instructions, sent in January 1916, were vague: be in Berlin by February to discuss the use of merchant U-boats in the United States. But to Paul Hilken, they came as a relief.

Hilken's only contact with the German government had been through von Rintelen, and he had heard nothing since von Rintelen had been expelled from the country. He continued to build the Baltimore-based spy network, distributing the vast amount of money von Rintelen had left him and regularly meeting with Hinsch in Baltimore and Hoppenburg in New York. This was the only way he knew to prove his commitment to the kaiser. It was an act of desperation by a man who was worried about his future. With the work of the German Lloyd suspended, he had nothing else to do.

Eighteen months into the war, the Germans were still devising innovative strategies to beat the advancing Allies. Because of the *Lusitania* disaster, the whole world knew of the power of the German submarines. In addition, on January 29, 1916, German zeppelins air-bombed Paris. But such innovations were insufficient; the Germans needed raw materials such as rubber, gunpowder, and coal, as well as food, fertilizer, and manpower. Most able-bodied farmers were fighting in France and Russia, and German agricultural production had dropped almost 30 percent, with nearly eight hundred Germans dying each day from starvation. Women desperate to feed their families fought in the stores over a single egg or potato. Food riots were common, with the kaiser's army often being dispatched to haul away the most violent offenders, who were then sent to the front. German citizens gathered in the plaza of the Reichstag to protest the war. Gray and forbidding, the Reichstag was home to the German parliament, war offices, and publicity and censorship departments. More than the kaiser's palace, it had become the symbol of German power. But to those protesting, it was also a symbol of waste and corruption.

Even so, as Hilken entered the Reichstag, he couldn't help but feel proud. The foyer was suffused with light—an ethereal glow created by the sun streaming through the glass and steel dome atop the center of the building. He had been called by the highest authority in Germany. This is what he'd wanted from the moment he'd met von Rintelen: a chance to prove his loyalty and his worth to the kaiser.

Hilken's first meeting on February 18, 1916, was with a lieutenant in the raw materials office of the war department. The Germans wanted Hilken to arrange for the procurement of goods such as rubber, oil, and grain; to find a staff to load and guard a submarine that would secretly smuggle the stash back to Germany; and to handle the money needed to run this operation. As they spoke, von Papen "dropped in to say, 'How do you do?'" said Hilken many years later. The two knew each other from von Papen's years in the United States. As they finished catching up, either von Papen or the lieutenant, Hilken never remembered which one, suggested that Hilken go to the other side of the Reichstag and visit the Sektion Politik, aka Section III-B, a branch of the German secret service. Years later, Hilken said, "The thought came up that I, being in charge of the U-boat services, might also act as banker for all of their agents in America."

In the Section III-B offices Hilken met two men. The first, Hans Marguerre, was a major in the German army who had been injured fighting on the front lines just weeks into the war. After a two-month recuperation, he had been assigned to Section III-B, where, he once said, his job was to "organize, prepare and carry through actions against establishments essential for war and situated in countries at war with us. To ascertain, through our agents whom we had inside, sites of ammunition plants, arms and powder factories, chemical plants. . . . These data were collected by us for the purpose of having essential establishments in belligerent countries attacked by our agents."

Marguerre reported to Captain Rudolf Nadolny, the acting General Staff of Section III-B and the second man Hilken met in the III-B offices. Neither Marguerre nor Nadolny acted surprised to see the American. As Hilken said years later, "They undoubtedly had been informed of my coming." The men were friendly, if not obsequious, telling Hilken how valuable he could be to them and to Germany. Their words flattered and reassured him, filling him with confidence.

Fred Herrmann and Anton Dilger arrived at the Section III-B offices together in February 1916, both of them cocksure, fair-haired, and dashing. Herrmann was the younger and more daring of the two. He was just twenty years old, the son of a first-generation German-American father and a second-generation German-American mother. Tall and slender, the blond-haired Brooklyn native had already spent more than a year working for the German secret service by 1916. He had more aliases, twenty-one, than he had years on earth.

Herrmann had become a spy by chance. In January 1915, while sailing on a Dutch steamer from New York to Holland to visit his grandmother in Bederkesa, Germany, he had met a German named William Kottkamp. Transatlantic cruises were long trips, and passengers were entertained with formal evenings centered on decadent dinners and plenty of drink. The war was always a topic of debate, and casual acquaintances often became close friends as they bonded over shared loyalties. After one too many late nights, Kottkamp told his new friend that he worked for the German secret service. He recounted stories of adventures in the United States that were full of intrigue and danger. When the ship docked in Holland, the two men went their separate ways, but shortly after arriving at his grandmother's in Bederkesa, Herrmann received a wire from Kottkamp asking him to come to Berlin. The Germans, he learned when he got there, wanted him to be a spy. He accepted their offer, he said, "just for kicks."

Herrmann's first assignment was in England. Using an emergency passport issued by the United States, given under the pretext that he'd be working for a textile company, Herrmann spent June, July, and August 1915 monitoring the British fleet as it left the English coast. He returned to Germany briefly, then traveled to Scotland, where he enrolled at Edinburgh University as a forestry student. Herrmann spent most of his days monitoring the ships sailing down the Firth of Forth, an estuary that connects with the North Sea. By December of that year, his interest in departing British ships had begun to draw suspicion from Scotland Yard detectives. All of Great Britain was on high alert for foreigners who acted strangely, and unlike Wilson, the British wasted no time in dispatching anyone they thought posed a threat. Before Christmas, Herrmann was expelled from Scotland and sent back to New

York. He was there a little more than a week before being called to Berlin for a meeting at Section III-B.

Herrmann boarded a ship headed for Norway. During the long voyage, he met a young doctor from outside Washington, D.C., named Anton Dilger. Herrmann never revealed the purpose of his trip; Dilger was equally cagey. Once in Norway, each man separately boarded a train headed south through Denmark and then on to Germany. During a stopover in Copenhagen, Herrmann checked in at the Danish branch of Germany's naval intelligence office. Standing in the doorway was Dilger. Like Herrmann, the doctor was a spy, headed to Berlin for a meeting at the Foreign Office. They spent the night in Copenhagen, laughing about how clever they had been in concealing their identities on the trip from New York.

The next morning, they boarded a train for Berlin. Watching the snow-covered fields zip by, the thirty-two-year-old Dilger found his fellow agent charming. Herrmann didn't seem like a German loyalist so much as a young man in it for the adventure. He told Dilger stories about growing up in Brooklyn with three brothers, and he recalled times while working in England that his cover had been nearly blown. Herrmann laughed everything off, as if getting caught for spying would incur no worse a punishment than if he were caught stealing a gumball.

Dilger was much more serious. The son of a German immigrant who had fought with distinction for the Union army during the Civil War, Dilger had been born in Virginia in 1884. He'd attended Johns Hopkins medical school and then, looking to learn more about his German heritage, continued studying medicine at the University of Heidelberg in Germany, specializing in surgery. When the Balkan Wars broke out in 1912, he volunteered to work in the Red Cross for the Bulgarian army.

When World War I began, Dilger was back in Germany. Like his father, who had joined the Union army out of a sense of loyalty to his new country, Dilger felt that it was his duty to offer his services to the kaiser. For a short time, he headed the surgical section of the military hospital in Karlsruhe. Early in 1915, however, he returned home to Front Royal, Virginia. He told his parents that he needed to recuperate from the trauma he had seen, explaining that he had been on duty when a French plane bombed a nearby German church full of children. Dilger vividly described how he had helped carry the wounded and the dead back to the hospital.

It was all a cover story, which Dilger's brother, Carl, helped him pull off. Taking advantage of Dilger's status as an American, the Germans had sent him back to the United States to advance their sabotage efforts. In his trunk, he had packed cultures of various toxic germs. His targets were livestock, such as the horses and mules being sent to the British and French troops in Europe. Dilger cultivated a stockpile of the bacteria that cause anthrax and glanders, which is particularly lethal to horses, in a house Carl rented in Chevy Chase, Maryland, less than ten miles from Washington, D.C. The Germans nicknamed the house "Tony's Lab." Throughout 1915, Dilger supplied von Rintelen, Koenig, and Hinsch with the bacteria, which could be put in needles, then injected into horses by dockhands loading the animals onto ships or simply dropped into the animals' food and water.

Dilger's operation had been efficient and undetected. As a result, Marguerre and Nadolny had summoned him back to Section III-B. They had another plot in mind.

Hilken knew Dilger from their work on the East Coast, but Herrmann needed an introduction. Marguerre told Hilken that Herrmann had been working for the German navy's secret service and was being transferred to Section III-B. It would be Hilken's job to pay Herrmann from a $50,000 fund to be deposited in accounts at the Corn Exchange Bank, Baltimore Trust Company, Guaranty Trust, and Continental Bank. Marguerre emphasized that Herrmann reported to no one. He should never be denied an advance, and he could use the funds any way he pleased, without any accounting.

Then Marguerre turned to Herrmann. The young spy looked confident, eager, and willing. Marguerre instructed him to identify every U.S. munitions plant or factory that was supplying the Allies. He wanted to know how well guarded these establishments were, their accessibility, and, most important, the possibilities for attacking them. Every plant had its weak point, Marguerre told him. Herrmann would be responsible for finding his own help, or he could consult Hinsch in the United States.

Herrmann listened as Marguerre continued with his instructions. "I told him we had to be prepared for all possibilities," Marguerre said later, "and elaborated in great detail that the preparation should advance so far that sabotage against the establishments essential for war could be started immediately." Marguerre noticed the color rising in Herrmann's boyish face and thought that he was "flush with enthusiasm."

After a long pause, Herrmann responded simply, "Yes, everything will go into the air."

Once he had laid out his plan, Marguerre reached underneath his desk and pulled out a crate filled with what appeared to be blue, green, and red colored pencils. Herrmann remembered them looking "like crayons." There were thirty in the box. For nearly a year, German saboteurs in the United States had been using Walter Scheele's cigar bombs to ignite fires on boats and at munitions plants. Hilken and Dilger were familiar with Scheele's small lead cylinders, but no one had ever seen these "pencils" before. The outer shell was made of thick colored glass. Inside were the same chemical-filled compartments used in Scheele's cigars. Marguerre called these pencils "glasses" and explained that the Germans had improved on Scheele's design out of necessity. So many cigars had been discovered undetonated that the police, the U.S. Secret Service, and even some dockhands knew what they were when they saw them. The new bombs would be more effective.

Marguerre pulled out another crate, showing the men sixty glasses in all, and explained that production was now done in Germany. Herrmann didn't believe that the glasses could be so potent, but Hilken assured him that if they were anything like the cigars, they would be powerful. Hinsch had built a capable network and was introducing his men into factories all over the country, Hilken said. Already they had destroyed DuPont plants in New Jersey and Delaware and a factory in Pennsylvania. From these little tubes would come great destruction.

Marguerre gave the two cases to Herrmann, who later recalled, "He told me to take these tubes and go to the United States and upon my arrival start immediately using these tubes for the destruction of munitions plants, ships, piers, anything to do with the shipping of supplies to the Allies." During the entire meeting, Marguerre was concise and calm in his directions, while Nadolny said nothing. The next day, Herrmann left Germany with a false-bottomed trunk containing the glasses.

Back in Baltimore, in March 1916, Hinsch anxiously awaited Hilken's return. The two would have much to talk about. Hinsch needed more money and supplies and hoped that Hilken would come back from Berlin with both. One afternoon, while Hinsch was working on the *Neckar* in Baltimore Harbor, one of Hilken's employees told the captain that Hilken was back and that he wanted to see Hinsch. The German Lloyd offices were in a building called the Hansa Haus, just a short distance from the piers. "I took my car with which I had come to the pier in the morning and drove at once to the office," Hinsch said years later.

The Hansa Haus was a quaint, three-story, gingerbread building with a shingled roof on the corner of Charles and Redwood streets. Built in the middle of a growing city, it was modeled after a seventeenth-century German courthouse and decorated with thirty-seven plaques, representing the German and Baltic cities served by the German Lloyd. Hilken had a private study in the attic. When Hinsch arrived at the building, he walked up the three flights of stairs and opened the door. The curtains were open, but the late-afternoon sun wasn't high enough to light the room, and shadows crossed the floor at a low angle. Inside, Hilken was waiting, alone.

Hilken told Hinsch that the Germans were building six submarines with the intention of sailing for America. They would have neither armaments nor a naval crew, which would help them pass through a British blockade inspection if they were spotted. Once docked in Baltimore, the subs would be loaded with nickel, tin, and rubber before sneaking back to Germany under cover of the sea.

Hilken then explained that Hinsch would have to find a tugboat, as well as a pier to accommodate the submarines. He'd be responsible for supervising the loading and unloading of the subs, as well as their protection at night. Meanwhile, Hilken would find and buy the raw materials Germany needed. Because of the restrictions placed on German companies owning or operating boats in the harbor, Hilken would set up the Eastern Forwarding Company, an American business of which he'd be president. The Germans would give them $50,000 to help finance this new venture.

For the first several minutes of their meeting, Hilken avoided the topic of sabotage, instead emphasizing the importance of these submarine runs. But Hinsch understood force and violence. Sure, he'd find a pier for the subs, protect them, and do the grunt work to fill them with supplies. But what he really wanted to know was how the sabotage operation would move forward.

"During these next few days somebody named Herrmann is coming from the General Staff," Hilken told him. "An alert young fellow who has been spying three times in England. He also brings new things along."

Before calling on Hilken, Herrmann visited Anton Dilger, with whom he had now become very close, at what the *Washington Star* reported was "an innocent looking house in the quiet and dignified residential section near the Chevy Chase Country Club." Inside, Dilger was cooking up anthrax and glanders cultures for distribution to dockworkers hired by Hinsch. The procedure seemed relatively simple. Dilger filled small glass bottles, each about two inches long, with bacteria. He stuck the dull end of an inch-long, hollow steel needle into the bottom of a cork and then used the cork as a stopper in the bottle. The hollow needle rested in the liquid.

Herrmann toured Tony's Lab, making a mental checklist of what he saw. The shelves were stocked with cultures, needles, corks, and bottles. But there was also a stockpile of sugar, sulfuric acid, and chloride of potassium—all the ingredients he'd been told he needed to fill his glasses. The lab had become an all-purpose sabotage warehouse.

When the two had roomed together in Berlin, Herrmann had grown to admire Dilger's brilliance, his commitment to the kaiser, and his daring, the quality Herrmann identified most easily with. But walking around the lab, he was humbled by Dilger's accomplishment—and his nerve. Von Papen, Boy-Ed, and von Rintelen had all been kicked out of the United States or recalled by the Germans. Prejudice against Germans, from the press and the government, was at its height. For his lab, Dilger could have chosen someplace near his home in Virginia or in Baltimore, where Hilken would have given him a cover story. But instead he had settled on a part of Washington, D.C., that was popular with congressmen, senators, and government bureaucrats and was just a few miles from where President Wilson slept. "He thought the nearer they got to the center," Herrmann said years later, "the less suspicion there would be."

Even with his detour through Chevy Chase, Herrmann beat Hilken to Baltimore by several days. While awaiting Hilken's arrival, Herrmann stayed at the Hotel Emerson, one of the most regal and ornate lodgings in the city. He spent his days wandering around the harbor, keeping to himself, speaking with no one except the German Lloyd staff at the Hansa Haus, and then only to ask if Hilken had returned.

One late-March morning, Herrmann headed to Hilken's office. Spring had yet to arrive, and a wet, cold breeze swept off the harbor. Herrmann pulled up the collar of his overcoat to cover the back of his neck and cinched the front tight around his thin body. As he opened the Hansa Haus door, he recognized Hilken standing in the front office. They shook hands, greeting each other with a familiarity born of sharing a secret. Hilken told one of his staff to find Hinsch and bring him back to the office immediately.

"Let's go upstairs," Hilken said to Herrmann.

Almost as soon as they'd reached the attic, Hinsch came sprinting up the stairs behind them. His breath was heavy, his thick chest and belly heaving as a result of his having run from the piers. Herrmann and Hinsch were an odd match. Hinsch appeared to be twice the width and depth of his counterpart. While one could glide through a crowd unnoticed, the other would divide it.

"Well, here is Herrmann from the General Staff," Hilken said to Hinsch.

"Have you told him?" Herrmann asked his new paymaster.

"I have told Hinsch about our instructions and so forth and he is to go on, keep right on doing what he is doing," Hilken answered.

"What's that exactly?" Herrmann asked.

Hilken didn't know that Herrmann had been to Tony's Lab, so he explained how Hinsch's men had been injecting horses and mules headed for the front with anthrax and glanders bacteria. He then let Hinsch expand on the sabotage missions. They discussed the cigar bombs they had been using, as well as another crude explosive called a "dumpling," made to look like a lump of coal, which Hinsch had been manufacturing at his house.

Then Herrmann put his briefcase on a table. Inside were two boxes, each about three inches wide, three inches long, and one inch deep. Both were heavily wrapped in brown tissue paper. He pulled one box out of his briefcase, unwrapped it, and opened the lid. The glasses were in tightly packed rows; there were close to thirty in the box. "I gave about half to Hinsch, who then gave them right back to me and told me to prepare them," Herrmann said years later. Having seen the sulfuric acid, chloride of potassium, and sugar at Dilger's house, he knew that Hinsch meant he should return to Tony's Lab.

Hinsch then handed Hilken a piece of paper. On it was a list of powder plants, screw works, and munitions depots. Black Tom

Island was included under its official title, Jersey City Terminal, as was a plant in Kingsland, New Jersey. There were close to twenty entries on the page, plus a separate listing of cities from which horses and mules were being shipped. Hinsch told Herrmann to look over the list and pick out the places he thought he could handle on his own, then put a check by them. Herrmann handed the list back to Hinsch and said, "I'll see what is up at these places and you see what is up at the others."

He left the space next to Black Tom blank. "That was Hinsch's," Herrmann said. "I had to leave him something."

Chapter Six

HINSCH AND HILKEN spent the spring of 1916 establishing the Eastern Forwarding Company and preparing for the arrival of the German submarines. These boats fascinated, and frightened, the world. They were stealthy killing machines, picking off Allied ships from underwater with no warning. In the Atlantic Ocean and North Sea around the British Isles, the Germans had twenty-one subs on patrol, and between February and September 1915, they had torpedoed and sunk fifty enemy boats. The waters between the United States and Europe were increasingly dangerous. Rumors of submarines heading for the United States sent newspaper reporters scrambling for the coast, watching for something they weren't sure they would even recognize. One report in Baltimore claimed that a sub was already hidden in the harbor. When local newspapermen walked the piers, asking German sailors for tips and leads about any newly interned vessels, Hinsch would whisper in their ears about numerous submarines en route from Germany. His plan, like Dilger's, was to hide in plain sight and thus be ignored. And that's exactly what he was doing.

•   •   •

Hinsch's initial purchase was a tugboat, a weather-beaten craft called the *Thomas F. Timmins,* with a motor that could barely whimper. He overhauled the engine, added an electric searchlight to the roof of its steering house, and made it strong and reliable enough to pull a German submarine into port.

On the piers that Hilken had rented under the name of the Eastern Forwarding Company, Hinsch's men enlarged the enclosures; dredged the channel leading to the ocean, adding thirty feet of depth; and surrounded the piers with heavy beams and barbed wire. There was only one entrance to the piers, so watchmen could control who entered.

Meanwhile, Hilken and Hinsch both made frequent trips to New York. There Hilken would visit with the jolly Hoppenburg at the German Lloyd's office to find out where he could buy the nickel, rubber, and tin to be transported in the subs. Hinsch would go to the Hotel McAlpin, a favorite German haunt on 34th Street and Broadway, checking in as Francis Graentnor, the alias he'd given Kristoff, who still knew him only by that name.

One afternoon in June, Hinsch, referring to himself as Graentnor, called Kristoff and asked him to come to the lobby of the hotel. The two men spoke briefly just inside the doors before walking to Hinsch's room. Once inside, Hinsch showed the poor factory worker a suitcase containing $5,000. Hinsch explained why he had carried those drawings, maps, and photos all over the country during their trip, admitting that he had hired men to blow up factories and set fire to ships. Then he told Kristoff that he had bigger plans.

Hinsch quickly fired a series of questions at Kristoff, barely giving him a chance to speak. Was he still working at the Eagle Iron Works? Did guards at the gate know who he was? Could he come and go as he pleased, or did people question why he was there? How often was he paid? How secure was the area? Kristoff became agitated by his inability to answer one question before Hinsch asked the next.

As Kristoff's frustration grew, Hinsch told him about the munitions depot at Black Tom. Hinsch knew how Kristoff felt about the war, and he knew that hearing about munitions being shipped right under his nose would further infuriate him. Hinsch told Kristoff that they could make it all disappear, that they could save German lives. He pulled $500 from the suitcase and spread it out in his thick fingers. Kristoff could have it, Hinsch told him, if he helped blow up Black Tom Island. Kristoff agreed. "This will be the best thing to stop the war," he said.

Hinsch knew that Kristoff would need help. The guards at Black Tom left the yard virtually unprotected because they were still on the German payroll. But since the expulsion of von Papen and the arrest of Koenig, the U.S. Secret Service and the local police had developed lengthy dossiers on likely German spies. German sailors who spent a lot of time around the harbor were under heavy surveillance. They could observe what was happening but not act out. Any help Hilken and Hinsch needed would have to come from outside New York.

In February 1916, Kurt Jahnke walked into the San Francisco branch of the U.S. Secret Service and offered himself up as a spy. He was five foot eleven, weighed 165 pounds, and had a small brown mustache that made him look distinguished beyond his thirty-four years. His two front teeth flashed with gold. Although he had moved to the United States from Germany several years earlier, had become a naturalized citizen, and even had spent time as a U.S. marine, he still spoke English with a distinctly German accent. A coworker at the Morse Detective Agency, a firm that supplied security guards, described him as "a charming gentleman. A man of the world."

Those traits were an asset when it came to espionage. Jahnke told the government agents that as a German, he could easily strike up an acquaintance with his country's consul in San Francisco. There had been a huge explosion in November at a San Francisco factory that was allegedly manufacturing munitions. Perhaps, Jahnke told them, he could be useful in tracking down clues. As proof of his willingness to spy on his countrymen, Jahnke told the agents about a plot to blow up the Mare Island Navy Yard, just thirty miles northeast of the city.

The agents listened in stunned disbelief. The man who just walked into their office and offered to help investigate an alleged case of sabotage was in fact the same man they suspected of blowing up the factory. As they understood things, Jahnke was one of the most clever German spies on the West Coast and the German consul's most trusted aide. Secret Service agents in San Francisco had been trailing him for weeks, talking to coworkers at the detective agency, checking his alibis. No one could ever place Jahnke at the jobs listed on his time card, but the Secret Service had found no evidence against him.

Jahnke knew all this and, short of disappearing, felt that his best option for thwarting their investigation was throwing them off balance. In fact, by brazenly walking into their office and announcing himself, he was following what had become standard protocol for German spies. A British intelligence officer during World War I once noted, "Calculating that a bold action would best divert suspicions, German agents were instructed how to act in the manner best designed to convince those watching them of their loyalty. The most popular plan was for the spy who felt that he had incurred suspicion to march boldly into the headquarters of the enemy and volunteer for service in their interests."

Met with hesitation, Jahnke walked out of the office. It was the closest the San Francisco agents ever came to him.

One of Jahnke's protégés was a twenty-year-old former lieutenant in the German navy named Lothar Witzke. Witzke was serving aboard the *Dresden* off the coast of Chile in late 1915 when his ship became engaged in a fierce battle with the Royal Navy. The *Dresden* was sunk, but Witzke survived, swimming, wading, and floating his way to Valparaiso with a broken leg. He spent two months recuperating, then escaped from South America on a steamer headed for Mexico City. From there, he hopped trains going north, finally settling in San Francisco. He immediately reported to the German consul, who put him under Jahnke's command.

Witzke, boyishly handsome with wavy, light brown hair, observed ship movements in San Francisco and made notes of what they were carrying and what they were made of. He worked for a chemist in Berkeley, learning how to mix highly combustible materials without blowing himself up. He cased factories that manufactured shells. He didn't look like a threat, was enthusiastic, and was dedicated to Jahnke, who believed in him.

At 6:00 a.m. on June 23, a crew assembled by Hinsch pointed the *Timmins* east toward the rising sun, then due south through the Chesapeake Bay. A storm was coming from the west, and it cooled the air, keeping the temperature in the low fifties, requiring the sailors to stay bundled in their wool coats. For sixteen days, a U-boat had been roaming the ocean. Unbeknownst to most of the men on the *Timmins,* they were about to rendezvous with it.

At 315 feet long, 30 feet wide, and 17 feet high, the *Deutschland* was the biggest submarine in the German fleet. It cruised at fourteen knots, carried a crew of twenty-nine men and two 600-horsepower diesel engines, and could fully submerge in ninety seconds. In the months after the sinking of the *Lusitania,* Americans had developed a paranoid fear of submarines. Underwater craft were not a new invention, but the widespread use of these dangerous vessels in war signaled a shift in the previously gentlemanly rules of engagement: U-boats didn't have the crew to rescue enemy seamen from sinking boats, nor did they have the space to house them. Once considered too inefficient for war, submarines were now quite the opposite: they guaranteed the destruction of everything in their path. And while the Germans hadn't built enough submarines to make a dent in the British fleet's blockade, they knew how to use what they had to their advantage.

Hinsch joined the *Timmins* in Norfolk, Virginia. He knew only that the *Deutschland* was scheduled to leave for the United States in June, but communication between Berlin and Hilken had slowed down that month, with both sides fearing that too much talk of a German sub headed for the United States, even if it was in coded language, was risky.

At noon on June 24, Hinsch captained the *Timmins* ten miles into the Atlantic, then announced the mission to his crew: they were on the lookout for a German submarine that had instructions to dock in Norfolk. They'd search as long and as far as daylight would allow. The first man to spot the sub would receive ten dollars.

The *Timmins* patrolled the ocean off Norfolk for three days before its coal supply ran low. There was no sign of the *Deutschland,* and when the boat pulled into the harbor to refuel, Hinsch called Hilken for an update. Hilken had heard nothing. To save fuel, and thus avoid heading back to the harbor every few days, Hinsch decided that the *Timmins* would search for an hour, anchor for an hour, and then search for an hour. For the next sixteen days, that was the routine, with the *Timmins* returning to Norfolk for fuel only twice.

At 1:00 a.m. on July 9, the *Timmins* was cruising off the coast of Cape Henry, the southernmost entrance to the Chesapeake Bay, just seventeen miles east of Norfolk. As Hinsch settled onto a bench in the *Timmins*'s rudder house for a nap, he heard a rustling on the bridge. Beneath a starlit summer sky, it was impossible not to see the top of the massive submarine just breaking the plane of the ocean. "We saw a long body with bright electric lights," Hinsch said.

Hinsch steered the *Timmins* as close to the *Deutschland* as possible. Even partially submerged, the U-boat dwarfed the tug, making it look no bigger than a lifeboat attached to the submarine's side. From the deck of his barge, Hinsch could see a man standing on the bridge of the sub, peering through a long spyglass. He called out to him in German, and the captain responded through a megaphone, "Is that you, Captain Hinsch?" Hinsch told him it was. The two crews let out a cheer and shook hands as some of the Germans boarded the *Timmins*. The captain of the sub was named Paul Koenig (not the same man who ran the War Intelligence Center for von Papen). He explained that the *Deutschland* had been submerged while traveling through the North Sea and then had risen for the Atlantic crossing. Two-thirds of the way across the ocean, a Dutch merchant ship had forced the U-boat to submerge again. Finally, six hundred miles from Virginia, an enemy warship had scared Koenig into taking the sub down one more time. Hinsch congratulated him for making it past the blockade and then apologized, explaining that, after Koenig and his men had endured such a long trip, the plans were being changed: the *Deutschland* was no longer headed for Norfolk; it should follow the *Timmins* up the coast, where it would eventually dock in Baltimore.

The two boats traveled in a slow crawl up the coast of Virginia. At Old Point Comfort, just twelve miles north of Norfolk, Hinsch instructed the *Deutschland* to anchor offshore and wait while he docked his tug. The *Timmins* needed four hours to refuel for the trip back to Baltimore. Hinsch also needed to let Hilken know that he had found the sub. As the *Timmins* pulled into Old Point Comfort, Hinsch wrote a note and handed it to a member of his crew. He instructed the man to find a phone and call Hilken immediately. The note read, "I caught the fish."

When the *Timmins* rejoined the *Deutschland* several miles offshore, Hinsch recognized a U.S. Coast Guard cutter, which had been on a standard patrol, floating next to the sub. There was nothing Hinsch or Koenig could do; the element of surprise was lost.

At 3:45 p.m. on July 9, the trio of ships, with the *Timmins* in front and the *Deutschland* close behind, snaked past Maryland's Cove Point Lighthouse. A government observer called the *Baltimore Sun,* notifying an editor that he had just seen what could only be a German submarine sailing up the Chesapeake Bay at a speed fast enough to put it in Baltimore Harbor, approximately sixty-five nautical miles away, sometime in the evening.

As the *Deutschland* neared Baltimore, battling sheets of rain, the sub cut through the whitecaps churning in the bay. The press waited on chartered ships and yachts. Steamers trained their searchlights on the German craft, making its dark hull stand out in the blackness of the stormy night. The sub was almost completely out of the water, with eight feet of its rounded sides showing. The word DEUTSCHLAND was painted on each side of the bow, while the stern read, DEUTSCHLAND, BREMEN. As the sub entered the bay, the crew of the *Deutschland,* most of them wearing oilskins, gathered on the narrow deck. The only man who looked dressed for an evening out was Captain Koenig. A small, stocky man, he wore a white cap, a blue coat, and white pants. He didn't seem to notice the rain that was pelting his face.

An Associated Press reporter riding in a yacht sailed up to Koenig as he led the *Deutschland* into the bay.

"Hello, *Deutschland,*" the reporter screamed above the storm.

"Hello. What do you want? Who are you?" Koenig replied in a sharp tone.

"Where do you come from and when?"

"June 23. Helgoland."

"Did you have any accidents coming over?"

"None."

"Did you see any British or French ships?"

"None."

"Were you chased by any British or French vessels near the coast?"

"No," Koenig answered angrily, adding, "I said I didn't see any enemy ships." The *Deutschland* then sped away, shooting sparks from its exhaust.

As the *Deutschland* docked and drew the breathless attention of America's major newspapers, Kurt Jahnke and Lothar Witzke got off a train at Penn Station. They traveled north to a residence hotel at 100 West 56th Street. Shortly after they unpacked their bags, they headed downtown to the harbor.

After spending the night anchored at a quarantine station, the *Deutschland* finally settled in at a pier at Fort McHenry, where Francis Scott Key had written "The Star-Spangled Banner." Hinsch had crafted a near-impervious border to protect the submarine. On one side of the ship was the pier itself, whose entrance was blocked by barbed wire and guarded by a sentry. The back of the sub was shielded by five barges, with the open spaces between them closed off by sheets of canvas. And on the other side was Hinsch's *Neckar*. The view of the *Deutschland* was blocked from all sides. Hinsch wasn't just keeping reporters away; he was also trying to frustrate the U.S. Navy. As soon as the *Deutschland* entered the harbor, it had become just another German ship subject to internment. The more Hinsch cloaked the ship in secrecy, the better were its chances of outrunning a patrol and getting back to Germany.

That morning, the *Baltimore Sun* ran a four-column headline across the front page: UNARMED GERMAN SUBMARINE WITH MERCHANDISE CARGO NOW LIES NEAR BALTIMORE. Two smaller headlines underneath declared, THE *DEUTSCHLAND,* THE GREATEST OF UNDERSEA CRAFT, ANCHORED OFF QUARANTINE, HAVING COME FROM BREMERHAVEN IN 16 DAYS and SHE IS NOT A WAR VESSEL— TO DOCK IN BALTIMORE THIS MORNING. The *Sun* further reported, "She is grounded there with a completeness that is in proportion to the acute and worldwide interest in her. Scows, high-board fences, barbed-wire fences, and chains of floating logs protect her from the numerous inquisitive and possibly dangerous visitors. Moreover, a cordon of determined looking officers constantly is about her."

For three weeks, as crews unloaded the *Deutschland* and then reloaded it with tons of nickel, tin, rubber, and oil, newspapermen patrolled the harbor in rented boats. They asked police when they thought the sub would try to make a run for it, but the police didn't know anything. They begged Koenig for a quote, but he always walked by, unwilling to answer their questions. Left to speculate, the newspapers reported with certainty on each of the last three days of July that the *Deutschland* would attempt to escape internment the next morning.

The sub's departure was made more complicated by an extra patrol at Cape Charles, near the southern entrance to the Chesapeake Bay, where the *Deutschland* had originally entered the bay. President Wilson was vacationing there in a yacht called the *Mayflower,* which was constantly shadowed by the armored navy cruiser *North Carolina.* On their way down the coast, the president and his family had spotted several sharks. A man-eater had been preying on vacationers near the New Jersey shore all summer, and the ocean predators were as much a source of fascination as the *Deutschland.* On board, Wilson worked on his acceptance speech for the Democratic nomination. He was campaigning for reelection as the man who had kept the United States out of war, and he planned to proclaim that his policy of internment had been one of the reasons for his success. The prospect of Wilson's yacht passing the *Deutschland* as it raced for freedom "excited great interest along the waterfront," reported the *New York Times.*

Early on the morning of July 29, Koenig and Hinsch took a trolley car to Hilken's office at the Hansa Haus. The three men met for more than an hour. It had been decided: the Germans would strike Black Tom that night.

Later that afternoon, not coincidentally, Koenig finally decided to speak to the throng of reporters trailing him. One of them asked him when he would leave. The captain responded, "Well, if any of you men from New York want to go to Germany tomorrow to attend church, we'll go today just to oblige you." Asked about his stay in Baltimore, Koenig, his bronzed cheeks crinkling with a smile, replied, "Everything has been done to make our stay pleasant. It will mean much when we get back and tell our friends, and of course the whole German nation, what American feeling toward Germany is."

"Captain," one reporter wondered, "do you Germans feel angry at us for selling munitions of war to the Allies?"

This was the question Koenig had been waiting for. For weeks, he had evaded reporters, but he chose now, the morning before he knew that Germans would attempt to blow Black Tom sky-high, to send a message. "No, no," he answered, throwing his head back in laughter. "There is no reason for them to be angry. If

Germany could come here after arms and munitions, you would sell them to her, wouldn't you?"

Three days later, on August 1, the *Deutschland* dashed south along the Chesapeake Bay, evaded the U.S. Navy, and made its way into the Atlantic, bound for Germany. By then, the big story had moved north, to New York.

Chapter Seven

On Friday night, July 28, a group of interned sailors and German spies met in the formal dining room of Martha Held's house. Jahnke and Witzke were there, too. Hinsch and Hilken were back in Baltimore, conveniently tending to the *Deutschland*. Suitcases filled with dynamite and explosive glasses had been stored in Held's bedroom closet.

Photos and maps of New York Harbor and Black Tom Island, drawn by Germans who had paced the yard, were spread out on the dining room table. Mena Reiss, a model for Eastman Kodak and a regular at Held's, remembered hearing the phrase "Jersey Terminal" spoken repeatedly. "There were to be three explosions," Reiss said, "one on the cars and the others in sheds, or barges or enclosures." Reiss had been one of von Papen's favorite companions before he was recalled. She was far from oblivious to the company she kept. At Held's, she had often seen men carrying orange-size dumpling bombs into the house. Wrapped in black tissue paper and pieces of gray wool, the bombs were packed tightly in a tin "to avoid vibration," Reiss said.

At the end of the night, after the maps and photos had been put away, the men who remained serenaded one another with old German songs meant to be sung before going off to war, including

"Deutschland über Alles" ("Germany above All Others") and "Die Wacht am Rhein" ("The Watch on the Rhine"). The time to strike had finally come.

Reiss became so scared by what she heard that the next morning she hopped a train for the New Jersey shore, where she would spend the weekend visiting a friend. She warned no one.

By 5:00 p.m. on Saturday, July 29, Black Tom was quiet. At the north end of the depot, trains and barges bearing signs that read INFLAMMABLE and HAZARDOUS were lined up side by side. During the previous year, nearly three thousand train cars and barges had been loaded with ammunition at Black Tom, and there hadn't been a single incident. Lehigh Valley Railroad, the owner of the depot, had been lulled into such a sense of security that it put only five guards on duty. Two of them were Barton Scott and Jesse Burns, Paul Koenig's old friends from the Communipaw Avenue station.

For the next several hours, the only sounds heard were the waves lapping at the piers and the occasional guard laughing. Black Tom was what the workers called "a dead yard."

Kristoff left his aunt Anne Rushnak's house in Bayonne after 11:00 p.m. on Saturday, telling her he was going to pick up his pay at the Eagle Iron Works. She thought it was odd that he'd go so late at night, odder still because her nephew hadn't been to work in almost a week, instead spending his days nervously pacing, twitching, and mumbling around the house. In the evenings, he had disappeared, usually until early the next morning. One night, Rushnak had gone into Kristoff's room and looked around. She saw a large amount of cash, maps with factory locations pinpointed, and a letter addressed to a man named Graentnor. In the letter, Kristoff had written that he wanted the money he felt he was owed. Rushnak had put the letter back, not wanting to know any more.

• • •

The boat, a dinghy, was tethered to a German merchant ship that had been moored in New York Harbor. Its bow pointed south, aimed like a missile at the Statue of Liberty, which was silhouetted beneath the moon. Against the backdrop of the new skyscrapers in downtown Manhattan and the merchant ships getting ready to set off for Europe, the rowboat seemed insignificant, almost impossible to spot unless you were looking for it. Nobody was.

As Jahnke and Witzke rowed toward the Statue of Liberty, and Black Tom Island beyond, they knew that Kristoff was walking toward the target. Jahnke and Witzke had been given explosives, detonators, a target, a patsy, a getaway route, and a safe house. They knew the weak joints on barges carrying supplies, and they knew which markings represented the most harmful ammunition being sent to the front lines. All three men carried several sticks of dynamite as well as the explosive glasses. Kristoff, a common face around Black Tom, would have no problem walking past the guards, in the unlikely event they were paying attention. The plan was for him to head straight for the north end of the yard, where he would meet Jahnke and Witzke.

Within half an hour after midnight, the three men had placed their ammunition on steamships and barges. Kristoff then walked away from Black Tom as easily as he walked on. Jahnke and Witzke got in their boat and began rowing toward Manhattan. Halfway back, they turned around to watch the fireworks.

At around 12:45 a.m. on Sunday, July 30, a captain of one of the barges docked at Black Tom returned from a night on the town in Newark. It was sixty-five degrees, a beautiful evening, and he strolled slowly along the seawall, past dozens of train cars and barges filled with hundreds of thousands of tons of ammunition. A soft breeze blew in from the harbor. In the distance, he could see the Statue of Liberty. Nothing seemed out of the ordinary. He spotted Jesse Burns on patrol, and the two men stopped to chat. About five minutes into the conversation, Burns noticed something odd over the captain's shoulder. "There's a fire," Burns screamed.

The captain turned around. Shooting over the tops of the railroad cars he had just passed were bright white and orange flames. "It was burning from the interior of the car, flaming out around the top and side edges of the door and up in the air," he said. "But there was no fire on the ground."

Burns ran to alert the other guards, stopping to pull the fire alarm along the way. When he turned his back, he could hear popping sounds from the direction of the fire. The shells were exploding.

By the time the Jersey City Fire Department pulled up to Black Tom at 1:20 a.m., the barge was so hot that the men couldn't get near the potential inferno. One of the firemen attached his hose to a hydrant, but when he turned the nozzle, there was no water pressure. Shells were now popping in all directions. The Jersey City fire chief ordered his men to pull back.

At 2:08 a.m., the *Johnson 17,* a barge carrying 100,000 pounds of TNT and 25,000 detonators, exploded. "It was like the discharge of a great cannon," reported the *New York Times.* A doctor, who was treating immigrants on Ellis Island and watched the destruction through a set of opera glasses, said, "A great light went up; it seemed to me from where I stood as if it filled the whole sky, not only in front of my vision, but everywhere, and from that great mass of fire there seemed to shoot out thousands of little stars. As I ran into the house fragments began to fall, thousands of pieces of wood, pieces of sheet metal and a heavy muddy rain." Firemen standing on the edge of the yard were actually blown out of their shoes.

Shells now launched toward the sea. Bullets flew through the air. The explosions were constant, reverberating throughout lower Manhattan, Brooklyn, and Jersey City, lighting up the sky. The *Johnson 17* had disappeared.

The thunder and shock of this first explosion devastated almost all of Jersey City. City Hall lost every window and glass door, and the ceilings of the assembly chamber and the courtroom caved in. The stained-glass windows of the city's most beautiful church, St. Patrick's, were blown out, as were the windows of All Saints Church. For five blocks along Ocean Avenue, one of the town's main arteries, every shop window was gone. At police headquarters, part of the ceiling collapsed on the head of the lieutenant dispatching men to the scene.

At 2:40 a.m., another massive explosion occurred, sending a pillar of flame shooting skyward and engulfing the yard in fire. The Jersey City Fire Department, drawing water from the harbor, was kept at bay on land by a hail of shrapnel. The New York City Fire Department hurried a fireboat to the scene, hoping to help the hundreds of people living on barges to the northwest of Black Tom. But the bullets flew so fast that the firemen were reduced to lying on their stomachs, protected by the boat's steel railing, and aiming their hoses blindly over the bow.

Across the harbor in downtown Manhattan, windows in the skyscrapers lining Broadway, Wall Street, Broad Street, and every other street were shattered, including every pane in the building that housed J. P. Morgan & Co. Farther uptown, the windows at the library on 42nd Street were blown out, as were the windows in nearly every store along Fifth Avenue. At the corner of 42nd and Fifth, ten fire trucks, responding to different alarms throughout the city, were gridlocked. The fire department was tied up for an hour trying to sort out and respond to false alarms as night watchmen panicked, convinced that their own buildings had been dynamited.

In Times Square, the explosion caused a water main break beneath 42nd Street and Sixth Avenue, flooding four square blocks. The guests at the Knickerbocker and other upscale hotels gathered in the streets, running barefoot over the shattered glass that littered the pavement. Police frantically blew their whistles and ran into stores, assuming that the windows had been blown by safecrackers. When they realized that no one was inside, they commandeered taxicabs and raced downtown, chasing the glow of Black Tom. The harbor burned a bright orange, and the *rat-a-tat-tat* of exploding gunpowder made people feel as if they were witness to a battlefield.

Outside Manhattan, chaos reigned as well. Shortly after the second explosion, James Dougherty, a twenty-eight-year-old patrolman with the Jersey City Police Department, sprinted into the burning yard. Almost instantly, flying bullets hit him in the head and neck. His partner dragged him to safety, and he was rushed to the hospital, where he was pronounced dead. The Brooklyn Bridge shook from the shockwaves, and the tubes under the Hudson River connecting New York and Hoboken rolled with the blast. Phone lines between New York and New Jersey went dead. Headstones in Jersey City were upturned. Shrapnel tore into the chest of the Statue of Liberty and pelted the foundation of buildings packed with immigrants on nearby Ellis Island. People as far south as Philadelphia felt the ground shake and thought they were in the middle of an earthquake. In Maryland, phone lines to police were jammed with people concerned about weird vibrations they felt in their homes. No one knew what had happened, what was happening, and no one felt safe.

At 3:00 a.m., nearly five hundred immigrants on Ellis Island were evacuated by ferry to Manhattan. The main building on the island had been nearly destroyed, its windows shattered, its frame ripped from the ground, and its iron door blown off. The terra-cotta roof of the hospital next door had caved in as though heavyweight champ "Jack Johnson had done it," reported the *New York Times*. Broken glass, charred wood, and cinders covered the walkways and lawns.

As the thin Ellis Island overnight security staff herded the immigrants onto the ferry, they radioed harbor patrol for help to prevent a riot. But by then the panic had died down. People in Manhattan realized that the fires were coming from across the harbor, and a crowd numbering in the tens of thousands converged on lower Broadway. People, afraid for their lives shortly before, were now mesmerized by the red-orange sky and the shells rocketing across it, brilliant gashes of light that continued until sunrise.

Not everyone stood outside to enjoy the spectacle. At 4:30 a.m., Anne Rushnak, nervous about the explosions that had shattered her windows and rattled her house, heard footsteps sprinting back and forth across her porch, as though someone were checking every corner of the house. The running suddenly stopped and gave way to a pounding at her front door. She hesitated to open it, until she heard her nephew Michael Kristoff yelling for help. When she let him in, he pushed her aside and sprinted up to his room, screaming, "What did I do? Oh God, what did I do?"

Once the sun was up, rescue workers sifting through the rubble where the main warehouse building had stood uncovered the badly mangled body of Cornelius Leyden, the forty-five-year-old chief of the Lehigh Valley Railroad's security force. It seemed that every bone in Leyden's body was broken.

Three months later, the body of Captain Johnson, the man whose boat had been the first to explode, washed ashore along the Hudson River.

Miraculously, the official death toll from the Black Tom blasts held steady at five: Arthur Tosson (a ten-week-old baby thrown from his crib), James Dougherty, Cornelius Leyden, Captain Johnson, and an unidentified man found underneath one of the remaining piers, whose watch read 2:08 a.m., the time of the first explosion. Police admitted, however, that there had been hundreds of people living on barges just northwest of Black Tom — immigrants, vagrants, and the poor — and that dozens of them surely should be counted among the dead.

By 6:00 a.m. Sunday, the early Mass at the Mission of Our Lady of the Rosary in Jersey City was the most crowded in the church's history, noted Father A. J. Gorgan. "I can assure you, there were many praying on their knees who had not been inside a place of worship for a long time," he added.

Thousands of people gathered at the perimeter of what was left of the railyard. Some were residents of Jersey City, but others took the first ferry available from lower Manhattan to the Communipaw Avenue station. At one point, they watched as a burned-out barge, pulled into the middle of the harbor, suddenly came to life as shells burst nonstop for nearly an hour. Just as quickly, the noise stopped, leaving the boat as still and lifeless as it had been before.

At the north end of the yard, where the first fire had been noticed, a lake 300 feet long and 130 feet wide had been carved out by the explosion. A gentle breeze sent ripples across the water and whistled through the blackened freight cars and metal rails that had been melted into grotesque sculptures. Of the seven piers that extended from Black Tom, four were destroyed, two were extensively damaged, and one, the southernmost pier, was unharmed. Thirteen of the twenty-four warehouses, each holding several hundred tons of dry goods such as borax, grain, and salt, were decimated. Piles of sugar continued to burn; it would take a month before all the fires were extinguished.

A hundred workmen had the grim task of cleaning up the site, looking for live shells that could be salvaged as well as bodies that couldn't. It was a hazardous job, with bullets and shells indiscriminately shooting out of the smoldering ruins. The workers had to remove each brick by hand, afraid that the tap of a pick or the scrape of a shovel would send them skyward. The shore of Bedloe's Island, the nearest piece of land to Black Tom and home to a small army base, was covered with shredded wooden cases, fragments of iron and brass casings, and various bits of shrapnel.

The area south of Canal Street in downtown Manhattan, which was usually deserted on Sundays, was overrun with vehicles headed for the Battery. Passengers hung from the sideboards of streetcars. Even so, it was eerily quiet. Nearly the entire roof of the aquarium in Battery Park had caved in, raining glass into the tanks holding the porpoises and other large fish. Employees worked desperately to remove the glass and keep the fish from eating it. Twisted window frames littered the streets. Ash from the fires across the harbor mixed with pulverized glass to create a fine black-and-white dust, which coated everything and glistened in the sun. Ironically, the landmark Whitehall Building, which housed Hilken's New York representative, Hoppenburg, suffered the most damage of any downtown skyscraper. The face of the building had an unobstructed view of the harbor, and the shock-waves from the blast had torn through it as though it were tissue paper. The plate-glass windows on the second floor were blown out, and more than five hundred smaller windows were broken into pieces no larger than a half-dollar. On some floors, office doors were torn from their hinges.

From the shattered windows all over New York and New Jersey to the ravaged warehouses, barges, railroad cars, tracks, ammunition, salt, sugar, and other dry goods, damage estimates totaled $20 million, the equivalent of nearly $350 million in 2005. People demanded to know who was responsible, and they demanded revenge.

The police were quick to affix blame to the men whose companies were in charge of the safety and security of Black Tom. By midnight Sunday, less than twenty-four hours after the *Johnson 17* exploded, Jersey City police arrested the superintendent of the National Dock and Storage Company, owners of the piers surrounding Black Tom, as well as the Black Tom agent for the Lehigh Valley Railroad. Both men were immediately thrown into Jersey City's Ocean Avenue jail. The next day, the president of the Johnson Lighterage and Storage Company, which owned the *Johnson 17,* was in custody, and the president of the National Dock and Storage Company was prepared to turn himself in. Arrest warrants had also been issued for the presidents of the Lehigh Valley Railroad and the Central Railroad. All of these executives, most of them living on estates located deep in the New Jersey wilderness, were booked for manslaughter.

The *New York Times* ran an article listing forty-two other factory explosions in the United States since the war began. But government officials refused to acknowledge publicly that these were planned attacks. Instead, the *Times* reported, "the investigating bodies agree . . . that the fire and subsequent explosions cannot be charged to the account of alien plotters against the neutrality of the United States, although it is admitted that the destruction of so large a quantity of allied war material must prove cheering news to Berlin and Vienna."

The preliminary government report from a special agent based in New York said that there was no evidence that the fire at Black Tom had been caused by saboteurs. "There is nothing to justify action now by the Department of Justice," Bruce Bielaski, the chief of the Bureau of Investigation, declared. "Our investigator there seems to think that the explosion was an accident."

Meanwhile, President Wilson, just returned from his vacation on the Chesapeake Bay, had what he considered more pressing concerns. The British government was blacklisting several high-profile, high-powered American firms suspected of trading with the Germans. That issue, much more than what he called "a regrettable incident at a private railroad terminal," needed his full attention.

August 4, 1916, was a perfect night to throw a party: breezy, clear, and softly lit by a late-summer moon. With the help of Hoppenburg, Hilken had arranged for the top of the Hotel Astor to be theirs for the evening. At the corner of Broadway and 44th Street, the Astor had an elaborate roof garden overlooking Times Square, giving Hilken and his men an opportunity to gaze down upon the masses and congratulate themselves for the secrets they kept.

Before they sat down to dinner, Hinsch approached Hilken,

who was standing near the balcony looking north, toward Central Park. There was still enough light to make out the colors of women's dresses on the sidewalks below and see the leaves swaying in the breeze.

Hilken and Hinsch had developed a good working relationship: Hinsch did the dirty work; Hilken paid the bills. And this was payday. With their backs to the rest of the party, Hinsch said to his boss, "How about that bonfire?"

Hilken began to press for details about who had planted the bombs, but Hinsch brushed him off. "It's better if you don't know too much," he said.

Hilken didn't disagree. The less he knew, the safer he'd be. Hilken casually handed Hinsch two $1,000 bills, his reward for arranging the explosion of Black Tom Island.

Part TWO

Chapter Eight

BY THE TIME John McCloy entered Harvard Law School in 1916, the Central powers and Allies had been killing each other for two years, the *Lusitania* had been torpedoed, American newspapers were reporting stories about German diplomats willingly engaged in passport fraud, and a wave of suspicious explosions had rocked the nation. Yet America still stood by and watched. McCloy was a year into law school when the Zimmermann telegram—a proposal from Germany to Mexico suggesting a secret alliance if the United States decided to join the Allies—was intercepted by Blinker Hall's Room 40 cryptographers. The telegram, leaked to American newspapers, further inflamed anti-German public opinion. Wilson had no choice; on April 6, 1917, the United States declared war on Germany and its allies.

McCloy dropped out of Harvard immediately and joined an officer training program at Fort Ethan Allen in Vermont. The training was rigorous—hours a day on horseback, lessons in trench warfare—but McCloy felt well prepared by his days at the military training camp in Plattsburgh. As usual, what he lacked in skill, he made up for in painstaking effort. After one particularly grueling day of riding, the back of his pants was covered with blood when he dismounted. General Guy Preston, a cavalryman who had fought at Wounded Knee, was impressed by McCloy's tolerance and dedication. "Any man who could keep riding in that much pain must be a damn good officer," he said.

Preston was so taken with McCloy that he made the young man his staff aide. McCloy considered it an honor, even though it kept him stateside and away from the front lines, where he was desperate to be. McCloy didn't make it overseas until July 1918, when he joined Preston in northeastern France and was put in command of a field artillery brigade. By then, the war was close to being won by the Allies, and the little combat McCloy saw in early November, just a few days before the Armistice, was, as he put it, "drab." The day after peace was declared, a bitter McCloy wrote to his mother, Anna:

> The war is a thing that will be talked of and dreamed of for the duration of time and I did not get in it. A great many of my friends were killed, a greater number are wounded, and still a greater number were actively engaged in it. I was a soldier before any of them. . . . It is a bitter shame that the people of Germany are not to see their towns sacked and their fields laid waste as the French have. People of Germany don't realize yet what war is, and until they do there will be no peace in Europe.

McCloy had been training to beat the Germans since his college days at Amherst, and he felt deprived.

After the war, McCloy returned to Harvard. Anna moved in with him to cook and clean. In 1921, five years after first entering law school, McCloy finally became what his mother had always expected him to be: a lawyer. He had attended the best schools, learned from the best teachers, competed against the best students, and made the best contacts. Anna McCloy's son, literally born on the wrong side of Philadelphia's tracks, finally had a pedigree.

•   •   •

McCloy's first job interview in Philadelphia was with George Wharton Pepper, his mother's ideal of a noble, gentlemanly, and refined lawyer. A longtime law professor at the University of Pennsylvania who would become a U.S. senator in 1922, Pepper was one of the city's most admired legal minds. An essay he wrote about the difference between state and federal jurisdictions when graduating from Penn's law school in 1889 had resonated so strongly throughout the legal community that Supreme Court justice Louis Brandeis would cite it when writing opinions decades later.

While John McCloy Sr. was alive, Pepper was one of the lawyers who represented his employer, Penn Mutual. The two became friendly, but patrician families like the Peppers didn't socialize with working-class folks like the McCloys. When John Sr. died, however, Anna relied on Pepper for advice, and his wife, Charlotte, became one of her best hairdressing clients. Anna often asked Pepper how to help her son get ahead, what he needed to study, and where he should go to school. It was Pepper, a strong believer in the preparedness movement, who had inspired McCloy to attend the training camps in Plattsburgh.

Despite all the support Pepper had given McCloy, he was blunt about the young man's prospects for a legal career in Philadelphia: "John," Pepper said, "I know your family well. When your mother wanted to send you away to school, I was against it. I didn't think she could afford it. I was wrong about that. But I am not wrong about this. I know Philadelphia. It is a city of blood ties. You have good grades, but they don't mean anything here. Family ties do. You were born north of the Chinese Wall, and they'll never take you seriously in this town. In New York, however, your grades will count for something." The next day, McCloy hopped a train for Manhattan. He never lived in Philadelphia again.

Pepper was right. McCloy's grades, his service in the war, and his degree from Harvard all counted for something in New York. Where he had been born was irrelevant; what he had done since then mattered more.

Indeed, McCloy had come to a town that was focused on the moment, on beauty as much as background—maybe more so. In the 1920s, everything was moving and shaking in New York. It was a place where a man could redefine himself. Slick glossies such as *The New Yorker* and *Vanity Fair* were filled with humor, jazz, liquor, stories of sweet girls with bob haircuts, and the Broadway sensations George and Ira Gershwin. The *New York Times,* writing about F. Scott Fitzgerald's 1925 novel *The Great Gatsby,* called this an age when "gin was the national drink and sex was the national obsession." After a brief recession, the economy boomed, as U.S. companies won contracts to rebuild Europe. Per family income grew by a third, and in McCloy's adopted hometown, buildings rose higher, their lobbies plated with gold and marble.

New York produced more than one-twelfth of the nation's manufactured goods. Oceangoing steamers entered or left the harbor every twenty minutes. Five million square feet of office space was added in the financial district. Late in the decade, two architects, partners turned rivals, were commissioned by separate companies to build the tallest building in the world. At 40 Wall Street, just down the block from von Papen's old War Intelligence Center, a tower shot seventy-one stories high. At 42nd Street and Lexington Avenue, the Chrysler Corporation commissioned an art deco masterpiece, topped with a silver needle that helped the building become the first in the world to exceed one thousand feet. And even before the Chrysler Building was finished, plans were announced for the Empire State Building, which would soar even higher. In the 1920s, the heavens were no longer something you prayed to reach; you could get there just by going to work. And looking down at the city streets, New Yorkers saw more evidence of the good life. With the help of the General Motors Acceptance Corporation, Americans leaped at the chance to buy on credit. Cars, once a luxury for the rich, choked New York's roadways, as the city simply could not build newer, wider, more accommodating streets fast enough.

Wall Street lawyers benefited from the boom as well. Firms

were billing more hours and making more money than ever before. Revenues at one of the most prestigious firms, Cadwalader, Wickersham & Taft, rose 30 percent between 1921 and 1922, from a little more than $700,000 to nearly $950,000 (equal to nearly $11 million in 2005). Young associates, many of them veterans who had interrupted law school to fight in World War I, were hungry to prove themselves and make up for lost time in their careers. Before the war, it had been rare for even the busiest young associate to work through the night. Now it was commonplace.

McCloy was among the most driven of this new breed. Shortly after arriving in New York, he received offers from seven of the top firms. Cadwalader was particularly appealing because of the political prominence of two of its partners, George Wickersham, who had been William Howard Taft's attorney general, and Henry Taft, the former president's brother. The other Cadwalader partners appealed to McCloy's desire to achieve a certain social status. They were members of the newly formed Council on Foreign Relations and served on the board of the Metropolitan Opera; they played tennis and had estates on Long Island. They were Fitzgerald characters come to life.

Early in his career at Cadwalader, McCloy worked on several securities deals, often involving bankrupt railroads that were being bailed out by investment banks such as J. P. Morgan & Co. or Kuhn, Loeb & Co. Along the way, he nurtured relationships with upstart bankers such as Benjamin Buttenweiser of Kuhn, Loeb, who became his companion for nights on the town. They double-dated, going to the theater and then hitting the city's best speakeasies.

More often than not, McCloy's social life was geared toward career advancement. He was his father's boy: never the smartest kid in class, just the hardest worker, a character trait his mother never stopped encouraging. Shortly after Anna visited him in New York, early in his legal career, she sent him a note, expressing concern that he looked tired. She wrote, "Save and eat good food. Sleep more, you look as though you need it. Don't play the stock market. And don't forget, work to win."

McCloy did just that. After three years at Cadwalader, he was recruited by Paul Cravath to work at Cravath, Henderson & de Gersdorff. Cravath represented Kuhn, Loeb and was increasingly hired by investment banks looking to tap into the ever-expanding European market. The opportunity to travel abroad appealed to McCloy, but so did the "Cravath system." Cravath refused to hire lawyers who had family connections to any of the firm's clients. He wanted men who had worked their way through school, not those who had been pampered, and he expected his hires to put aside their egos. While other firms handed new associates cases and let them work with minimal supervision, Cravath associates were more like apprentices. They trailed a senior partner, learning to master the most mundane components of a case before being allowed to work on their own.

The Cravath system, designed to develop lawyers who would spend their entire careers at the firm, was novel at the time, but no one dared tell Paul Cravath it wouldn't work. At six foot four and 240 pounds, with a thick, wavy mane of iron gray hair, Cravath was an intimidating man. Even into his sixties, he worked out with a personal trainer every morning on his Long Island estate. A *New Yorker* profile in 1932 described him as someone whose "irascibility and temper were a matter of legend. Most of the young men who worked in his offices disliked him heartily, not because of his brusqueness, but because his unfailing confidence in his own judgment demanded that everything be done his way." You either proved you could do the work, or you were pushed out, an ethos that suited McCloy's meticulous, dogged approach. From his days as a tennis player in college, he had learned how to carry himself with the confidence and grace of someone used to winning.

As he grew older, McCloy would become thick and stocky, but as a young man still in his early thirties, he was athletic, carrying 150 pounds on his five-foot seven-inch frame. He exuded hunger and drive. He almost always wore a black suit, black tie, and white shirt. He was a handwringer, constantly rubbing the palms of his powerful hands together, intertwining his long fingers in anticipation of work to be done. It was a gesture of a busy man, a plotter who constantly asked, "What's next?"

While other associates chafed at the rigidity of the Cravath system, McCloy thrived in it. He stayed at his desk through the night, ordering steak dinners at 10:00 p.m. and puffing away on cigars to stay awake. In 1925, Cravath was hired by the Chicago, Milwaukee and St. Paul Railway to handle its bankruptcy, and the thirty-year-old McCloy was the associate in charge of organizing the paperwork. "It didn't require legal genius," he would later say. "But it did require hard work." He worked so hard that in the days leading up to the railroad's dissolution—after all the execs had either resigned or been fired—he was made its president, the youngest ever of a railroad company.

The title was one of the perks McCloy enjoyed as his star rose at Cravath. Admittedly, his only ambition was to become a partner. To him, every sixteen-hour day brought him sixteen hours closer to achieving that goal. He kept a white tie and tails in his office so that he could sneak out for a night at the Met, where many of the firm's partners had season tickets, without having to go home and change. Afterward, he'd often drop off his date and head back to work. Even his weekends were geared toward career advancement. He joined the Heights Casino, a Brooklyn tennis club whose members included prominent bankers and lawyers. One afternoon, he took a set off of Wimbledon champion Bill Tilden. In the mythmaking alleys of Wall Street, McCloy's accomplishment was retold, distorted, and embellished enough by men who weren't even there that it eventually morphed into a triumph. He became known as that lawyer who had beaten "Big Bill."

As a boy, he had done chores for the wealthy at their summer homes in the Adirondacks. Now he was their guest. Trubee Davison, the son of Morgan partner Henry Davison, invited McCloy to his family's home on Long Island for tennis. Averell Harriman, who had inherited the Union Pacific from his father, invited McCloy to his estate for polo. It usually took ten years for a Cravath associate to become a partner, but McCloy did it in less than five.

It was the summer of 1929, and to celebrate, the thirty-four-year-old McCloy hopped a train for California. He had to work on a case.

When his train approached Flagstaff, Arizona, on the way back from California, McCloy decided to take advantage of his new status as a partner and gave himself a couple of days off. He had never seen the Grand Canyon, which was just a short train ride away. Who knew when he'd have the chance again?

Still in his suit, he wandered off the eastbound train, caught another one straight to the canyon, and looked over the edge of the South Rim. The alternating layers of red, black, and brown rocks shimmered in the heat, and a hot wind blew up from the bottom, as though the center of the earth were exhaling. The view was sublime, enticing, and alluring, and McCloy decided that he would hike to the bottom. Just like that, he hit the trail, his shoes and pants and skin picking up dust along the way. He emerged from the canyon late the next day with just enough time to get back to Flagstaff to catch his train. Covered with dirt, he settled into his seat and casually began reading a newspaper.

As the train rolled east, McCloy stood up to take a walk. He passed from one car to the next, shaking the stiffness from his legs. Strolling into one of the carriages, he recognized someone from behind. He didn't need to see the man's face to know it was Lew Douglas, his old rival from Amherst. McCloy hesitated before moving farther into the car. He wasn't sure he wanted to talk to Douglas, let alone be stuck sitting with him for part of a cross-country train ride. Then he noticed the woman seated across from Douglas. She had perfect posture, flawless skin, brilliant teeth, and hair the color of midnight. He didn't know it was Peggy Douglas, Lew's wife, until after he sat down.

This was not how McCloy would have chosen to see Douglas for the first time since college. He looked like a hobo — dirty, tired, and unshaven — not at all like the distinguished Wall Street lawyer he had become. Douglas, meanwhile, was on his way back east as a thirty-five-year-old congressman, Arizona's lone representative in the House.

Despite the differences in their appearance, McCloy and Douglas bantered as though they were still in college. They were competitive and playful, and Peggy Douglas found McCloy to be charming, accomplished, and important. A plan began to formulate in her mind; she couldn't wait to call her sister.

E llen Zinsser waited at the end of a Penn Station platform, exactly where her younger sister, Peggy, had told her to be. It was a hazy August afternoon in 1929. Peggy had called days earlier from New Mexico demanding that Ellen meet her at the station. Her voice practically screeched with excitement over the phone as she told Ellen, "I've met the man you're going to marry." Even in the moist heat of summer, Ellen couldn't be compelled to dress down. She wore a stylish dress and white gloves and tucked her black hair tight under her pillbox hat, which made it easier for people to see her hazel-brown eyes. She was a knockout, and she drew leering glances from the weary men passing by.

She didn't go to the station expecting to find a husband. At thirty-one years old, she had nearly given up on getting married. And it bothered her that she had resorted to waiting for a train, as though she were some desperate spinster. She was a college graduate, fluent in French and German, and worked as a buyer at Bergdorf Goodman. She had been a fixture on the New York social scene since her days as a student at Smith College. With her bellowing laugh and self-confidence, she was never without a date.

Before Peggy got married, both Zinsser girls were invited to every high-society party. They were beautiful, rich, and from a prominent family. Their father, Frederick Zinsser, ran a chemical company in their hometown of Hastings-on-Hudson. Their mother, Emma, gave Christmas presents to every child in town and cordoned off a portion of her garden for use by the women in Hastings who had none. The Zinssers lived in a big, yellow Victorian house at the top of a hill overlooking the Hudson. The third floor had five bedrooms, while the second had two living rooms, each with a grand piano. The ten-acre estate included a gardener's house, a separate garage, a tennis court made of mud dredged from the Hudson, and enough room for a maid, a cook, a nanny, and a chauffeur.

Within the family, Frederick played the absentminded professor, barreling out of his hilly driveway in his ascot and pearl pin without looking left or right, bringing all the other traffic to a screeching stop. Emma, while charitable with townsfolk, demanded a lot of her girls, and despite the staff at home, both girls had a full complement of chores. (Ellen earned the nickname "Diddy" for yelling out "Did it!" whenever Emma reminded her to do something.)

When they were both single, the two sisters were less-than-friendly rivals, constantly competing for suitors. While Peggy was prettier, Ellen was more personable. She was witty and brash and full of opinions. She enjoyed a bawdy joke. One year for Christmas, a cousin sent her a bath mat emblazoned with a pair of breasts, and she laughed so hard she started to cry. She appreciated men who flirted with her, and she flirted right back. Her life was charmed and privileged, but she never acted entitled. Her first instinct was to put those around her at ease, which, as she waited for her sister's train, was exactly the way she wanted to feel.

McCloy was smitten as soon as he saw Ellen on the platform. For the next several months, he pursued her with as much zeal as he had chased a partnership at Cravath. Their dinner dates gradually became more elegant and expensive. He took her to the opera, for which he donned white tie and tails and she wore flowing gowns that scraped the floor. He brought her to a Cravath partner's brownstone mansion for private parties with New York's business and legal elite. Douglas was now his greatest ally, and McCloy repeatedly pestered him for information about Ellen's other suitors. McCloy knew that Ellen had an affinity for doctors and that she was dating one who was anxious to marry her. The doctor drove a black-and-white Cadillac roadster with wire wheels, and Ellen thought that he was as dashing as a movie star. One afternoon, McCloy, desperate to win over Ellen, scraped together all the money he had and bought his own Cadillac roadster. It was the same model as the doctor's, only his was red. He drove it straight to the Zinssers' home in Hastings-on-Hudson. When he saw the doctor's Cadillac in the driveway, he pulled right up next to it.

Ellen and her dad, hearing a car pull into the gravel driveway, were watching from the window. Frederick Zinsser leaned over to his daughter and whispered, "This man is going to go somewhere, keep an eye on him." Shortly thereafter, the doctor was out of the picture.

To those outside their romance, they seemed like an unlikely pair. Ellen, a stylish brunette from a wealthy family, was always on the town with men whose stature matched their good looks. McCloy was already bald and still had no portfolio or property, despite his rise to partner. Most of his extra income went toward supporting his mother. When they announced their engagement in late 1929, friends of the Zinsser sisters joked that Peggy had won the marriage sweepstakes. Ellen just ignored them; they didn't know what she knew and couldn't see what she saw. Several men had proposed to her, but they had all worn their privilege too easily and approached their lives too casually, because they knew where they were going. McCloy had come from nowhere, and his destiny would be of his own making. "All you had to do was look in his eyes," Ellen said. "I never saw a man with more energy. It never occurred to me that he wasn't the most exciting man I had ever met."

They planned an April wedding, because McCloy had been asked to run Cravath's office in Paris. Their engagement was so brief that Frederick Zinsser feared that people might think this was a shotgun wedding. He wrote to every guest explaining that he and his wife were thrilled that their future son-in-law had been offered such an important job, even if it meant rushing the wedding. Anna McCloy, however, was less than thrilled with her son's choice of a bride. She was convinced that marrying into money made him vulnerable, that Ellen's friends would look down on her son because of where he came from. In fact, it was the opposite; Ellen enhanced McCloy's credibility. Anna never realized this. She even made her son promise to sell his Cadillac because she was irritated that he had spent so much money to impress a woman. To Ellen, meanwhile, it was obvious she had traded in one rival, her sister, for another: her new mother-in-law.

A freezing wind blew off the Hudson the morning of April 25, 1930. Snow squalls screamed over the hill toward the Zinsser mansion, settling in a fine white dust on the second-floor veranda. The house was already packed with relatives, anxious for the wedding between Ellen and John. While the staff prepared the grand, second-floor living rooms for the ceremony, setting up candelabras everywhere, Ellen spent the day playing with her nieces and nephews. She desperately wanted children. For years, she had been a warm presence in the lives of her friends' children, known to them as Aunt Ellen. She knew that she and John would begin trying to have a child as soon as they could, even if Anna McCloy was joining them on their honeymoon cruise from New York to Paris.

That morning, Ellen put together a scrapbook with her nephew John. Then she joined the rest of the kids in the frigid temperatures and played kick the wicket in front of the house. McCloy spent the day with Trubee Davison, now the assistant secretary of war, who had made a dramatic entrance the day before on a seaplane that had landed on the Hudson. But by 8:00 p.m., hundreds of candles had been lit, flooding the two second-floor rooms with light and setting the guests' faces aglow. A white pillow was laid in front of the altar for the bride and groom to kneel on while they took their vows. As Ellen finally made her way down the aisle in a white lace dress and carrying a bouquet of white orchids, she realized that this was the moment she had been waiting for.

• • •

After five days touring the French countryside, the newly-weds focused on getting settled in Paris. John left their hotel early each day for the office and often stayed late, while Ellen spent her time looking for a place to rent. One afternoon, she called on a member of the Tiffany family, who she heard was sub-letting her apartment on the Left Bank. Ellen took one look at the luxurious apartment, which seemed to be as big as her parents' house in Hastings, and was sure it would be too expensive. When she sat down with the owner for tea, both women put their cups on the antique table in front of them. As they discussed the apart-ment and what the McCloys could afford to pay, Ellen noticed drops of water clinging to the side of her host's cup and dripping toward the table. She took out a handkerchief, picked up the cup and wiped it, and then placed the cup back down on the table, on top of her handkerchief. Moved by this trivial act of grace, the other woman immediately offered Ellen the apartment, for what-ever she could pay.

All through the summer, the McCloys acted as though they were still on their honeymoon. They took long drives around the city in John's red Cadillac, which he had kept, despite his mother's wishes. Ellen hired a tutor to teach her husband French. John, al-ways trying to expand his connections, organized touch football games with the other American lawyers living in France. But by early fall, Ellen still wasn't pregnant, and visits to the top doctors in Paris didn't provide any answers. John worried about his bride because, while he merely wanted children, she absolutely needed them. She talked about a family endlessly and breathlessly, as if nothing else mattered. While he had his work with the firm, Ellen's ambitions consisted entirely of becoming a mother.

Both lives were about to become more complicated. In early September, John received a cable from Cravath's New York office. One of the firm's clients, the Lehigh Valley Railroad, had a case pending before the German-American Mixed Claims Commis-sion, a bilateral commission that was still doling out awards for damages during World War I. The cable explained that back in 1916, a munitions depot in New York Harbor called Black Tom had been destroyed. The U.S. government, representing the Lehigh Valley Railroad, claimed that Germany had been responsible. The Germans denied it. For five years, the two countries had parried back and forth, filing briefs, summaries, and motions. In 1929, they had spent ten days making oral arguments, which led to a request from the three-judge panel for even more briefs, summaries, and motions. The commission had resolved nearly twenty thousand disputes since its creation in 1922, but no one—not the judges, not the lawyers, not the two countries—had been able to determine who was responsible for blowing up Black Tom.

McCloy read that the commission's next round of oral arguments would begin on September 18 at the Peace Palace in The Hague. Cravath wanted him there to gauge how the case was going. He pulled a notecard from his desk, jotted down the relevant facts of the case, created a Black Tom file, and made plans to visit The Hague.

With those simple tasks, McCloy stepped into a maze that would take him decades to escape.

After the war, the United States, untouched by the devastation and separated from Europe by an ocean, felt little of the visceral hatred for Germany that its European allies did. The French, in particular, wanted more than mere victory. They believed that the Germans would remain a threat unless they were completely shattered, militarily, economically, and psychologically. The terms of the Treaty of Versailles, negotiated during the first six months of 1919, reflected their intent. The German military, which for some World War I battles had dispatched more than a million troops, was capped at 100,000 soldiers, its sole function to be a police force within its borders. The importing of munitions and firearms was prohibited, and the number of German battleships was not to exceed six. Germany's territory shrank by 13 percent, as it gave up Alsace-Lorraine and the coal-mining regions along the Rhine to the French and West Prussia to Poland. Despite a national food shortage that had begun during the war and continued to result in hundreds of deaths each day, Germany agreed to hand over 180,000 cows to France and Belgium over a six-year period.

Most devastating to the German national psyche was Article 231 of the treaty, which forced Germany to accept full responsibility for the losses and the damage caused by the war. Many German citizens had protested the conflict and hated the government for letting it go on for so long. German women had marched in the streets with empty pots and pans to show the government that they could not feed their families. Men in factories had put down their tools in defiance. Even in the Reichstag, politicians who had once voted in favor of the war had eventually pushed for peace. But once the war was over, the entire nation rallied around the idea that all of Europe was communally to blame for the aggression, not just Germany. Article 231 was dubbed the "war guilt" clause, and the new German leaders negotiating the treaty railed against it more than they did the forced disarmament, lost land, or billions in reparations they were told to pay. The Germans may have lost the war, but because the fighting stopped before fully penetrating their borders, they still retained their dignity. Admitting sole fault would deprive them of that.

Many Americans on the Versailles delegation felt as strongly about the treaty's failings as the Germans did. Herbert Hoover, the American relief administrator, thought the consequences of the treaty would ultimately be more destruction. Secretary of State Robert Lansing wrote President Wilson a memo calling the treaty "immeasurably harsh and humiliating." Another member of the delegation organized the resignation of himself and a dozen other colleagues, simply stating that the final agreement wasn't "a treaty of peace."

Wilson, hailed as a hero and awarded the 1919 Nobel Peace Prize for bringing the warring factions to the table and creating the League of Nations, couldn't sell the treaty to a pragmatic Congress. Germany no longer represented an enemy, but an opportunity: it would need to be rebuilt and recapitalized, to import materials and food. American politicians recognized that the new German government, a product of the people, would never succeed if its citizens didn't believe that better times were ahead. So while Germany's European enemies ratified the Treaty of Versailles, the U.S. Senate debated it through the summer and fall of 1919. Congress wanted Germany as an economic partner, not an indentured servant. This desire, combined with fierce opposition to the League of Nations, meant that the treaty would never be ratified. The senators' message was simple: let the Europeans live for vengeance; Americans lived for the future.

After the war, vagrants crowded Berlin's streets, pulling wagons holding everything they owned from one corner to the next, before policemen shooed them away. During the summer, with nowhere to escape the heat, families crowded into Schiller Park at the north end of the city, where children without toys played in depleted sandboxes. In the autumn, with most of the country's coal being exported to Belgium and France as reparations, the poor gathered fallen leaves from the parks' trees to burn as fuel. Immigrants, many of them from war-torn parts of the Ukraine and Russia, flooded Germany looking for work. But there was no work to be found, and even fewer places to call home. People of all ages—old men with long beards, young men looking angry and scared, women in torn clothing—crowded into shelters. Each person was given a paper blanket and a bowl of soup. Families were placed inside wooden cubicles lining the hallways, each with a small gas burner in the corner. They would hang their wet clothes from ropes running across the tops of the cubbyholes, where the clothes picked up the smells of cooking food and sweating refugees that lingered in the hallway.

The shelters closed at 9:00 p.m., leaving the steam baths on Friedrichstrasse as the only housing option for anyone who still lacked a place to sleep. Before the war, the baths had been the domain of the wealthy, a place where men came after a night on the town to get a shave and sweat away the toxins. They were the break between the sin of the evening and the work of the day. Now they were nothing more than a home for the displaced. The men inside were sad, pathetic, and hopeless. After a night spent in the baths, the Austrian journalist Joseph Roth wrote, "I don't know if the people in hell look as ridiculous as the people here."

On July 2, 1921, Congress approved the Treaty of Berlin, a separate peace negotiated between the United States and Germany. Unlike the Versailles treaty, this agreement included no clauses accusing Germany of starting the war; its sole purpose was economic compensation. The United States took possession of all German property it had seized during the war. None of it would be returned until the Germans settled every claim filed against Germany for wartime damages. In August of the next year, the two countries established the bilateral Mixed Claims Commission (MCC) to arbitrate the settlements.

The first item on the agenda was choosing the three-member panel. The German strategy was shrewd and smart: play on the Americans' sympathies and their inherent need to prove themselves as both kind and powerful. There would be two commissioners—one an American, the other a German. At the Germans' request, the third member, the umpire, would be an American. Under the commission's bylaws, the umpire would never hear a case unless the two commissioners had dissenting opinions. Although the Germans took a risk in requesting an American umpire, they calculated that an impartial American would bend over backward to avoid any appearance of favoritism, especially when making a final judgment on what would likely be the most difficult, controversial, and expensive cases.

The Americans took their fair and just role seriously. The American commissioner, Edwin H. Parker, suggested that he and his German counterpart, Wilhelm Kiesselbach, share a Washington, D.C., office. Parker said that it would help them come to conclusions on cases more quickly. In addition, because the United States was already paying rent on the space, Germany wouldn't have to contribute a cent. Kiesselbach appreciated the gesture; so did the German politicians. The new Weimar government (named for the German state where the meetings to hammer out a new constitution had been held) actually offered cash bonuses and lucrative private-sector opportunities to government attorneys for bringing all the cases to closure as soon as possible. It was convinced that the sooner these debts were settled, the sooner normal relations with the United States would begin and the sooner it would again be recognized on the world stage—and in their own country—as legitimate.

President Warren Harding, who came to office in 1921, named Supreme Court justice William H. Day as umpire. He sent a note to his secretary of state, Charles Evans Hughes, asking Hughes, when making the announcement to the press, to "emphasize the request to us to name the umpire. It is so unusual that its significance is worth bringing well to the fore."

The rules of the commission had been established with expediency in mind. While any attorney in private practice could file a claim, only government-appointed lawyers, called agents, could argue a case. The commission did not have subpoena power, meaning that the agents could not force key witnesses to testify. The agents would not have the benefit of eyewitness testimony either. Because of the logistics of shuttling potential witnesses around the globe for hearings, it was agreed that only written testimony and affidavits would be accepted. The assigning or assuaging of German guilt was entirely dependent on the agents' legal briefs and arguments in front of the commissioners. The debates could be theatrical, contentious, and funny, with agents lambasting each other while trying to influence the commissioners. Even so, the atmosphere was more collegial than confrontational.

In May 1923, less than a year into his term, the seventy-four-year-old Day resigned, citing failing health and the overwhelming workload. (He would die two months later.) Parker was promoted to umpire, and a man named Chandler Anderson was appointed as the American commissioner in Parker's place. Throughout these transitions, the spirit of the commission was cooperative, with the Germans making sacrifices to keep the cases moving.

For the first three years of its existence, the MCC worked

smoothly and under the radar. By June 1925, more than 12,000 cases had been filed, more than 6,700 had been settled, and nearly $81 million had been paid out to American claimants. Of the 6,000 cases that remained, nearly all of them fell into one of several categories that had already been ruled on and could easily be settled.

But there was one case, filed in March 1924, that lingered on the MCC's docket.

A former Republican congressman from Colorado, Robert Bonynge, had been named by Harding as the MCC's American agent, responsible for representing all the American interests before the commission. Bonynge was a blunt, abrasive, demanding sixty-year-old, who had been raised in New York City and was prone to outrageously bold statements. He made his name as a lawyer in Denver at the turn of the century, as the last of the Wild West was being tamed. With his smooth pate, heavy-lidded eyes, circular wire-rimmed glasses, and tightly pursed lips, Bonynge looked serious and enjoyed the challenge of convincing people that he was right.

Initially, the Germans feared that Bonynge was interested only in using the commission to advance his own cause. (For years after his stint in Congress, he had stumped around the country on behalf of the National Monetary Commission, which had led to the formation of the Federal Reserve. He was never quite able to get preaching and grandstanding out of his system.) But the Germans realized early on that they were wrong. By the time of his appointment to the MCC, Bonynge had mellowed. While he still enjoyed sparring verbally with his German counterpart in front of the commissioners and he never passed up an opportunity to comment publicly about the commission's progress, his attitude toward the MCC was the same as that of the commissioners: he wanted the cases settled quickly. At the time of his appointment, he had been happily working in private practice in New York, and living in an apartment overlooking Central Park. He and his wife had been married for thirty-seven years. They were childless and enjoying their twilight years together. He had taken the job as American agent not because he wanted to get back in the game, but because the president of the United States had asked him to.

If Bonynge was the MCC's American showman, Harold Martin was the figure behind the curtain. He was a career government lawyer in Washington, D.C.—a company man in a company town—and he adored it. A native of tiny Atchison, Kansas, the slightly built, bookish Martin loved that everything in a bureaucracy had its place and process. He loved sitting at his desk in the State Department—his white shirt sleeves rolled up above his elbows, several strands of fine silver hair dangling over his glasses—writing lengthy briefs and sifting through arcane laws. He loved the stability of his job and putting $100 every month into the Civil Service Retirement and Disability Fund.

Martin had spent nearly fourteen years in the navy solicitor's office, starting as a clerk and rising to the level of assistant to the solicitor. He was valued for what he wasn't: ambitious and political. Other young lawyers in the solicitor's office used it as a stepping-stone to private practice or to make their own political power grabs. But Martin would never be a man who led; he was a man leaders wanted. He did the grunt work no one else would do. During World War I, he had put together a handbook of maritime warfare laws that served as the navy's rule book. When the navy was commandeering real estate for military purposes, he became an expert on land values from Virginia to California. He then represented the navy when property owners sued for more money. These weren't glamorous jobs, but they had substance. And the way he went about them endeared him to those he worked for—and those he worked against.

Martin heard about the job on the commission from his sister-in-law, a State Department secretary, and it immediately piqued his interest. He was married and had two young daughters. The fact that his salary would nearly double, from $3,000 to $5,000 a year, made the job attractive. The subject matter also appealed to him. So many of the claims before the MCC involved assessing property damage, which Martin felt uniquely qualified to do. It was a testament to his character that when he inquired about the job, he included as references not just big names such as Robert H. Lovett, the assistant attorney general at the time, but five attorneys he had beaten after their clients had sued the navy for taking their land. When Martin was hired in 1922, the commander of the Great Lakes Naval Station, whom Martin had worked with, immediately wrote to his old friend, saying, "You were hiding your very brilliant light under a bushel in the Solicitor's office." Martin, however, wasn't looking to shine. He saw his role in humbler terms, as another chance to serve greatness.

Thorough, selfless, and dedicated, Martin took the lead in drafting briefs for the commission. He grouped the thousands of cases, ranging from personal property lawsuits to those filed by large corporations, into categories, then acted as the point man for all the attorneys whose cases were being argued or presented by Bonynge. Within a year of being hired, he was promoted to Bonynge's chief counsel. He was so loyal to his boss that over the fifteen years they worked together, he always closed his letters to Bonynge with the words "Dutifully yours." He'd do things as menial as picking up Bonynge's watch from the repair shop, sending flowers to funerals on Bonynge's behalf, and donating five dollars to a secretary's wedding gift pool in Bonynge's name.

But Martin was not without faults. When he took the job, he assumed it would be temporary but worthwhile. "It will probably last about four years," he wrote to a friend. He had no idea how wrong he was.

Chapter **Nine**

I N M ARCH 1924, Karl von Lewinski, Robert Bonynge's counterpart as the German agent for the commission, received a peculiar notice from a lawyer. He received dozens of notices like this every day from every attorney filing a claim with the commission. Usually he didn't give them more than a cursory glance, just enough to understand the nature of the case, who was filing, and how much the claimant wanted. After nearly two years of doing the commission's work, he could tell almost immediately what kind of settlement it would take to close the case.

But the tone of this particular notice surprised him. It was aggressive and threatening and gave no hint that the attorney filing it was interested in a settlement. He wrote that he represented the Lehigh Valley Railroad, which planned to sue Germany for the destruction of Black Tom Island, as well as a charred munitions plant in Kingsland, New Jersey. The lawyer wrote that he would use any means to win these cases, including feeding evidence proving Germany's guilt to the press.

Von Lewinski had studied at Columbia and Harvard. One of the reasons the Weimar government had appointed him as the German agent was his familiarity and comfort not just with U.S. law but also with American social customs. He was almost com-

pletely bald, with sunken eyes framed by dark circles. Yet his dour
face belied his friendly demeanor. He was a regular on the Washington social circuit and was highly regarded for his understanding
of the nuances of American politics. His ability to translate American interests to his German bosses had helped the commission settle nearly seven thousand cases during its first two years. Some
were as small as a $25 settlement for a New York couple who had
lost property on a ship crossing the Atlantic. Others were larger,
such as the $175,000 paid to the International Mercantile Marine
Company for one of its sunken ships. Von Lewinski knew immediately that the Black Tom notice meant trouble.

The Lehigh Valley lawyer didn't reveal his evidence or officially submit anything to Martin or anyone else in Bonynge's
office. When von Lewinski reported back to the Foreign Office in
Berlin, he wrote, "It is indeed possible that this is simply an attempt to blackmail money from the German government." But
von Lewinski was keenly aware that the Weimar government's
hold on the country was tenuous. So far, the average claim Germany had paid out was just $12,000, and it had been easy to per-
suade German citizens that that was a cheap price to pay for
respectability. Black Tom was not a bit of lost property, however;
it was a still-unsolved crime that millions of Americans remembered. This wasn't an attack during a declared war; at the time,
America had been a neutral party — or at least that's how Americans would see it. To admit guilt in the Black Tom case would be
to admit a preemptive first strike. It would be an acknowledgment
that Germany was the instigator. For those who doubted the official story — that the explosions had been an accident — the destruction of Black Tom symbolized the duplicity of the kaiser's
government, which Weimar was desperate to distance itself from.

In some ways, it was succeeding. The economy was improv-
ing, and Berlin was undergoing a cultural and architectural renaissance that rivaled New York's. The city was building its first
skyscraper, and developers talked of outfitting the new building
with a movie theater, a dance hall, a jazz club, and a vaudeville
theater. The nightclubs at the west end of Berlin were filled with

laughter, music, and the sounds of the elite drinking brightly colored drinks while smoking luxury cigarettes.

Even so, most people in Germany felt that the revival was happening in spite of Weimar, not because of it. They were so angry with their politicians that by 1924, after just five years of democracy, the ruling party had already changed four times. German chancellors came and went with every change in public opinion. Even the most mundane policy changes were met with harsh criticism. When antiquated, mostly empty streetcars clogged Berlin's thoroughfares and interfered with the increasing number of cars, the government suggested removing the streetcars. Newspapers in Berlin ran letters from chauffeurs, bus drivers, and motorists—people who no longer rode the trolleys and were most inconvenienced by the traffic—protesting the government's proposal. Logic mattered not; it was rebellion for the sake of rebellion. Eventually, the idea was dropped.

With this kind of public resistance to the removal of useless streetcars, von Lewinski knew settling Black Tom would be nearly impossible.

By the time the suit was filed in 1924, debating who blew up Black Tom had become a parlor game. Theories were passed around from Upper East Side bars to the trading pits on Wall Street, all of which led back to the Germans. In reality, investigators from the U.S. government, the New York Police Department's bomb squad, the Jersey City Police Department, and the Lehigh Valley Railroad had been trying for eight years to find out who was responsible, and their leads had all turned out to be dead ends.

The day of the explosion, Michael Kristoff's aunt Anne Rushnak had told her married daughter Anna Chapman about Kristoff's frightening screams earlier that morning. She had seen the maps and factory blueprints in her nephew's room. She knew that after years of being broke, he was suddenly flush with cash. All of this made her feel unsafe in her own home. Chapman had passed along what her mother had told her to the Jersey City police, adding that the night of the explosion, Kristoff had stopped by her house in Jersey City. He had told her that he was on his way to the Eagle Iron Works to collect two days' pay. Chapman had noted that the late hour was an inappropriate time for a visit, and an even stranger time to be on one's way to work. The police interviewed Rushnak and spent the next three weeks tracking Kristoff's every move.

Finally, on September 3, 1916, Jersey City police arrested Kristoff on suspicion of blowing up Black Tom, based mainly on his aunt's accusations. Kristoff told them that he had been in Yonkers that night visiting friends and that he had noticed "a great deal of glass lying on the sidewalks when I got off the subway in Jersey City," but he hadn't thought anything of it.

When police asked Kristoff what he did for a living, he didn't mention the Eagle Iron Works. Instead, he told them that he used to carry luggage for a man named Francis Graentnor. He even admitted looking inside one of the man's briefcases and seeing that it was filled with maps and factory blueprints. But before he could truly examine them, Graentnor had walked in and "severely rebuked" him for looking in the briefcase. Kristoff was thrown into the county lockup, where he stayed for ten days, as police tried to track down Graentnor. The search was futile, and what had seemed like a promising lead was abandoned.

In August 1919, Paul Altendorf, a former U.S. Secret Service agent, wrote a series of articles, syndicated in newspapers throughout the country, claiming that he had heard Lothar Witzke, the German saboteur, admit his part in the destruction. Hearsay made for good copy, but it was useless in a court of law.

The lack of concrete evidence against the Germans meant that von Lewinski's first instincts were right. The lawyers for Lehigh Valley were trying to frighten Germany, to bluff their way to a settlement. They knew that there was very little evidence linking the Germans to the sabotage. Indeed, when Lehigh Valley executives had approached dozens of law firms, hoping to persuade one of them to file a case on their behalf with the MCC, most had turned them down. The chances of winning were too slim, the firms said, and building a case would be too expensive.

Only one lawyer agreed that the case could be worthwhile, thirty-seven-year-old Amos Peaslee. A former associate at Cravath, a World War I veteran, and a former army judge advocate, Peaslee was experienced in international law and had already won several other MCC claims. His prewar work as a lawyer and service in the army had won him a spot on the American negotiating team at Versailles, and back home he had become the honorary secretary of the International Law Association of America.

Peaslee's tolerance for risk was higher than that at Wall Street's white-shoe law firms. He had left Cravath in 1917 to join the army, and when he'd returned, he'd opened his own firm with an office on Fifth Avenue. He worked on a contingency basis, and when the Lehigh Valley lawyers reminded him that there had been $20 million worth of damage done to their property, he needed but a minute to calculate what his fee would be if the case was settled for $20 million: nearly $2 million. Any reservations he had about a lack of evidence or trails that had gone cold promptly disappeared.

Peaslee was just five foot six, was completely bald, and had ears that jutted out from his head as though they were standing at attention. But he projected an image that made his awkward looks invisible. He stood with his shoulders back, a habit from his Quaker schooling. He spoke with force, as if using a megaphone, gesturing wildly while making his points. He wore custom-tailored suits and bright ties that complemented his personality, and he drank rum daiquiris at parties—but just one at each event.

He was not the philosophical type; he just acted—which was another reason he hadn't lasted at Cravath. He'd chafed at the workload, at the tedium of researching briefs for more senior attorneys. Peaslee's strength was in the pitch. He could convince a jury to believe what they hadn't seen and forget what they had. He wanted to be in court, to be making decisions, and, most important, to keep the money he made, not spread it around to the partners.

Peaslee had always been an entrepreneur as much as a lawyer. During World War I, he had started the Silver Greyhounds, an army messenger unit responsible for getting communications from headquarters to the front more quickly. Raised on a New Jersey farm outside Philadelphia, Peaslee had put himself through Swarthmore College by convincing vaudeville theater owners to let him show silent movies and keep a percentage of the nickel admission. He could afford Columbia Law School only by volunteering at an orphanage in exchange for room and board.

Having the freedom to take on a case like Black Tom was exactly why Peaslee had started his own practice. He was willing to gamble that the MCC would handle it no differently than it had the previous cases he had filed with it. Claims were being settled in bulk, with both countries anxious to wrap up the work. While lawyers at bigger firms saw Black Tom as a black hole, Peaslee saw it as a big score.

Shortly after being hired, Peaslee met with Bonynge at his apartment on Central Park West. Peaslee told Bonynge that he had heard there were some documents proving that the German government had been responsible for acts of sabotage in the United States. Bonynge practically laughed him out of the apartment. He'd heard the rumors, too, and twice he had asked the Justice Department to comb through its files and give him anything connecting the Germans to Black Tom so he could bring a case before the MCC. Both times, he had been told that no such records existed. But Bonynge and his staff were handling thousands of cases and didn't have time to make more than superficial inquiries. Peaslee had just one major case, Black Tom. When he asked Bonynge if he could do some digging himself, the American agent, almost condescendingly, told him to go ahead; maybe he'd get lucky.

On May 24, 1924, Peaslee took the train from New York to Washington, D.C., for a meeting with the chief of the Bureau of Investigation, the precursor of the FBI. He wasn't deterred by

Bonynge's lack of encouragement. When he had been on the front lines fighting the Central powers, he'd seen the evil in their soldiers' eyes. Germans were Germans, Peaslee felt. That didn't change with a new government or a peace treaty.

At the Justice Department, Peaslee listened calmly as the chief of the Bureau of Investigation told him the same thing Bonynge had said: the documents that Peaslee wanted didn't exist. "Many attorneys had asked about them in the past few years, and they had all received the same replies, that the Department of Justice did not have them," Peaslee later recalled. But the chief indicated that that might not be the problem at all. In the nearly eight years since Black Tom had blown up, all the files in the Justice Department had been completely reorganized. "Efficiency experts," the chief said sourly. Since then, no one could find anything.

Peaslee wasn't amused. "These are some pretty extraordinary charges," he said. "I urge you, in view of these charges, to have a complete and thorough investigation."

Empty-handed, Peaslee took the next train back to New York.

A few days later, Peaslee met in his midtown Manhattan office with Bruce Bielaski, the former head of the Bureau of Investigation. In 1916, Bielaski's first statement after the Black Tom explosion had made the front page of the *New York Times,* as he tried to calm people's fears by telling them that sabotage had not been a factor. But even he was skeptical. During his conference with Peaslee, Bielaski mentioned that the Department of Justice had confiscated thousands of files from Heinrich Albert, Franz von Papen, and Wolf von Igel, von Papen's replacement. "Mr. Bielaski and I went at once to Washington," Peaslee later wrote, "and conferred again with the Chief of the Bureau of Investigation."

This time, the new chief was more sanguine. He had asked someone to search again for the German documents seized before the war. They had been found in an old government warehouse on Virginia Street in Washington. For years, the thirty large filing cabinets, filled with thousands of folders, books, and ledgers and hundreds of loose pieces of paper, had been overlooked. Most of the material was from Heinrich Albert, and Peaslee figured that every file in the former commercial attaché's office must have been hauled away, put in this warehouse, and then forgotten.

In one of the cabinets was an index in Albert's handwriting, detailing what files he had and where, including an entry for Black Tom. Peaslee, grateful that German order and efficiency could be found even when it came to nefarious activities, could see the case coming together right there, as he stood knee-deep in a pile of papers no one had seen for years. He picked the most incriminating documents he could find, memos in which Albert generally discussed paying saboteurs and buying boatloads of munitions. Every scrap of paper felt like another dollar shoved into Peaslee's pocket.

The amount of material in the warehouse was overwhelming. Peaslee and Bielaski had two file clerks helping them, but even then, there was only so much they could sift through. Peaslee went back to New York that night, feeling confident and rich, anxious to get started on his brief.

For the next week, the two file clerks waded through Albert's papers, looking for the Black Tom file, searching for a link between the German government and the sabotage in New York Harbor. They found nothing. Peaslee was not deterred, and over the next two months, he continued to work on his brief for the MCC. In the end, it would be more than a hundred pages long and include a three-hundred-page digest of the evidence. None of this evidence linked Germany directly to the sabotage in New York, but Peaslee did have proof that Germany had authorized the use of sabotage against munitions plants and depots in the United States during World War I. Albert's papers were littered with incriminating cables sent to and from various offices in Berlin. In fact, Peaslee was so convinced of Germany's guilt that he submitted only a sampling of the damaging messages he had found in Albert's files. In his brief, which he gave to Bonynge and von Lewinski in August 1924, he wrote:

The evidence is so overwhelming and convincing that it was not deemed necessary to burden the record unduly by a multiplicity of documents.... Indeed this evidence, which has recently been discovered ... is of such an overwhelming and convincing character that it does not seem that there can be any question but that the German government ordered and directed the destruction of all possible stores of munitions in the United States.... If the Commission desires further data, however, certainly the burden of establishing a defense has been thrown upon the German government.

Von Lewinski's review of the brief hadn't changed his initial opinion. He cabled the Foreign Office in Berlin, writing that the Americans could certainly prove that Germany had established sabotage networks in the United States. But convincing the commission of an indirect link between Germany and sabotage agents in general was different from fingering the specific saboteurs who had blown up Black Tom. That made von Lewinski confident that the United States would rather settle the case than argue it.

But the Weimar government still had no interest in settling. Paying off the Americans for a relationship between the German government and sabotage agents who had violated neutrality laws before World War I was tantamount to admitting that they had started the war. To be sure, the war had been in progress when Black Tom had been destroyed. But America had not technically been involved, and admitting the attack would cast Germany in an unpleasant light—if not in Washington, then certainly in Berlin.

The German ambassador, Otto Wiedfeldt, agreed with his bosses, but for an entirely different reason. He argued that everyone in the United States believed that Germany had been responsible for blowing up Black Tom, as well as for several other acts of sabotage. It had been written about in the newspapers. If everyone already thought the Germans were guilty, he said, Weimar had nothing to gain by making the case go away. In a public battle,

Germany would either lose and still be considered the war's aggressor (no worse off, really) or win and be vindicated (much better off, especially at home). Even Wilhelm Kiesselbach, the MCC's German commissioner, opposed settling the case. In a conference with his American counterpart, Chandler Anderson, he argued that current American textbooks accused the Germans of violating neutrality laws in the United States before the war. This was a chance to prove Germany's innocence.

Von Lewinski was surprised by the reaction, especially from Kiesselbach. Thus far, the German-American relationship overall had improved, partially because of the collegial attitude forged by those working on the MCC. Peaslee's brief had been a departure, attacking the Germans on an issue they took personally, and von Lewinski felt that his countrymen were taking the bait. He warned, "A bungling of the defense would be very disadvantageous politically. It must be considered that a great deal more material is undoubtedly still available and can be brought forward by the participating parties or the American government." He demanded a full investigation from the Foreign Office, not just of internal documents but also of interviews with the main players accused in Peaslee's brief. His compatriots, he feared, had played a dangerous game once and were about to play another. He did not know whether the truth could be discovered, but if it could, he needed to find it first.

As Peaslee waited for an official response, his confidence in his brief faded. Several months passed, as fall turned to winter and 1924 turned to 1925. When Bonynge broached the topic with von Lewinski, the German agent coolly answered that his government was still considering its options. The regular business of the commission continued, and cases were settled at a rapid rate, but the tone had become more adversarial. The commissioners, Anderson and Kiesselbach, still shared an office, but they spent little time together. The umpire, Edwin Parker, announced that if Black Tom was eventually argued before the commission, he would break protocol and listen to the debate. All the while, Peaslee waited and worried. He was beginning to get the same feeling an attorney has when a jury has reached a verdict against him and won't look him in the eye. By early January, he no longer expected a settlement. He knew he'd have to work the case; he'd have to fight the Germans again. He'd have to find the Black Tom connection.

Bielaski continued to assist Peaslee on the case, digging through old files at the warehouse on Virginia Street, looking for clues. One afternoon, the ex–bureau chief casually mentioned that the British secret service had been active in the United States before World War I, constantly monitoring the docks around New York Harbor, making sure German ships didn't escape internment, and keeping its eye on alleged German spies. A lot of those spies had tried sailing through the British blockade under false passports, only to end up in Scotland Yard. Peaslee hadn't even considered visiting London, but now it seemed obvious. He'd go that spring, when the weather, and perhaps his case, would be warmer.

Nearly every day through the winter and early spring of 1925, von Lewinski conducted interviews with the men who had represented German interests in the United States before World War I. They appeared honorable and beyond reproach. Many of them, such as von Papen, had deftly made the transition from one of the kaiser's warmongers to a proud member of the Weimar government, with a place in the Reichstag. Every accusation that was corroborated by material from Albert's, von Papen's, or von Igel's files was admitted to. But every accusation Peaslee made without proof was met with a denial. The German testimonies were expansive and dovetailed perfectly. They were also clever and well crafted. Denying the existence of a spy network in the United States was impossible, but admitting to it made their denials of Black Tom seem more credible.

The former ambassador, Johann von Bernstorff, admitted that the embassy had used "legal means" to thwart munitions production in the United States. He didn't clarify what that meant, but he did add that he had never seen any orders from his government authorizing sabotage. And, he claimed, whenever anarchist groups, usually those affiliated with the Irish, had suggested destroying munitions plants, he, von Papen, or Karl Boy-Ed had flatly rejected the idea. Even though von Bernstorff admitted that Germany had sent agents to the United States, he said that they had been assigned relatively harmless tasks, such as causing labor strikes on the docks, running forged passport operations, or helping Franz von Rintelen buy supplies such as cotton and food. "What is false," von Bernstorff said, "is to tie this with sabotage in the United States."

Boy-Ed backed up the former ambassador, saying, "Never were we in any way disposed towards sabotage during my stay in the United States." Instead, he said, any cables suggesting sabotage had been directed at Canada and Mexico, which also had businesses shipping munitions to the Allies. Boy-Ed emphasized that all the agents in the United States had been told to obey the law and to "do everything to avoid what in any way could be interpreted as a violation of this hospitality." Wolf von Igel testified, "I have never given any payment of any kind for sabotage." He acted as though he were insulted by the question, emphasizing that the Germans had desperately wanted to keep the Americans out of the war, not provoke them into joining it. Kurt Jahnke, one of the alleged Black Tom saboteurs, said that neither he nor his partner, Lothar Witzke, had been instructed to commit sabotage "in America, that is on American ground and soil."

Von Lewinski, wary of arguing the case at first, was now more confident. In the eight months since Peaslee had filed his brief, nothing new had been uncovered. Although the German government had settled thousands of cases, von Lewinski told Bonynge that there would be no such resolution regarding Black Tom.

Detective work was not Amos Peaslee's strong point. He was a showman, a salesman with a gifted tongue. He worked hard at building a case, but he worked harder at selling it, making it palatable. He thought he had done that with Black Tom, but he had misread his opponents. Now, in the spring of 1925, he arrived in London and headed for Scotland Yard.

The red and white brick police headquarters, built on the site of a former palace where Scottish royalty had stayed when visiting England, was set along the Thames River. The perfectly manicured trees planted in front of Scotland Yard were just beginning to bloom when Peaslee arrived, their white buds giving way to green leaves that looked bright and bold against the building's bricks. Peaslee noticed this in passing as he walked into the building, then quickly put the images out of his mind. Back home, he had a young wife, a two-year-old son, and a three-year-old daughter. His small firm couldn't support a never-ending case that might require experts, frequent trips to Europe, and translators. He had been foolhardy and blinded by the promise of a huge payday when he had taken on Black Tom. Within months, he had gone from cocky to desperate.

Peaslee was led to a dank, windowless room. Inside, the officer escorting him opened a cabinet and handed him a folder, just a single thin file. Peaslee opened it. He saw a yellowed clipping from the *New York Times* with the headline MUNITIONS EXPLOSIONS SHAKE NEW YORK. There was nothing else in the file.

Peaslee realized that he would be sailing back to New York as clueless as when he had left.

Faced with the task of researching the case even more, Peaslee resorted to what he did best: he sold the idea of it. His connections in the international law and diplomatic communities were numerous, and he began to tap his contacts aggressively, selling them on the importance of the case, of justice being done and of setting a precedent that America could not be a target. But his friends knew him too well. After he'd made his speech, they'd tease him that as good as his pitch might be, he couldn't hide the fact that his own agenda came first, sticking it to the Germans second. Still, those friends also couldn't stop themselves from helping him. Peaslee pushed hard, but he was endearing. And those working for big firms especially admired that he gambled on the kinds of cases they were too comfortable to consider.

It was during one of Peaslee's breathless pitches that a colleague mentioned the name Blinker Hall.

On July 29, Peaslee wrote to Wilson's secretary of state, Robert Lansing, asking for an introduction to Hall: "You will perhaps remember that I was associated with the American Commission to Negotiate Peace in Paris and from December 1918 to September 1919 served as a major in the army and as director of courier services."

Lansing did remember Peaslee and led him to Admiral William Sims, who had been commander of the navy in European waters during the war, and who also happened to be Hall's best friend in the United States. On August 14, at Sims's home in Newport, Rhode Island, Peaslee earnestly explained his dilemma. Sims was sympathetic and gave Peaslee a letter of introduction to give to Hall. Anxious to get to England, Peaslee boarded a ship for Europe four days later.

Peaslee called on Hall, now fifty-five years old, at noon on August 27. The admiral was retired from the British navy and had become a member of England's elite. He had been knighted by King George V for his work during World War I, was an elected member of Parliament, and lived comfortably on Cadogan Gardens in a posh section of London. Hall's five-story redbrick home was topped with an attic and a pitched roof, which made it taller than most London row houses. Despite being just a few feet off King's Road, one of the city's busiest thoroughfares, the block was tranquil, the street sounds absorbed by the lush green garden across the way.

Hall didn't like to be disturbed, and he had reluctantly agreed to meet with Peaslee as a favor to Sims. Even then, he wasn't sure he would help the American lawyer. That afternoon, they sat in

Hall's parlor, looking through three floor-to-ceiling windows into the park. As Peaslee presented his credentials and his case, Hall seemed to stare straight through him. The war had been over for almost seven years, but Hall's first instinct was still to size a man up, decide whether he was ally or enemy, before trusting him. He sat silently as Peaslee continued to talk about the case. Peaslee was nervous, not just because Hall's eyes, despite the incessant blinking, remained locked on his but also because he needed Hall's co-operation. Hall was his last chance.

Peaslee filled the gaps in the conversation with minor details of the investigation, unsure whether he was convincing the expressionless Hall that he should help. The less Hall said, the more Peaslee felt compelled to talk, and since Hall said little, Peaslee prattled on like a ticker. Finally, Hall cut Peaslee off and said, "Well, I will do it."

Hall walked Peaslee down to his cellar, where windows in the front of the room led to a dog's-eye view of the Cadogan Gardens' sidewalk. The walls were lined with tightly sealed tin boxes piled deep and high. Inside were ten thousand decoded German cables and radiograms, the products of Hall's handiwork. Peaslee could barely believe his eyes, and for the first time a smile registered on Hall's face. "I sealed up these boxes with instructions that they were not to be opened for twenty years," he said. "However, you have caused me to change my mind. I will open them up for you. I am going on a shooting trip to Scotland, but my house and servants are yours and you may live here while you are working."

Peaslee stayed in Hall's cellar for the next five days. He eye-balled every cable, copying by hand the ones that appeared to be valuable. One was from Jahnke to the Foreign Office, dated April 3, 1918. After the United States had entered the war, the German agents in America had been told to make a run for Mexico, where they would reorganize. Originally, the Foreign Office had named Frederick Hinsch the head of all Mexican sabotage operations, which had drawn Jahnke's anger. Over the course of several months in early 1918, Jahnke had pestered Berlin to reconsider its decision, citing his sabotage successes in the United States as proof that he should report to no one. On April 3, he wrote, "The destruction of war factories and provisions in the U.S.A is satisfactory. . . . My success justifies the confidence which has been placed in me. . . . Hinsch has absolutely no organization; it is out of the question placing my services at his disposal. . . . He is tactless and works with characteristic pettiness and personal spite." Three days later, Berlin relented, allowing Jahnke to work on his own in Mexico.

Peaslee copied another message, this one written on April 12, 1917, from the German ambassador in Mexico to Hans Marguerre and Rudolf Nadolny: "Frederick Herrmann professes to have received from General Staff a year ago, and renewed in January by Paul Hilken, a commission to set fire to the Tampico Oil Field and proposes now to carry it out."

For Peaslee, the names mentioned in the messages were as important as the content. He already had cables from the top layer of German diplomats—von Bernstorff, von Papen, von Igel, Albert—about agents in the United States and general acts of sabotage, but they weren't specific enough to frighten Germany into a settlement. He had heard rumors about who some of those agents might have been (Witzke and Kristoff), but they remained unsubstantiated. With Hall's files, he had concrete information—names of agents, such as Hilken, Hinsch, and Herrmann, who were working in the United States at the time. He had the foundation for the second layer of names he had been looking for. Now he had to dig deeper.

Following protocol, Bonynge sent von Lewinski copies of the Hall cables that Peaslee brought back from England. The American agent thought that they were good leads, but none mentioned Black Tom, and therefore the evidence wouldn't scare von Lewinski into settling the case. He was wrong. With the cables laid out before him, von Lewinski knew where the Americans were headed. He did not know where Herrmann, Hilken, and Hinsch were, but he knew that Peaslee could track them down.

And unlike the former ambassadors and diplomats whom von Lewinski could prepare before their testimony, he couldn't be sure that Herrmann, Hilken, and Hinsch would deny Peaslee's claims of German sabotage.

Von Lewinski again approached the Foreign Office, now pleading with them to settle the case. At the very least, he argued, they should formally suggest settling in order to slow down the American investigation. Negotiations would consume and distract the Americans, diverting their attention from finding the agents. This time, armed with more specific evidence, he was more persuasive. In the winter of 1925, he told Bonynge that the Germans were ready to talk.

Peaslee immediately stopped looking for Hilken, Herrmann, and Hinsch and instead focused on determining a fair settlement. If Peaslee added the $20 million in Black Tom damages to the Kingsland fire and nine years of interest, his tally ran to nearly $40 million. It was a staggering figure that even he knew he couldn't sell.

On February 26, 1926, he visited von Lewinski's office in Washington. When Peaslee's first settlement offer came in at more than $20 million plus interest, von Lewinski didn't bother to negotiate. Instead, he politely told Peaslee to come back with a new offer. When he returned, von Lewinski dismissed him again. And again. And again. Peaslee visited von Lewinski five times that day before the German agent finally accepted his proposal. Germany would pay the Americans $12 million plus $6 million in interest, $18 million total.

For a moment, it seemed, both countries were satisfied. But word of the pending settlement soon spread through the Reichstag. A majority of the members were opposed to settling a case that sullied Germany's reputation, but one in particular was furious: Franz von Papen. In early March, the former German military attaché railed against the settlement on the floor of the Reichstag: "I have personally suffered enough from the poison of public opinion until now. My record is clean. I most positively demand a hearing of this lawsuit with the broadest publicity, so that I can once and for all draw the line and end these procedures from the American side. A cowardly compromise can never be considered. I would come forward in the German public against such a compromise with all the means that were available to me."

Von Papen's colleagues rallied behind him, and his political star began to rise. Meanwhile, over the next several months, negotiations stalled. Von Lewinski strung the Americans along with promises that his government would accept their proposal soon. The Americans complained to Parker that the Germans were deliberately delaying the matter. Finally, in early 1927, Parker informed Bonynge that Germany had decided not to settle the case. In March, nearly three years after Peaslee's preliminary brief had been given to the German agent as a courtesy, Bonynge officially submitted the Black Tom and Kingsland cases to the MCC. There would be no more negotiation; the battle over who had destroyed Black Tom had officially begun.

Chapter **Ten**

HAROLD MARTIN'S HOME life reflected what he appreciated about his bureaucratic career: it was predictable, secure, and comforting. During the summers, he'd rent a cottage for his wife, Alcie, and their teenage daughters somewhere on the beach in Maine, Virginia, or Maryland. They'd go for two weeks; he'd go for one, using the time alone in Washington, D.C., to dig through the piles of work on his desk.

The summer of 1928 was no different. The Martins had a cottage outside Portland, Maine, for the first half of August. Particularly busy at the MCC office preparing for a trip to Europe at the end of September, Martin considered skipping his vacation altogether until he got an urgent call from his older daughter, Francesca, telling him he needed to get to Portland right away.

Alcie had fallen ill. A sickness was racing through her system, inflaming the marrow in her spine. Within twenty-four hours, she would lose the use of her legs and her reflexes. Her illness was called transverse myelitis, and it robbed Alcie of the feeling of her husband's touch as he massaged her limbs. She couldn't swat away the mosquitoes that settled on her listless arms. Her children's voices became faint, until she heard nothing at all. Seven days after contracting the disease, Alcie Martin died.

His wife's death left Martin feeling hollow, cold, and, most disorienting for him, frayed. He wrapped himself in his work to keep warm. Before Alcie died, he was a pious man. Now he put his faith in his caseload, in the steady logic of the law. Peaslee was still the lead attorney on the sabotage claims (as the Black Tom and Kingsland cases were casually called), but because they had been officially filed with the MCC, Martin took a more active role. The work focused his energy, helping him to channel his anger at whatever, or whomever, had rearranged his life.

On September 29, a chilly, rainy day in Manhattan, Martin left New York Harbor for a five-day trip across the Atlantic on the *Ile de France.* He was headed for London to meet with Blinker Hall and examine more of his secret service records, which the British government had decided only an official agent of the MCC could review. The commission was low on funds, and Martin, now making $7,500 a year, couldn't pay out of his own pocket and hope to be reimbursed. Peaslee had offered to pay for the trip, and special permission from the State Department had been granted. Armed with $200 in cash, a $1,000 line of credit, a diplomatic passport, and a letter from Francesca, Martin set sail for England. He tucked the note from his daughter inside the breast pocket of his jacket. She was a freshman at George Washington University, but she still called her father "Daddykins." In the days after his wife's death, she had put aside her grief to help him get over his. On the front of the envelope, she had written, "Do not open for two days."

The trip was rough, with high seas slamming the massive bow of the cruise liner. On the second day, suffering from a bout of seasickness, Martin was confined to his room. He had been waiting to open Francesca's letter, and settling into a small chair near the porthole, he began reading. She offered her prescription for nausea: taking a long stroll. She also included a picture of Alcie, writing:

I'm sure it will help you. It's the picture I love best of Mother. It just seems as if we can see her looking down and smiling on us all and it makes us determined to do our best, our very best for her sake.

Remember Jesus is always with us and ready to listen to our prayers. If we ever feel discouraged or sad, we must just go to him and he will hear our prayers, "Lo I am with you always."

Daddy take care of yourself and enjoy your trip as I know you will. I hope you'll meet just lots and lots of lovely people and maybe get to Paris. Please enjoy your trip just as much as you can. You must come home well and fine. You mustn't worry about us. We can get along all right until you come back again. We'll take care of ourselves and each other.

Feeling better, Martin decided to go for a long stroll.

The Germans had taken their time replying to the Americans' official MCC filing, waiting until December 1927 to submit their response. While Bonynge had included nineteen volumes of evidence with his original brief, the Germans had offered none. Instead, they waited until late spring 1928 to send any evidence backing up their defense.

The Americans built their case around a cable, sent from the Foreign Office to the German attaché offices in the United States on January 26, 1915, which authorized acts of sabotage. "In United States sabotage can reach to all kinds of factories for war deliveries," it read. "Under no circumstances compromise Embassy." The authorization, the Americans claimed, begat the payments from Albert, von Papen, and von Igel to men like Hilken, who begat agents like Hinsch, Herrmann, Jahnke, and Witzke, who begat explosions like Black Tom.

While it seemed so clear-cut on the surface, Bonynge, Martin, and Peaslee all worried about von Lewinski and his defense. If the cable itself was the black-and-white piece of evidence the American lawyers believed it to be, the case would have settled in 1924, 1926, or at any other point in the four years since Peaslee filed his preliminary brief.

Heinrich Albert, the German commercial attaché, solicited millions in investments from German-American companies, ensuring that Germany's sabotage operations were always well funded. CREDIT: COURTESY OF THE LIBRARY OF CONGRESS

German Ambassador Johann von Bernstorff charmed President Wilson's aides and was a regular at high-society parties, all while overseeing the activities of German spies. CREDIT: COURTESY OF THE LIBRARY OF CONGRESS

Franz von Papen's position as military attaché to the United States was largely ceremonial. But when the war in Europe began, he created Germany's War Intelligence Center in New York. CREDIT: © BROWN BROTHERS, STERLING, PA.

Paul Hilken's status as a member of Baltimore's elite provided the perfect cover for financing a network of German agents. CREDIT: HENRY LANDAU, *The Enemy Within*

Frederick Hinsch, captain of a German merchant ship interned in Baltimore Harbor and Hilken's top lieutenant. CREDIT: HENRY LANDAU, *The Enemy Within*

The U-boat *Deutschland*'s arrival in Baltimore Harbor created a sensation on the East Coast, with reporters from Baltimore to New York renting yachts to get closer looks at the well-guarded ship. CREDIT: © BROWN BROTHERS, STERLING, PA

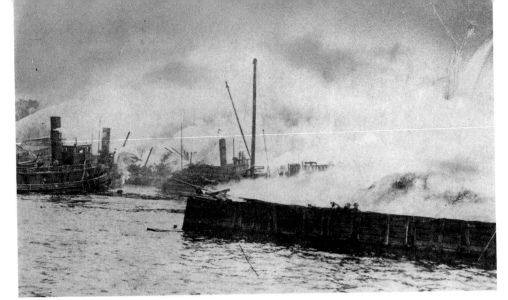

The Black Tom explosion leveled nearly all the buildings within a mile of its center and turned barges into ashes. During the first days of sifting through the wreckage, workers dodged bullets as they uncovered smoldering hot spots.
CREDIT: © BROWN BROTHERS, STERLING, PA

Lothar Witzke *(above)* and Kurt
Jahnke, the German saboteurs assigned
to blow up Black Tom. CREDIT: ©
BROWN BROTHERS, STERLING, PA
(WITZKE); HENRY LANDAU, *The Enemy
Within* (JAHNKE)

Fred Herrmann *(left)* and Adam Siegel in Mexico in 1917, shortly after being told that war with the United States was imminent and all German spies should flee. CREDIT: HENRY LANDAU, *The Enemy Within*

Harold Martin *(left)* and Robert Bonynge, the American agents before the commission. Bonynge, the U.S. face of the sabotage cases, counted on Martin to make him look good. CREDIT: REGINALD HALL AND AMOS PEASLEE, *Three Wars with Germany* (MARTIN); © *The New York Times* (BONYNGE)

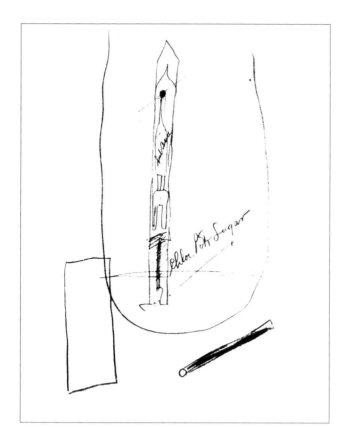

Herrmann's diagram of the deadly pencil bombs, known as "glasses." CREDIT: COURTESY OF THE NATIONAL ARCHIVES

A page from Herrmann's secret *Blue Book* message written to Hilken in 1917. Originally written in lemon juice, the message was invisible until Hilken heated the page with an iron. CREDIT: COURTESY OF THE NATIONAL ARCHIVES

John and Ellen McCloy on the steps of the Supreme Court Building in 1939, posing with copies of the final Black Tom brief. CREDIT: COURTESY OF ELLEN McCLOY HALL

Amos Peaslee photographed in the mid-1930s, more than a decade after first agreeing to accept the Black Tom case. CREDIT: COURTESY OF DICK PEASLEE

Von Lewinski knew how to play the MCC. For starters, he took advantage of the fact that witnesses were not allowed to testify in front of the commissioners and the umpire. He knew that the panel would never get to hear someone struggle through an explanation, stammering to remember his story, getting tripped up by a cross-examination. He knew the panelists would never get to judge someone's credibility with their own eyes, never see if a witness shifted uncomfortably in his seat or looked to his attorney for direction. The texture and tone of what people said would be stripped away.

In October 1928, while Martin was culling the files of the British secret service, von Lewinski met with Rudolf Nadolny, the head of Section III-B in Germany's Foreign Office during the war. Twelve years earlier, Nadolny had sat quiet as a ghost in the III-B offices as his aide, Hans Marguerre, had delivered sabotage instructions to Herrmann, Hilken, and Anton Dilger. He was now fifty-five years old and four years into a nine-year reign as Germany's ambassador to Turkey. Like von Papen, he had made the transition from a prominent role in the kaiser's government to one in the Weimar regime. And like von Papen, he had been adamant that the Germans not settle the Black Tom case, for the good of Germany's psyche and his own reputation.

The January 26, 1915, cable had been sent from Nadolny's office, which meant that he was the first person von Lewinski used to minimize its significance. Nadolny began by humbly identifying himself as a former captain in the reserves, not as Germany's current ambassador to Turkey. He then continued, "The telegram of January 26, 1915—according to information received by me in 1916—had not been followed out, and the fact that neither before nor afterwards were similar communications or instructions issued, seemed to me to prove . . . that neither the telegram nor other steps of the office in my charge had resulted in sabotage in the United States.

"Whether the message was formulated in my section or whether the text was brought to me I can no longer recall. . . . The telegram contained, I want to emphasize, no order but merely information that certain sabotage acts could be transacted in the United States. . . . [From] the fact the telegram did not contain an order, it follows as a matter of course that Mr. von Papen, if he did not agree with it, had the right to disregard it altogether.

"Mr. von Papen, in a conference soon after his recall from the United States, discussed the principles which controlled his actions. He related that he refused, in agreement with the Ambassador, to suggest or undertake sabotage. . . . After the telegram had been sent, I was told in the Foreign Office that sabotage in the United States must by no means be undertaken."

Nadolny's testimony was deft and duplicitous, and without a chance to cross-examine, the Americans had no easy means to react. But the sabotage cable was just a starting point. Since his first visit to Hall's cellar, Peaslee had been sitting on the names of potential agents. With no settlement in sight, he had to find them.

Paul Hilken had become something less than what his father had intended. Once considered royalty in heavily German Baltimore, he was now divorced and living alone in an apartment on West 183rd Street in Manhattan. A tire business he had invested in had gone under, as had a trucking company he'd begun. Now Hilken worked as a paint salesman for a company whose office was, coincidentally, in the Whitehall Building. Every time he went to work, he was reminded of the power he'd once wielded. He had celebrated the destruction of Black Tom with Hoppenburg, Hinsch, and Herrmann in this building. Now he carried a sense of failure with him when he walked through the doors.

Peaslee got to Hilken at a time when he was disenchanted, disengaged, and ready to come clean. Sitting with Peaslee in the lawyer's Fifth Avenue office in October 1928, Hilken recalled how he had first met von Rintelen at the Ritz in Philadelphia. After hearing about von Rintelen's daring acts of espionage, Hilken had been anxious to volunteer his services. At first, he said, von Rintelen had made him the paymaster in Baltimore, responsible for recruiting and funding Hinsch. Then he described the February

1916 meeting with Nadolny and Marguerre in Berlin. He remembered Nadolny as a spooky man who said little as Marguerre gave each man—Dilger, Herrmann, and Hilken—an assignment. Marguerre's message, Hilken said, was clear: they were to begin sabotage activities immediately. The Germans wired cash to the United States for Hilken to use, gave Herrmann a case of explosive glasses, and handed Dilger vials of anthrax. Hilken admitted that he had paid Hinsch and Herrmann $70,000 combined once they were back in the United States. And he remembered a specific payment he had made to Hinsch.

"Shortly after Black Tom we met in New York," Hilken told Peaslee.

"When you say 'met in New York,' who do you mean?" Peaslee asked.

"Hinsch, Herrmann and myself, and I remember a dinner that we had at the Astor at that time . . . and I remember giving Hinsch a payment which I think was $2,000."

"That was about what date?"

"That was in early August 1916."

"What did Hinsch say he wanted the money for?"

"Well, Hinsch told me at that time that he had hired the men that set fire to Black Tom."

"He told you that at that time?"

"He told me that. . . . I remember perfectly asking Hinsch about Black Tom and his saying, when I wanted details of how it was done, 'Oh, it is better, much better, for you to know nothing about that.' I remember that perfectly."

The case was back on track.

That November, Peaslee had even more luck. He found Fred Herrmann's brothers living in Roselle Park, New Jersey, less than an hour from Manhattan. After the war, he learned, Herrmann had moved to Chile and was now living in Santiago. He married a Chilean woman, had children, and found a job in a bank. He had become a good man, they told Peaslee. He'd tell the truth.

On the last day of November, Peaslee cabled Herrmann at the National City Bank in Santiago. He explained who he was, that he was representing claimants in the sabotage cases before the Mixed Claims Commission, and that he understood Herrmann may have some relevant information. "Your cooperation," he added, "would be greatly appreciated by our government."

Herrmann wasn't the same carefree teenage spy he had been at the start of World War I. His blond hair was nearly white now, bleached by the South American sun. His once mischievous grin came less easily to him. He had, after all, run away from the United States. When he read the cable, he stood motionless for a moment, staring at the words, as if his past had a stranglehold on his throat. His mind jumped through several scenarios. All of them ended badly.

For several days, he pondered what he would do next. He spoke with a friend, told him all about his past—his spying; his trips across the Atlantic, beating the barricade; the sabotage. He told his friend how much he feared losing his job in Chile and having his family find out about his past. He feared, more than anything, going back to America and being charged for what he had done. On December 5, he cabled Peaslee: "Received your cable. Believe you are mistaken. Don't see how I can be of assistance to you. Cannot leave Chile as my business is here."

But Herrmann underestimated his American correspondent. In early January, Peaslee wired Herrmann that Paul Hilken, who was now cooperating with the investigation, would "arrive Valparaiso on Steamer *Santa Marie* January 10th. Will bring interesting data to show you."

Herrmann could do nothing but wait anxiously.

Von Lewinski unveiled his "mosquito defense" in January 1929, just four months before the first round of oral arguments.

It had become standard practice for the American and German agents to submit testimony as they received it, giving both sides a chance to review the evidence and rebut it. It also gave them the opportunity to argue their cases in the court of public opinion, which continued to drive how their governments approached these claims.

Von Lewinski had found a barge captain whose ship had been docked at Black Tom on the night of the explosion. The captain, named John Grundman, gave von Lewinski an affidavit in which he swore that, at the end of the pier, near the watchman's shanty, he had seen a smoldering fire—the kind that came from burning rubbish, not wood; the kind that produced more smoke than flame. The reason for such a blaze was simple: "To drive away the mosquitoes," Grundman testified. "It was about the worst place in Jersey, on account of the swamps." The fire, erupting out of control, must have been what caused the explosions, he concluded.

As von Lewinski had expected, reporters lapped up the story. It didn't matter that the Americans almost immediately produced rebuttal testimony from the guards on duty at Black Tom that night, all of whom claimed that there had been no rubbish fire and no watchman's shanty where Grundman had said he'd seen one. The rebuttals didn't get reported. For now, as far as the press was concerned, the Black Tom disaster had been caused by the determined New Jersey mosquito.

The *Santa Marie* pulled into Valparaiso at 7:30 a.m. on January 10. The South American port was located in the shadow of the Andes, and as the ship docked, the sun was just beginning to peak over the mountains. To Hilken, it felt a very long way from Berlin or Baltimore.

Herrmann arrived at the docks a little past 8:00 a.m. with a friend he called Mr. Lemberg. He didn't feel comfortable meeting Hilken alone, nor did he want to meet Hilken on board the *Santa Marie*. Instead, Herrmann asked Lemberg to go on board, find Hilken, and tell him that Herrmann was waiting on the dock. When Lemberg returned alone, he reported that Hilken wanted Herrmann to come on board because Hilken wasn't finished shaving. They may once have been coconspirators, but now neither man entirely trusted the other. Herrmann told Lemberg to go back and tell Hilken that they could meet at the Hotel Astor in Valparaiso at 10:00 a.m. Hilken agreed.

Together for the first time in a decade, the suspicions seemed to evaporate and the two men acted like old friends. Herrmann asked Hilken about his kids, whom he hadn't seen since they were young, and Hilken congratulated Herrmann on his wife and two children. Herrmann was now thirty-four, the same age Hilken had been when the two had met. Back then, Herrmann had been a brash and cocky adventurer; now he was a grown man, pale and nervous.

"What brings you down to Chile?" Herrman asked.

"I'd rather talk to you alone," Hilken said, staring at Lemberg.

Herrmann refused. He preferred that Lemberg stay, and Hilken was in no position to negotiate. Hilken told Herrmann that he had decided to come clean with the Americans about his role in German-sponsored sabotage. But he had no credibility and only scant evidence to offer the lawyers. He needed Herrmann to corroborate his story.

Hilken asked Herrmann if he would go to the United States to testify. Herrmann said, "I cannot." Hilken explained that he had already testified and that Peaslee had "papers to identify my activities. And they found your name and had connected both of us." Hilken thought he was giving the Americans just enough "to win the case," saying that he had refused to tell everything he knew — specifically, "I've disclosed nothing about your connection with sabotage activities."

Hilken then handed Herrmann a list of questions that Peaslee had prepared. Herrmann read the questions. He could see that Hilken had made it seem as if he had been nothing more than a banker and didn't know what anyone had done with the money he'd doled out. "That would shift the responsibility onto me," Herrmann concluded uneasily.

Once more, Hilken asked Herrmann to testify and to sign his testimony before the American consul in Valparaiso. Herrmann had no intention of doing so, but instead of refusing outright, he asked Hilken, "What kind of reward would I get for testifying? What did you get?"

"Nothing," Hilken answered. He said that he was just glad to "get out of this mess as easy as it appears I'm doing by giving testimony more or less in private."

Then Herrmann brought up the one thing that Hilken had ignored, the one thing that made Herrmann most reluctant to testify: People had been killed as a consequence of Black Tom. It was possible the two of them could be charged with murder. If he signed a statement and answered these questions, he asked, would he get immunity? Hilken said he didn't know.

"I then left Paul," Herrmann remembered, "and I reported to the German consul at Valparaiso." Herrmann's reasoning was simple: the Germans had gotten him into this situation, and they should get him out. He told the German consul that he had been implicated in sabotage activities in the United States, then "I asked him what he was going to do about it."

Flustered and frightened by Herrmann's demands and demeanor, the consul sent Herrmann to the German ambassador in Santiago, sixty-five miles away. The drive did little to calm Herrmann's nerves.

In Santiago, Herrmann recounted his meeting with Hilken for the ambassador. The Germans had yet to establish a permanent residence in Chile, and their temporary embassy was a shoddy, one-story house in which the ambassador and his aide shared an office. As he walked in, Herrmann couldn't help but notice what terrible shape the building was in. "It looked as if they did not have the money to keep the place going," he recalled. He handed over the questionnaire and a pamphlet that Hilken had left him. The pamphlet contained estimates of what the Americans thought the case was worth. The ambassador was stunned by the figures.

"How can this be?" he asked.

"It's true, they are dollars," Herrmann answered. "Not pesos."

The more Herrmann spoke, the less lucid he became. He jumped from one subject to another and from past to present, making connections that only he could see. Nadolny, he said, was the man who had given the sabotage instructions. He repeated Nadolny's name again and again, as though he were in a trance.

The ambassador finally interrupted Herrmann. "Nadolny is the ambassador to Turkey," he said. "You must never mention Nadolny with the activities you just told me about."

The ambassador promised to cable Berlin for instructions and said that everything would work out. Then he asked Herrmann what he was going to do about Hilken and the Americans.

"I'm not going to do anything," Herrmann answered. "It's up to you to do something. You're to get in touch with Berlin and I will follow their instructions, but I'm not going to do anything on my own."

Several weeks later, on February 20, 1929, Herrmann was called back to the German Embassy. The ambassador asked Herrmann to sit down and showed him statements that had been prepared in Berlin by von Lewinski. "I didn't want to go back to the States," Herrmann later testified. "I wanted to keep my position with the bank. I didn't want to be mixed up in it, and the easiest way out was to sign these statements. What was in them, I didn't know."

Without bothering to read them, he quickly signed and hoped his troubles were behind him.

Hilken's testimony had rattled the normally unshakable von Lewinski. For the first time, the Americans were presenting specific details linking German agents to Black Tom. Hilken's testimony about paying $2,000 to Hinsch for arranging the explosion would, if credible, be enough to persuade even the lenient and sympathetic MCC of Germany's guilt.

Von Lewinski showed a copy of Hilken's testimony to John Schroeder, the German head of the North German Lloyd shipping company in the United States, Hilken's employer during the war. Schroeder relayed both his and the German agent's concerns to his bosses in Bremen. "This testimony is, I am sorry to say, painful for us, as Mr. Hilken accuses indirectly our former captain, Mr. Hinsch, to have participated. Mr. von Lewinski says that this testimony is nearly catastrophic for the German government, and he feels that this testimony will be decisive if he should not succeed to overcome it."

To do this, von Lewinski needed to discredit the supposed $2,000 payment to Hinsch. Submitting an affidavit from Hinsch, a German whose motives could be questioned, wouldn't suffice. Von Lewinski needed the one man Hilken had trusted most during the war, the only other man who had had access to Hilken's spymaster accounts and his permission to make payments. Even better for von Lewinski, the man was an American.

A month after Herrmann signed the affidavit the German ambassador had prepared for him, an emissary from the American Embassy in Santiago, named Mr. Green, visited the National City Bank where Herrmann worked. The diplomat's tone was even and calm. He asked Herrmann to explain his whereabouts during the war. Herrmann said that he had been in Chile. Green looked confused and asked Herrmann if he was sure he had been in Chile during the war. Herrmann didn't hesitate.

"I'm positive," Herrmann said. "What do you want to know?"

"A Mr. F. L. Herrmann was implicated in sabotage in the explosion of different munitions factories in the United States. You fit the description. What kind of citizenship papers do you have?"

"Chilean."

"Do you know Paul Hilken? Or Frederick Hinsch?"

"No," Herrmann answered. "You've made a mistake. I'm not the Herrmann you are looking for."

"Do you know any others?"

"Yes, there is a druggist in Valparaiso," Herrmann said. He didn't tell Green that the man was seventy years old.

Green politely dismissed Herrmann, telling him he had nothing to worry about. But bank manager Douglas Allen, an American, wasn't as comforting. After he walked the diplomat to the door, Allen paused at Herrmann's desk. He asked Herrmann, in a manner less friendly than Green's, if he had been involved in anything that had just been discussed. Herrmann coolly replied, "No."

A week later, Herrmann heard from Green again. This time, the diplomat asked if Herrmann would visit the embassy that afternoon. He arrived at four o'clock, and immediately the questioning took on a less friendly tone than before. Green was pointed and confrontational, demanding to know what Herrmann knew about Black Tom. Herrmann didn't bother answering. Instead, he criticized Green, telling him that it wasn't very tactful to put him on the spot, as he had the week before, in front of his boss. "If you had any questions for me," Herrmann said, "you should have asked me personally and alone and perhaps I would have been able to help you out."

Green pulled back, telling Herrmann he had nothing to fear at the bank as long as he admitted what he knew.

"Admit what?" Herrmann asked.

"Admit the truth," Green answered.

Herrmann apologized. He said he didn't know anything. He said it was a case of mistaken identity.

Green again told him that his job was safe, but Herrmann refused to answer any more questions, and the meeting ended.

Back at the bank, Allen began regularly asking about the case, always in an accusatory tone. He also increasingly found fault with Herrmann's performance. In early May, Allen asked Herrmann if he would resign. Herrmann refused. If he left, he wanted to be fired. They repeated this routine daily until mid-July, when Herrmann was finally let go.

Later that day, Herrmann sued the National City Bank for overtime. The next day, the Germans put him on their payroll.

When Hilken failed with Herrmann, he moved on to Carl Ahrendt. His former protégé had done well at the German Lloyd. In 1929, Ahrendt was living outside Detroit, where he was the shipping company's representative. During a visit to New

York, Hilken tried to convince him that testifying truthfully was in the best interests of Germany. Ahrendt acted annoyed. The notion of his former boss, a man he had once admired, pleading with him to testify was unsettling. He found Hilken's tactics — trying to fool him into believing that his affidavit would help Germany — insulting. Ahrendt warned his bosses that Hilken would likely contact other German Lloyd employees.

If Ahrendt was unwilling to help the Americans, he was more than willing to lend von Lewinski a hand. Hilken's claim that he had paid Hinsch $2,000 after Black Tom had exploded was still unchallenged by von Lewinski, and he was counting on Ahrendt to discredit his old boss. No one else had had access to Hilken's German Lloyd accounts. No one else could have made payments on his behalf.

In mid-March of 1929, two weeks before oral arguments began, Ahrendt sat down in his German Lloyd office as a witness for the Germans. "Sometime in the month of January 1916," Ahrendt began, "Captain Hinsch called me on a long distance telephone from New York, I then being in Baltimore, and asked me to bring to him in New York immediately the sum of $2,000, which he said would be provided to me by the cashier. I applied to the cashier, who furnished me with $2,000, in the form of two $1,000 bills, with which I departed for New York on the next train. I arrived in New York sometime after five o'clock in the afternoon, and proceeded to Captain Hinsch's hotel, where I delivered the money. I did not ask what the money was for, nor did he tell me, except that in calling me over the telephone to ask me to bring the money he said, 'I want to show some people here that I am able to get money when I want it.' He told me that he had asked the North German Lloyd's agent in New York for the $2,000 and the agent had refused to give it to him.

"I am able to fix my time of this event as in January 1916 because of the following circumstance, that impressed the matter on my memory. An intimate friend of mine was an automobile salesman, and had to attend the automobile show then being held in Baltimore. During the evening session of the show he had to wear a tuxedo. I had a very good overcoat while my friend's was shabby. To enable him to make a better appearance at the show, we exchanged overcoats for that week, and I therefore had to go to New York wearing a rather shabby overcoat, the sleeves of which were too short for me. That the incident occurred in cold weather is further fixed in my memory by reason of the fact that, as Captain Hinsch and I were walking along Fifth Avenue together, going out somewhere in the evening after I had delivered the money to him, I remarked that I was shivering with an overcoat on, while he was apparently comfortable, although not wearing any overcoat. He said, 'You young fellows don't have any blood in you.'"

Hilken said that he had paid Hinsch the money in August at a dinner party. Now Ahrendt testified that he had done so in January at a hotel. Such divergences were good for the German case. Ahrendt's detailed testimony was enough to cast doubt, and with the commission doubt was better than proof. There was no hard evidence, such as Hilken's 1916 checkbook, to prove who was lying. Von Lewinski began to breathe easier.

Chapter Eleven

THE FIRST ROUND of Black Tom oral arguments began on April 3, 1929, in Washington, D.C. After five years of waiting to be heard and negotiating settlements that had ended in bitter disappointment, Bonynge took this case very personally. He wanted to embarrass von Lewinski, not just beat him, by proving that the German government had been duplicitous. "The duty that devolves upon me today is not an agreeable or pleasant one," Bonynge said during his opening statement. Throughout the arguments, both lawyers would feign disappointment when pointing out their opponent's fallacies. "But I shall call attention to a number of instances where there is in possession of the German government evidence which, if produced, would very materially aid and assist this Commission in arriving at the truth, but which the German government so far has failed to produce. . . . If the German government persists in refusing to produce that evidence, you will be justified in drawing the proper conclusions and presumptions from its failures."

Bonynge's strategy was to prejudice the commission against the Germans and then follow up with lengthy expositions about the evidence he'd happily submit. Primary among them was the January 26, 1915, cable from the Foreign Office authorizing sabotage in the United States, which read, "In United States sabotage can reach to all kinds of factories for war deliveries. . . . Under no circumstances compromise Embassy."

Nadolny had already given an affidavit admitting that these instructions had come from his office, which proved, argued Bonynge, "they had a direct animus—a spite—against ammunitions supplies being furnished by American nationals to those at war with Germany." Bonynge spent the next two days outlining his case. He traced the path of von Rintelen from Germany to the United States, quoting von Rintelen as admitting that he had given instructions to "bomb, burn and destroy." He pointed out that Heinrich Albert had deposited nearly $30 million into accounts in American banks and that "many of the deposits must relate to these acts of sabotage." It was Albert who had lost his briefcase on the subway, Bonynge reminded the judges, a briefcase whose contents had made their way to President Wilson and had alerted the U.S. government to the Germans' subterfuge. Bonynge then read aloud from one of the memos found in Albert's possession: "I have received a cablegram from the foreign minister of Germany advising me where I can obtain agents to carry on sabotage work and destroy factories in the United States. Under that telegram that I received on January 26th, 1915, I am to go and do anything and everything necessary to accomplish that purpose." After reading this excerpt, Bonynge asked rhetorically, "What better evidence could we have as to what Albert was doing?"

But there was more. Von Papen and Boy-Ed had been deemed such threats to the United States that Wilson, who everyone knew had been indulgent toward all but the worst German transgressions, had had them expelled. Von Papen, when interviewed by von Lewinski for the sabotage cases, had admitted that he had worked with German spies and even named one, Paul Koenig. Bonynge now told the judges that Koenig had been the head of the War Intelligence Center and that he had built a network of German spies working on what he'd labeled "D" cases—"destruction cases," Bonynge called them. The implication was clear.

But Bonynge's star was Hilken. He was the only man who could connect German saboteurs to members of the German government. Bonynge knew that much of what he had said during the previous two days, though dramatic, served only as a compelling case for intent. The sabotage cable and Albert's papers were too general for his purposes. There was still no paper trail for Black Tom. Hilken's explanation and proximity to German agents would have to be enough. "He acted as a banker for the organization," Bonynge declared. "We have his testimony. He received money from the General Staff, he was to pay it to others designated, and he was not to ask any questions. He also testifies that after the Black Tom explosion he asked Captain Hinsch about details and Hinsch replied, 'You had better not know anything.'"

In fact, Bonynge needed the judges to believe that Hilken actually knew everything.

Von Lewinski waited his turn, anxiously and angrily. He had been taken aback by Bonynge's opening argument, especially the accusations that he had withheld evidence. He saw it as grandstanding, a manipulative ploy to poison the commission against the Germans, and he wanted to explain himself. "The present claims have been presented to this Commission with an aggressiveness which is unusual in the proceedings before the Commission," von Lewinski said moments into his opening statement. "The American agent has charged the German authorities with eliminating documentary proof by destroying it. It is true that a great many documents were destroyed because of the circumstances that grew out of the war.

"The American acts as if Germany could be held responsible for not being in a position at that time to keep all her records in order. The German military destroyed a great many records in many places before the Bolsheviks, who were at that time in control of Germany, got a hold of them. They did not destroy them because they had in mind the Black Tom claim. They did not destroy them by picking out one or the other piece of evidence. They burned them wholesale. This is regrettable, but it is the fact."

Von Lewinski then focused on the evidence, mainly trying to explain away the January 26, 1915, cable. Von Lewinski felt that this was the most credible piece of evidence linking the German government to sabotage. Hilken, without any paper to back up his claims, was merely a nuisance to him, and in five straight days of making his argument, he mentioned Hilken's name just once, during his summation.

The cable required delicacy. Von Lewinski wouldn't deny its existence. Instead, he would argue that it had been misinterpreted. "It was certainly meant seriously by Nadolny," von Lewinski argued. "There is no question about that. But the contents of the cable show that the matter which is in dispute was not an order, not a command, to the embassy." He then repeated the cable out loud for effect, emphasizing the first two words in the message: "*Sabotage can* be carried out. . . ."

Von Lewinski said that the original German could also be translated to mean "Sabotage is permissible." He repeated the phrase over and over, making eye contact with the judges as he repeated, "Sabotage is permissible. Sabotage is permitted.

"It was not an order," he continued. "Not a command. And it could not be a command to the military attaché because Nadolny, the General Staff, had no power to give any orders or commands to the military attachés. . . . When von Papen received this cablegram he knew he had the permission from an authority to commit sabotage in the United States. Von Papen and von Bernstorff had discussed this question and both reached the conclusion that sabotage must, by no means, be committed in the United States. It was their firm conviction."

Parker interjected, "Those were political considerations?"

"Yes, they were purely political considerations," von Lewinski answered.

"From the purely military point of view, it would have been desirable to have destroyed all the munitions possible?"

"Leaving out all other considerations, it is certainly advantageous to a belligerent to eliminate all the munitions in the world except his own," von Lewinski said. "But political considerations were considered, indeed, by von Papen himself, who could not act only from the military viewpoint in the United States, but had to consider everything in connection with the U.S., also political matters.

"The claimants doubt the veracity and truthfulness of Bernstorff's, Papen's, and Nadolny's statements. That is their right. I can only say these three gentlemen have sworn to their testimony, and we consider it true."

After nine days of arguments, Parker asked for more documents from both sides, hoping that someone would deliver some concrete proof, as opposed to what he felt were merely unsubstantiated accusations. He gave them until August 1 to file the new evidence and until September 15 to submit their briefs in response. While Bonynge readily agreed to the order, von Lewinski objected: "We have made a full disclosure. . . . I know that the former German General Staff had to burn most of these records. . . . It was an obligation imposed by Versailles. The General Staff was abolished and everything the General Staff had had to be abolished."

"It was incumbent upon Germany to destroy her records?" Parker asked incredulously.

"Yes," von Lewinski said. "We either had to deliver, or upon the command of the Inter-Allied Commission, destroy them. . . . Very often, in our opinion, these orders were not quite in accordance with the treaty, but the conditions at that time were such that they had to be complied with. . . . It was absolutely important to show that Germany was willing to disarm."

"Did that include the records of what the military authorities of Germany had done during the war?"

"It included the records of the German General Staff about activities during the war; war papers and war records."

"What was the purpose of destroying them?"

"It was the opinion of the Inter-Allied Commission in charge of Germany after the war that everything which had to do with military activities in Germany was doomed and had to be destroyed. That referred not only to papers and records, but to everything else, telephones used at that time and wireless apparatus used by military authorities."

Parker was skeptical of von Lewinski's claims (after the arguments, the former head of the Inter-Allied Commission in Berlin told Parker that von Lewinski's story was untrue), but he hadn't been swayed by the evidence the Americans had produced either. Meanwhile, the German commissioner, Kiesselbach, was obviously partial. The American commissioner, Anderson, who had served as a jurist or lawyer for five other international commissions, appeared to be just plain uninterested.

At times, it seemed that Parker was the only member of the commission who genuinely wanted to see justice served. His interpretation of the MCC's bylaws reflected the pragmatic and informal way he handled the cases. But it also reflected his idealistic belief in what the law could achieve. During World War I, he had been awarded medals of honor from the United States, France, Belgium, Italy, and Poland for the impartial way he had arbitrated claims between the United States and its allies over the allocation of resources. He saw the MCC as a model for how countries could settle their disputes in the future. And because of that, he pushed for its powers to be broader. He wanted it to subpoena witnesses. He wanted it to have the final word on a case, leaving no room for second-guessing or appeals from either side. Rather than sticking to arbitrary deadlines, he had been lenient toward both sides when they had been late filing briefs or submitting evidence that was vital to their cases. Ultimately, *when* someone filed didn't matter to Parker; he only cared about *what* they filed.

The Americans thought he was frustratingly evenhanded. The Germans thought he was a pushover. Parker knew what the two sides thought and laughed it off. He wanted the MCC to work much more than he wanted to know who had blown up Black Tom.

● ● ●

By August 29, nearly a month after the deadline Parker had set, the Germans still had not filed all of their new evidence. Von Lewinski claimed that he couldn't supply the government documents Parker ordered, so he filed affidavits from random government officials from that era instead. Bonynge was on vacation. Anderson was on vacation. Parker had just come back from a stretch in Maine. And von Lewinski was away. Meanwhile, Martin had postponed his trip to the Maryland shore to finish his brief by September 15. He was nearly done and did not look forward to writing a new one once von Lewinski submitted whatever evidence remained.

Martin ran into Parker at the State Department that afternoon. The umpire did not look well. His face was red from the heat, and he looked tired, despite having just come back from vacation. During their brief conversation, Parker told Martin that the climate in Maine, even during the summer, had been cold.

In the three days he'd been back, Parker had been at his MCC office early every morning, poring over the briefs that had piled up on his desk. Martin was glad to hear that he was working and requested a meeting with him the next morning to discuss the sabotage cases.

Martin always spoke in a measured and respectful tone, no matter whom he was talking to. But his voice during his meeting with Parker was tight with frustration. He told Parker that the Germans had put him in a difficult position. Von Lewinski was filing evidence that had nothing to do with any of the arguments made that April. Already Martin had seen new alibis for Jahnke and Witzke, stories whose veracity he hadn't had the time or the resources to investigate. One of the German motions was actually missing three pages from the middle, making it impossible to respond to or research independently. Martin's voice rose with each complaint, making it clear he didn't appreciate the fact that Parker had given the Germans such latitude without recognizing the efforts Martin had made to honor the deadline.

Parker did his best to soothe the panicked lawyer. He even

tried to call von Lewinski while Martin was still in his office. It was a Friday morning, and Parker was told that von Lewinski was taking a long weekend and wouldn't be available until Monday. Martin did his best to contain his rage. His voice still taut, he argued that it was unfair that he should have to write two or three more briefs based on evidence submitted past the commission's deadline. Parker tried to assuage Martin by telling him that wouldn't be the case, but Martin cut him off, saying, "I cannot help but feel that the Commission will not deny the German agent the right to file this new evidence and that if it is filed it would require considerable time on our part to discuss it."

The judge dismissed Martin's disrespectful tone and instead tried to defuse the situation with a joke about his health. "If there is a much further postponement in these claims," he said, "it might result in a decision by the Commission that didn't include me."

Parker was prescient. On October 30, 1929, he died at his home in Washington after a "lingering illness," wrote the *Washington Post*. Martin represented the American agent's office at the funeral, a service he described in a letter to Bonynge as "simple but impressive and touching." As Bonynge requested, Martin also sent two dozen roses to Parker's family. The bouquet included a condolence card signed by Martin on behalf of his boss.

With Parker's death, the agents and the commissioners were now more concerned about who would take his place than about missed deadlines. Kiesselbach had spent years cultivating a relationship with Parker and had convinced the umpire of Germany's good intentions. Martin wrote that he thought the State Department would have "a difficult time finding a successor. . . . Judge Parker was unquestionably a very unusual and able man in the position that he so competently filled." The Americans and the Germans felt that although Parker could be maddening, he was at least predictably and equally maddening to both sides.

As they had when the commission was first formed, the German government deferred to the Americans in the appointment of Parker's replacement. Undersecretary of State William Castle said at the time that Weimar did it because "in 1922 Germany got a lot of kudos by suggesting the arbiter should be an American." This time, though, the U.S. government was less diplomatic. Its choice for the new umpire was Roland Boyden, a sixty-six-year-old Boston attorney, whose experience in international law was highlighted by his work as a member of the U.S. reparations commission at Versailles. The fact that he had had a hand in dictating some of the terms that so debilitated the Weimar government was insulting to the Germans, especially since they had conceded the umpireship to the Americans.

Boyden wasn't overjoyed with the assignment, waiting two months, until the end of January 1930, to accept. He took it because President Hoover, whom he had worked for in 1917 as a lawyer in the Food Administration, had asked him to. Boyden stressed that he didn't want to make a "job out of the umpireship." He had been promised that the work of the MCC was almost done and that the sabotage claims would not keep him away from his law practice in Boston.

While the commission went on hiatus during the search for Parker's successor, Peaslee frantically looked for more compelling and credible witnesses. The man he needed most was Fred Herrmann, who Peaslee knew wouldn't be easily compelled to testify. Although Herrmann had signed four affidavits between early 1929 and early 1930 claiming he knew nothing about Black Tom, Kingsland, or Hilken's accusations, Peaslee didn't believe him. He remembered one of the first conversations he had had with Fred's brother Carl, who lived in New Jersey. Carl told Peaslee that a few nights after the explosion at the Kingsland factory, he had gone to see the building. The wreckage had been massive, and the chemicals had still shot flames into the sky, casting a glow that lured visitors from towns all over New Jersey. (The crowds had been so large that police set up a one-square-mile perimeter around the site of the blast.) Carl mentioned his visit to Fred, who angrily warned him never to go there again and not to answer any questions about it if he was asked. Both Carl and his brother Edwin knew that Fred had worked for Germany while in Europe; it was the family's dirty little secret. Once Fred had returned home, however, they had closed their eyes to what they suspected. When Fred snapped at Carl about Kingsland, Carl had been compelled to ask, "Fred, did you have anything to do with it?" Fred told him it was none of his business, and it had never come up again.

Even after Hilken's failed attempt to convince Fred Herrmann to testify, Peaslee stayed in touch with his brothers, keeping them up to date regarding the case, telling them about the statement he had signed, and dropping hints that Fred was hurting himself and the Americans by continuing to side with Germany. Finally, in January 1930, Peaslee told the brothers that he needed their help: they had to convince Fred to tell the truth.

On January 30, Edwin sent Fred a telegram that read, "Carl and self sailing *Santa Eliza.* Hope you can meet us or leave message where we can find you. Do nothing further Kingsland matter until we arrive. Regards to all. Edwin."

An upset Fred Herrmann read the cable and then called the German Embassy. Herrmann's stipend of one thousand pesos a month had been cut off in December. The Germans told him that they would hold his monthly payments in an account and pay him the lump sum when the sabotage cases were settled. Despite promises from the German ambassador to find him a job with the government, Herrmann was working as a truck driver. He worried that with the South American winter less than six months away, that job would soon disappear.

When Herrmann told the ambassador about his brothers' impending visit and reminded him how he had lied to protect the Germans, the ambassador suggested that he leave Chile: "Why don't you go over to Germany? If you want to go over there, say so, and I will fix it up." The ambassador looked up the steamer schedule and offered to book Herrmann on a ship leaving in two weeks.

"What will I do over there?" Herrmann asked.

"Well, there you will be in closer communication and touch

with the people on this thing. Hell, they have got to support you over there. You can count on me, that I will send in a report to Berlin personally on this matter."

Herrmann's thoughts drifted off as the ambassador spoke. He thought of Anton Dilger, the doctor who had created the anthrax lab in Maryland. In 1918, shortly after being interviewed and then released by U.S. investigators who suspected he was a German spy, Dilger had accepted an assignment from Section III-B in Spain, where he mysteriously died. When Herrmann had been on assignment in Mexico during the war, a fellow German agent told him that "a deadly poison had removed Dilger."

Herrmann decided that he was safer in Chile. And that he'd meet with his brothers.

By early January 1930, with Boyden's appointment all but official, both sides were back at work. They soon began filing hundreds of pages of new evidence and reply briefs. Then one of the attorneys representing the Lehigh Valley Railroad leaked details of the new material to the press.

On January 31, the *New York Times* and the *New York Herald Tribune* ran stories about the sabotage cases. One headline declared that the United States would FIGHT NEW EVIDENCE IN BLACK TOM CLAIM. According to the *Times*, "This argument will refute new evidence brought forward by the German agent, Dr. Karl von Lewinski, absolving Kurt Jahnke . . . and implicate more deeply other German agents in outrages against the neutrality of the United States."

Von Lewinski was waiting for Martin when the American lawyer arrived at his cramped office that morning. Martin's desk was covered with neatly stacked piles of briefs and memos, leaving no room for the newspapers von Lewinski held. Instead, the German agent folded the copies onto his lap. His displeasure with the articles was visible, but so was his embarrassment at getting beat. Throughout the case, he had been the savvy one in using the press to his advantage. Now he looked like a fool, and he wanted to know how it had happened. But he wouldn't ask outright. The two attorneys danced around the topic, choosing their words carefully. Von Lewinski told Martin how upset he was by the stories, but he felt even worse for Bonynge, because one of the attorneys working for the claimants had obviously been talking to the papers. "It's a disloyal act to give a statement out that could only be construed as coming from Bonynge," von Lewinski said.

"I assure you," Martin replied, "that I have not given out any interviews to newspaper men and neither has Mr. Bonynge. The agency has always been averse to trying these claims in the newspapers. It was unfortunate that newspaper stories had gotten out when you filed evidence last summer, because this revived newspaper interest in these claims."

Von Lewinski understood what Martin was talking about. The August before, he had given a young woman working for the Associated Press a peek at the new evidence he'd be filing, knowing that she would follow up with Martin. Sure enough, Martin received a call from the reporter, who had been in an "excited state of mind," he recalled. She had been given copies of the new German evidence filed with the commission and was anxious to write about it. Martin had calmly said, "What you do with the evidence is a matter that you have to decide for yourself." The next day, he read that the Americans were unprepared and outmatched.

"I agree that incident was unfortunate," von Lewinski said. "We tried to prevent those stories from being published, but that young woman representing the AP had gotten the story and we could not prevent its publication."

Martin, forever a subordinate, took a measure of joy in seeing von Lewinski backtrack. He stayed silent for a moment. Then the German agent quickly changed the subject. He was equally upset with the *New York Times* article, which included references to the germs German agents had allegedly spread during the war.

"That part of the story was just a rehash of the oral arguments," Martin said. "Those are public property."

"It's true," von Lewinski said. "But it is unfortunate that they've been revived again."

"I agree, but newspaper stories have to have a dramatic feature." Martin was not himself. He spoke as though he was giving a naive young attorney a lesson in legal politics, and it frustrated von Lewinski.

"The ordinary reader will take these two stories as having emanated directly from Mr. Bonynge," von Lewinski said. "Of course, I know this is not true. If I thought it was, I would not have said anything about it."

Martin again said nothing, and von Lewinski left his office.

Carl and Edwin Herrmann arrived in Valparaiso in late February, then traveled east to Santiago. It was summer in South America, and the weather was hot and still. Branches of tall green pines canopied the city streets, and all along the sidewalks, nuts and cones that had been shaken loose from the trees cracked and popped beneath the Herrmanns' shoes.

The brothers were armed with the one thing they knew Fred would want in exchange for testifying: immunity. "At first I thought there might be a hitch in it," Fred said later. "I told Carl I would think it over and for him to have the written offer sent down through the American Consul. I wanted to have a look at it, see how it was worded and so forth."

Several days later, Fred was called to the American Embassy. The diplomat in charge said that he had been given instructions from the State Department to offer Fred immunity. Still, Fred wanted the offer in writing. "I was rather suspicious," he said years later. "I told him, 'Seeing is believing.'"

That wasn't all he wanted. Going back to America to testify was out of the question. Instead, he suggested Havana, demanding $4,000 for travel expenses, money to cover his family's expenses during the weeks he was away, and a guarantee of safe conduct from Chile to Cuba and back. For all of that, plus immunity, he would tell his story.

Peaslee wired the money. Bonynge sent the immunity in writing. In early March, Fred Herrmann sailed for Havana.

• • •

The U.S. contingent in Havana included Peaslee, Carl Herrmann (who had sailed ahead of his brother), and Leonard Peto, a vice president at the Canadian Car & Foundry, which had suffered damages in the Kingsland explosion. They stayed at the Sevilla Biltmore on the Prado, whose sidewalks were lined with upscale boutiques and well-off vacationers. The lemon-drop yellow hotel, with its arched entryways leading to a lobby filled with moist and salty air, seemed to be painted with Cuban sunshine.

Carl met his brother at the pier and assured him that the proper arrangements had been made. A member of the U.S. Consulate was there as well, reiterating to Fred that he had been granted immunity. The diplomat spoke loudly, drawing looks from other passengers disembarking from the steamer. Herrmann felt them staring from all around, wondering what he had done.

It was nearing 5:00 p.m. when they pulled up to the hotel. The sun was low, casting orange streaks across the facade of the Biltmore, making it look as though it were in flames. Fred Herrmann walked through the arches into the breezy, Spanish-style lobby and for the first time met the man who had been chasing him. Peaslee and Herrmann said almost nothing at first, each taking his time to get a feel for the other. Herrmann could unlock Peaslee's windfall. Peaslee was forcing Herrmann to confront who he had been and what he had done.

Peaslee—tense, anxious, and at Herrmann's mercy—began by downplaying the importance of Herrmann's testimony, telling him, "In our judgment, the cases are already completely proved." Herrmann knew better. Peaslee had sent Hilken after him. He'd sent his brothers after him. He'd traveled to Cuba to meet him. But instead of walking away, Herrmann decided to be magnanimous. Confident and self-satisfied, he promised Peaslee he'd like what he heard. But he expected their conversations to be private, and he mentioned the diplomat's indiscretion at the pier. Peaslee told the former spy that nothing would be—or could be—on the record unless he swore to an affidavit in front of the American agents in Washington.

Peto joined them in the lobby a few minutes later, and only after he arrived did the two attorneys begin asking Herrmann what he knew. When Peto asked whether Herrmann would be willing to testify in front of Bonynge and Martin in Washington, Herrmann balked. His immunity, he said, covered him only for the trip to Cuba. This was true, so while Peto questioned Herrmann about Kingsland, Peaslee wired Bonynge, who then wired the U.S. Consulate, extending Herrmann's immunity to the United States. When Peaslee rejoined the conversation, he blurted out, "Do you know who Graentnor is?"

"Of course," said Herrmann. "That's Captain Hinsch."

As soon as he said it, he wished he could take it back. Before he'd left for Cuba, he'd decided to tell all he knew about Kingsland, since it was clear the lawyers already had evidence linking him to the explosion. But, still worried about murder charges, he'd keep his distance from Black Tom. Before Peaslee could follow up, however, Peto had moved on to his next question. Herrmann continued answering coolly, filling in the blanks in Peto's case. But for the rest of the interview, Herrmann never stopped thinking about Hinsch.

Over the next two days, whenever the subject of Black Tom was broached, Herrmann's responses were vague. Nevertheless, his knowledge of the Kingsland fire alone made him invaluable to the sabotage cases. That made getting him to the United States even more crucial. "We're not interested in a question of morals," Peaslee told him. "We appreciate that you were a young lad whose sympathies were with Germany and you had done what others who were older justified as being necessary. Those are questions outside this present discussion and the only thing that matters now is Germany paying for what she's done."

That was precisely what Herrmann wanted to hear. The next day, he was on a boat to Miami, where he'd catch a train to Washington.

• • •

Herrmann's train from Miami pulled into Washington's Union Station at 9:00 a.m. on April 3. Peaslee didn't bother taking him to his hotel; instead he brought the prize witness straight to Bonynge's MCC office at the Investment Building, just a couple of blocks from Lafayette Park and the White House. Martin was there, joining Peaslee, Peto, Bonynge, and Herrmann. Later that morning, Herrmann gave an affidavit in front of Bonynge and von Lewinski. But before the German agent arrived, Herrmann was asked to write a full history of his activities from 1916 to the end of the war. Martin, Bonynge, Peaslee, and Peto then looked through it, attempting to guess how von Lewinski would attack Herrmann's story.

Peaslee also knew that von Lewinski would make Herrmann's duplicity the centerpiece of his defense. He'd point out that the American case was built on the words of two men who were traitors to their country, including one who was obviously trading his allegiance for the best deal possible. On the trip from Cuba, Herrmann had told Peaslee that he had signed four affidavits for the Germans swearing he knew nothing about Black Tom. He was worried that this would affect his immunity. It never occurred to him that it might render the truthful testimony he promised the Americans totally useless.

While the lawyers studied Herrmann's written history of his activities, he pulled Bonynge aside. "Are you positive my immunity is good?" he asked. "They cannot start any proceedings against me?"

"Of course, it is good," Bonynge answered. "Why do you ask?"

"Well, I just wanted to convince myself."

Bonynge patted Herrmann on the shoulder, the way an adult would soothe a confused and frightened child. Then he changed the subject.

"Where are you going after the hearing?" Bonynge asked. "Are you going back to Chile?"

"I'd like to go to New Jersey and visit my family."

"Listen, Herrmann," Bonynge said, suddenly sounding serious. "I wouldn't advise you to go to Jersey."

"Why?"

"There is something up there with the prosecutor in Jersey City, and I am afraid they might arrest you on account of the Black Tom affair. I would not advise you to go through Jersey."

"But I have immunity," Herrmann said.

"That immunity is all right. They might lock you up, but we would get you out in a very short time."

Suddenly, Herrmann didn't feel very reassured.

Bonynge spent the first several minutes of the questioning asking Herrmann to explain where his parents were from, where he had grown up, how many siblings he had, where he worked after high school, and the like. Bonynge hoped to make Herrmann comfortable as he recounted his life story, from his childhood in New Jersey to his days as a young spy in Germany. Eventually, the path Bonynge laid down led to the February 1916 meeting at Section III-B in Berlin.

"What conversation, if any, did you have with Mr. Marguerre and Mr. Nadolny?" Bonynge asked.

"He brought up the thing about the destruction of munitions plants in the States," Herrmann answered. "I told them it was a pretty hard job and Marguerre said, 'Oh it is very easy.' He told me about different methods they had tried. He told us about these glass tubes."

Bonynge interrupted him. "What did he tell you about these glass tubes?"

"That they were to be given to workmen."

"What were they to do?"

"They were to be shown how to use them."

Bonynge's strategy of putting Herrmann at ease seemed to be working as he readily answered any question asked. As he did so, von Lewinski watched impassively.

"Did he describe what other things they had been using?" Bonynge continued.

"No, I did not know anything about the other things until I got to the States. Hinsch explained that to me. They did not work very well."

"Who did Hilken say Captain Hinsch was?"

"He told me he was a good man. That he had been on different jobs and had planned different things. They used something called dumplings and he said they did not work."

"Did you have any conversation with Hinsch about the use of these tubes?"

"I showed him, yes."

"Did you tell him the instructions you had from Germany?"

"Absolutely."

"To whom, if anybody, did you make a report of what you were doing?"

"To Hilken. Hinsch was kind of a funny character and I would not be responsible to him. Although we worked together on a good many things."

"Did Hinsch ever mention Black Tom to you?"

"Yes."

"What did he say?"

"He took all the credit. I think his men did it."

"Did you know a man named Graentnor or Granson?"

"I do not remember."

Suddenly, Peaslee stood up from his chair and fixed his gaze on Herrmann. Naming Hinsch as Graentnor was vital to the Americans' case. And during Herrmann's interview in Havana, he had admitted to Peaslee that Graentnor was, in fact, an alias Hinsch often used. "May I interrupt?" Peaslee asked.

"Yes," said Bonynge.

"I think the witness has forgotten something. When we first met I asked him about four or five names without any details, as to whether or not he knew certain men. In the course of that conversation, I said, 'Do you know Graentnor?' And his reply was that that was Captain Hinsch."

"That is right," said Herrmann, now backtracking. "But I could not recall for a moment just now if that was Captain Hinsch or someone else. But in thinking this whole thing over, that is clear."

Bonynge continued with his interrogation, but what Herrmann answered from then on wouldn't matter. Von Lewinski had witnessed Peaslee's outburst, the way he had coaxed the answer he wanted out of Herrmann. It was precisely what the German agent would need to discredit all of the testimony.

During his stay in Washington, Herrmann was visited by Paul Hilken. Their testimony had liberated them, and they reminisced about their days as saboteurs as though their actions had been nothing more than mischievous pranks. They laughed at Hinsch's temper and joked about how he had married the maid who cleaned his house in Baltimore. And they remembered Carl Ahrendt. He was six years older than Herrmann, but even the world-weary, twenty-one-year-old spy had thought of Ahrendt as an innocent, a young naif. Hilken mentioned that Ahrendt was now the Detroit agent for the North German Lloyd and that he had changed since Herrmann had last seen him. He was harder, and when Hilken confronted him about the sabotage cases, he had treated Hilken with disdain. Ahrendt believed in Germany more than ever and couldn't be convinced that telling the truth would help both countries.

The American lawyers had listened to Herrmann and Hilken recount their stories, laughing along but always listening for clues. When Herrmann mentioned he'd like to see Ahrendt again and "have a chat with him," Peto interrupted. He was going to Detroit on business in a few days, and he invited Herrmann to come along.

Herrmann and Peto left Washington in the late afternoon of April 8, traveling overnight and arriving in Detroit early the next morning. They checked into their hotel, and while Peto attended meetings, Herrmann called Ahrendt.

When they had worked together in 1916, Hilken had been the man Ahrendt most wanted to become later in life. He had status in the community, the idyllic family, and a comfort with money that came only from handling so much of it. But Herrmann—dashing, fearless, and fighting for a cause—was who Ahrendt wanted to be at that moment. When his old friend called that morning and invited him to lunch at the hotel, Ahrendt said yes right away.

The next call Ahrendt made was to John Schroeder, still his boss. Schroeder told him that he was right to schedule the meeting and that Schroeder would call von Lewinski to find out whose side Herrmann was on.

When Peto returned to the hotel at one o'clock that afternoon, he found a note underneath his door from Herrmann. He and Ahrendt were in the dining room, Herrmann wrote; come down. But as Peto walked in, he could see that Herrmann and Ahrendt were nearly finished with their meal. He sat at a small table nearby, waiting until Herrmann waved him over before joining them.

Ahrendt was immediately suspicious of Peto, barely waiting for Herrmann to finish introducing the attorney before asking if he was from Washington. Peto answered yes, that he was representing the company whose Kingsland plant had been destroyed by saboteurs. He mentioned that he had been instrumental in convincing Herrmann to come from Chile to testify. He also said that he had once considered asking Ahrendt to testify as well but realized that would be unlikely given his employer. Herrmann couldn't resist adding, "Enough people have lost their jobs over these cases already."

Peto made his pitch, explaining how the commission worked, how "each government was obligated to lay its cards faceup on the table . . . but Germany is not fully complying." Peto kept talking—giving Ahrendt a taste of the evidence they had gathered, his guess of the case's outcome, and whom they had been speaking to—and hoping Ahrendt would indicate his sympathy. Peto mentioned that several years earlier, von Lewinski had offered a settlement that had unfortunately been voted down by Berlin. When Ahrendt suggested that he thought it would be best if the cases were settled, Peto pushed forward, making his questions more specific. Did he know Witzke? Had he heard that Hinsch used the name Graentnor?

But Peto had misread Ahrendt's agreement as a willingness to help. Ahrendt said that he'd never heard Hinsch refer to himself as Graentnor. Once, however, with a woman who hadn't been his wife, he heard Hinsch check into a hotel as Mr. and Mrs. Fred Herrmann. "That son of a gun," Herrmann said. "I never knew that."

Irked, Peto announced that the meeting was over. Ahrendt tried to ease the tension by offering to host Herrmann and Peto for the night: they could have dinner at his home, then he'd take them to the German Club for some real German lager. Peto declined. It was 2:30 in the afternoon, and he and Herrmann were headed back to Washington on a train that evening. Ahrendt insisted on taking them to the station, promising to be back to pick them up by 3:45. They acquiesced and said they would see him later.

Returning to his office, Ahrendt heard from Schroeder, who had spoken with von Lewinski.

"Herrmann is against us," Schroeder said.

"Well, that is all I wanted to know," said Ahrendt.

Schroeder then instructed Ahrendt to leave for Washington immediately. The Germans needed him to give an affidavit.

At four o'clock, as a storm rained down on their heads, Herrmann and Peto were still waiting in front of the hotel.

The Germans knew from Ahrendt's conversation with Peto that the Americans wanted to prove that Graentnor was Hinsch and that Hinsch had organized the sabotage at Black Tom. And von Lewinski knew from listening to Herrmann's testimony that the

explosive glasses were the Germans' weapons of choice. The
Germans needed Ahrendt to disprove both claims.

Less than twenty-four hours after his meeting with Herrmann
and Peto, Ahrendt sat down with von Lewinski's assistant,
Wilhelm Tannenberg, and Harold Martin in Washington, D.C.

"During the time you were together with Hinsch, you were in
close contact with him," Tannenberg said.

"Oh yes," Ahrendt replied. After all, they had lived together
in Baltimore.

"Did you get the impression from what he was doing to
prepare for the *Deutschland*'s arrival that he attended to other
matters?"

"No."

"Did Captain Hinsch show you at any time during the years
1915, 1916, or 1917 any explosive tubes, little glass tubes?"

"No."

"Did he show you at any time pencils that contained little glass
tubes?"

"No."

"There is testimony in the record that certain men had glass
tubes containing sulphuric acid and other material which could be
put into pencils. These glass tubes or pencils, it is claimed, were to
be used in order to start fires. . . . It is said that after the sulphuric
acid had run down and had ignited some material in this pencil,
then there would be a flame about one foot to two feet long. Did
you ever hear anything about such devices?"

"No."

"Did you ever see such devices in Captain Hinsch's possession?"

"No. Not at all."

"Did he ever tell you about such devices?"

"No."

"Have you any reason to believe that he had such devices?"

"No, I have not."

"You stated that you met Fred Herrmann in Baltimore while

the *Deutschland* was there in July and the beginning of August 1916."

"Yes."

"Did Herrmann tell you at any time about those explosive tubes or pencils?"

"No."

"Did you ever see in his possession any of such pencils or tubes?"

"No, not at all."

"Did he ever tell you he had such devices?"

"No, he didn't."

"Did he ever tell you that Captain Hinsch had such explosive devices?"

"No."

"And did you ever see such devices?"

"No, I have never. To this day, I have never seen anything like that."

"Did Captain Hinsch ever talk to you about destroying American factories?"

"No."

"Did he ever mention that it was a good thing to do that?"

"No, not at all. He didn't like the idea of America sending so much ammunition abroad, but many other people in the United States thought the same way about that. People that were not even Germans didn't think that was a nice thing to do, or consider it neutral."

"Did he ever say that one should do something that should destroy the factories?"

"No."

"Did he ever tell you that he had other people working for him that would destroy American munitions factories?"

"No."

"Did Captain Hinsch ever mention the Black Tom explosion to you?"

"Never."

"Did you ever hear from somebody else that Captain Hinsch had something to do with the Black Tom explosion or Kingsland fire?"

"No."

"That is all," Tannenberg said. Ahrendt had given the Germans what they wanted.

Chapter Twelve

B Y THE SUMMER of 1930, the atmosphere surrounding the
MCC had turned dark, reflecting the mood of the world.
The hopes for an economic partnership between the two countries
buckled under the weight of the global depression. No country depended more on U.S. loans than Germany, and when desperate
American banks asked for repayments in the fall of 1929, the Germans had nothing to give. On the heels of mutual financial collapse, the dreams of a political alliance faded as well. The Weimar
government, eleven years into its democratic experiment, still
struggled. Between September 1928 and September 1930, the
number of unemployed Germans increased from 650,000 to more
than 3 million. And the challenges to Weimar's power were growing. Members of the Nazi Party roamed the country, preaching a
return to military dominance and a repeal of the Treaty of Versailles. Two years earlier, the Nazi Party had nearly disintegrated
from a lack of support, both financially and at the polls. But the
psyche of the country had changed. Disenfranchised and desperate Germans now listened and cheered and believed in the Nazis.
The anger toward the Weimar government became tangible during the September 1930 Reichstag elections, when the Nazis
picked up 107 seats in the German parliament, making it the sec-

ond most powerful political party in the country. Those Americans who wanted better relations with Germany no longer knew which party to court.

Against this turmoil, once innocuous issues before the MCC became contentiously debated. In June, von Lewinski notified Bonynge that three important German witnesses—Hinsch, Marguerre, and a former spy named Willie Woehst—would testify in Berlin that month. But the depositions would be given in German, a language neither Bonynge nor Martin spoke. Not wanting to rely on a translator misinterpreting their questions, they asked a German attorney who had worked on other MCC claims for them to handle the cross-examination. However, one of the MCC's rules stipulated that only official commission agents, or those approved by the opposition, could examine witnesses. Von Lewinski rejected Bonynge's candidate, saying he couldn't be impartial. Chandler Anderson, the American commissioner, didn't argue when his German counterpart convinced the umpire to rule in favor of von Lewinski. Bonynge and Martin would not get to challenge the German witnesses.

A month later, the commission announced that the second round of oral arguments in the sabotage claims would take place in Hamburg from September 18 to 30. Bonynge, still burning, immediately protested that the Americans couldn't possibly get a fair trial in Germany. This time, Anderson helped plead his case, and the site of the hearing was moved to the Peace Palace in The Hague.

For weeks, von Lewinski let Marguerre and Hinsch study the testimony of Herrmann and Hilken. When Marguerre was finally examined on July 30, 1930, he admitted that during his time at Section III-B, he had "decided to extend our agent-service to such countries which were still neutral, whose entry into the war, however, had to be counted on or whose entry into the war was considered a possibility . . . but they were not to cause any destructions or to commit sabotage acts of any kind, as long as the country was not at war with us. It is true that as soon as the neutral country entered the war, the agents were immediately to start action. . . . It is true that I sent agents to America and provided them with instructions and material to stop American establishments, essential for war, from working, if possible. These instructions however were to be followed out only in the event of America entering the war."

Hinsch was deposed by Tannenberg on August 4, just six weeks before the start of oral arguments. Fourteen years after Black Tom, he was still uncomfortably huge. The skin around his face was soft as jelly, with a pallor that suggested very little blood reached his cheeks. He was as smug, arrogant, and committed to Germany as he was large. He was also von Lewinski's best solution to the problem of Herrmann and Hilken.

For several hours, Tannenberg grilled Hinsch about his activities in the United States in 1916. Tannenberg asked about his work on the *Neckar* and his responsibilities regarding the submarine *Deutschland*. Hinsch answered with convincing detail, recounting conversations he had with Hilken about what should be bought for the sub, where he should get it, and even how the boat should be packed. "You had to visualize every detail," said Hinsch of his preparations. "Even how the heavy nickel-cargo was to be stowed in the U-boat. I had several samples made of small bags into which we intended to pack the nickel. Paul Hilken had told me that on the other side there was a great scarcity of sand-bags needed for the trenches. I therefore had to select bags which could be used on the other side."

Through the first day of testimony, there was no mention of Black Tom or even of sabotage, just a pleasant meandering conversation about Hinsch's duties in Baltimore. But shortly after the second day, August 5, began, following a question and answer concerning how much material Hinsch had stored away in anticipation of the U-boat's arrival, Tannenberg asked, "Did you have anything to do with the Black Tom explosion, that explosion which occurred end of July on the Black Tom Terminal of the Lehigh Valley Railroad Company in New York Harbor?"

"No," Hinsch answered.

"Did you hear anything about this Black Tom explosion during your stay in the United States?"

"Yes, I learned it from newspaper reports which were published at that time."

"Do you remember that?"

"Yes, the explosion was described at that time in the papers at great length and with big headlines. For days it was the general topic of conversation, but I did not follow the matter up because my head was full with other things."

"Do you remember where you were on those days?"

"In Baltimore at my pier, because that was immediately prior to the departure of the *U-Deutschland* from Baltimore. We were figuring day by day how he could get the *Deutschland* out of Chesapeake Bay."

"Did you ever, during the war, plan sabotage acts of any kind against Black Tom?"

"No."

"Did you ever hire people and instruct them to take action against that Black Tom Terminal?"

"No, never."

Then Tannenberg presented Hinsch with a postcard-size, black-and-white photo. The man in the picture wore a long-billed beret, pulled low, that pushed out his ears. His face sloped down toward a point, as though his chin were the bottom of a V-shaped vase. His top lip pushed over the bottom of his mouth, creating a perpetually dumbfounded look. It was nature's cruel joke to give this man a face that so perfectly matched his natural state of mind.

"Do you know this man?" Tannenberg asked.

"No, I do not know that man," Hinsch said.

"Do you feel sure that you never met that man during the war?"

"Yes, quite sure."

"Did you ever, during your stay in the United States during the war, employ a man by the name of Michael Kristoff?"

"No."

"Are you perfectly sure that you never had relations with this man, whose picture I showed you?"

"Yes, absolutely sure."

The Germans had their denial.

That same day, half a world away, as Bonynge sat in his downtown New York office, a feeling of panic set in. Oral arguments were six weeks away, and his floor, his desk, and his mind were cluttered with seemingly random pieces of evidence he'd spent hours trying to link. He could not escape the case, even if he wanted to. His office was at 50 Broadway, directly across the street from 45 Broadway, where Heinrich Albert, the World War I German commercial attaché, had laundered money that had financed the first network of German spies in the United States. A five-minute walk took him to 60 Wall Street, the building that had once housed von Papen's War Intelligence Center. All around him, the ghosts of German espionage lingered. And in front of him, amid the piles and stacks of files, a mystery remained.

By early August, 760 German affidavits and pieces of evidence had been filed, but between August 9 and 25, von Lewinski would file 56 new depositions, including the vital testimonies of Marguerre and Hinsch, some several hundred pages long combined. As more and more material poured in, all of which needed to be researched and rebutted, Martin became as nervous as Bonynge. "Personally," he wrote to Bonynge on August 18, "I do not see how it is going to be humanly possible for the final argument of these claims to begin on September 15."

Although the workload was overwhelming, the testimony was at least encouraging, especially Marguerre's, whose logic Martin found laughable. He wrote to Bonynge:

Marguerre confirms in remarkable detail substantially all of Herrmann's story with the sole exception of the time when he was to begin work on his notorious plans. For an official of a modern government to solemnly admit under oath that he was engaged in a conspiracy with nationals of a friendly neutral government looking to overthrow their own government is almost unbelievable. It certainly harks back to the political intrigues and treacheries of alleged statesmen of medieval times; that for their own personal or national gains they were perfectly willing to drench the world in blood.

But whatever optimism Martin had now would soon fade. In early September, after the American contingent had already set sail for The Hague, the Germans filed bills and memos from the North German Lloyd. Among them was a receipt for a $2,000 payment from Hilken to Hinsch made in January 1916, corroborating Ahrendt's testimony. Not present was any proof of a $2,000 payment from Hilken to Hinsch in August, shortly after Black Tom. Hilken told Peaslee, "I know I paid Hinsch another $2,000 for Black Tom. I was distributing funds to Hinsch all the time."

"Hilken," Peaslee responded, "the Commission will never believe that. Worse than that, they now won't believe any of your testimony. This evidence will defeat the United States in this trial unless you produce documents to explain it."

Hilken could not.

The scent of roses perfumed the air of the Peace Palace in The Hague. Noble and purposeful-looking, the palace had a large clock tower at one end, arched entrances, and marble floors that echoed with every step. Not yet twenty years old, the court there was a foal, its role in the world's system of justice still evolving.

Shortly before 10:00 a.m. on Friday, September 19, 1930, Bonynge walked into the smaller courtroom at the Peace Palace. He passed through a doorway, above which was inscribed the message PEACE HAS EXTINGUISHED THE FLAMES OF WAR.

Alone in the courtroom, he tacked two poster-size white placards to the wall nearest the commissioners' table. Side by side, they formed an intricate chart that attempted to trace the Black Tom and Kingsland explosions back to the imperial German government. Then he sat at his table, facing the commissioners' seats, and stared straight ahead.

Slowly, the other chairs around him were filled. First, von Lewinski arrived with Tannenberg. Then Martin, then Peaslee and Peto, who both sat in the small gallery. Bonynge recognized a reporter from the *New York Times*, and he also saw a man he didn't know, dressed in a black suit. He was bald, with a ring of fading black hair clinging to the sides of his head. He looked like a lawyer, Bonynge thought.

At exactly 10:30, the two commissioners and the umpire entered the courtroom, and Bonynge was asked to begin. "May it please the honorable commission," he said, "it seems to me very fitting and appropriate that a meeting of the Mixed Claims Commission should be held at this imposing edifice, dedicated by its donor to the cause of peace. These are serious charges to be made against a government. I appreciate the full extent of the seriousness of the charges. But, notwithstanding the seriousness, notwithstanding the evidence that has been produced—overwhelming evidence in my judgment—that fixes the responsibility of Germany for these disasters, permit me to assure the honorable members of this Commission that my government, nevertheless, does not present these claims in any spirit of enmity or hostility to Germany or the German government."

And then Bonynge launched into four days of arguments, nearly six hours every day of nonstop talking, which characterized the actions of the German government, past and present, as duplicitous and hostile. Early in his opening statement, he said, "The task of the American agent has been made infinitely more difficult and onerous because of the lack of assistance from the German Government in presenting the real facts in this case. I submit to you, gentlemen of the Commission, that there has not been a single admission made by Germany of any fact material to these cases that has not been forced from Germany by the overwhelming evidence introduced on behalf of the United States."

Bonynge's trail began with the sabotage cable of January 1915, sent from the Foreign Office in Berlin to Germany's military attaché in Washington, Franz von Papen. "That cablegram is the very link in the chain of evidence, as demonstrated by these maps upon the wall, from the time the policy of sabotage was announced until men like Jahnke and Hilken, with the aid of German agents, blew up Black Tom," Bonynge argued. Then, for dramatic effect, he paraphrased part of the cable aloud: "For Military Attaché. You can obtain particulars as to persons suitable for carrying out sabotage in the U.S. and Canada. . . . In the U.S. sabotage may be carried out against all kinds of factories which supply war materials."

Bonynge paused to let the words of the cable settle in. "The fact is," he continued, "that Germany did not regard the United States as a neutral country, that it regarded the fact that the United States was furnishing these war materials to the Allies as making the U.S. a belligerent country. They commenced their warfare against the United States at that time, a secret warfare instead of an open declaration of war, because that cablegram of January 26th, 1915 was nothing but a declaration of war against the United States. . . .

"One year after the cablegram was issued, Nadolny and Marguerre admit that they met, in the office of the Section III-B, with Herrmann and Hilken; that they authorized Hilken to pay Herrmann and then urged him to get to America as fast as he could, not even to wait to go with Hilken, but to get there as rapidly as possible. They admit they gave him incendiary tubes. . . . The only difference between their testimony and Herrmann's is that Herrmann says there was no restriction placed upon him as to when he was to use these incendiary tubes, whereas Mr. Marguerre says that he told him that he was not to use them unless the United States entered the war.

"Stop and think, gentlemen, what an extraordinary situation this is."

The bald man in the black suit was worried. He had come from Paris and was watching from the gallery to look out for the best interests of one of his firm's biggest clients, the Lehigh Valley Railroad. What he had heard so far from Bonynge was circumstantial and weak, not the sort of case he, John McCloy, would feel comfortable making.

During a brief recess, McCloy pulled aside Peaslee, whom he knew from mutual friends at Cravath, and told him he didn't think the cable alone was enough to win the case. It proved intent, McCloy cautioned, but not action. Peaslee told him not to be too concerned; Bonynge had the names to prove how the cablegram led to the destruction of Black Tom.

When the hearings recommenced, Bonynge started from the bottom, naming Michael Kristoff as the man who had blown up the island and Frederick Hinsch, aka Graentnor, as the man who provided him with the means to do it.

Kristoff, a convicted petty thief, had died of tuberculosis in 1928. But working off of the interview Jersey City police had conducted with Kristoff when they interrogated him in September 1916, Bonynge painted him as a cunning and cold-blooded saboteur. At the time, he had admitted to traveling around the country in early 1916 with a man named Graentnor. He said that he had carried Graentnor's briefcases, which contained books, maps, factory blueprints, and cash. "It is admitted by Germany that it had a large number of its agents making what they call 'legal observations' at this time, traveling around the country, making observations of the various munitions plants so that, if America entered the war, the Germans would be prepared to blow up these factories," Bonynge told the commission. "What other reasonable inferences can be drawn from this testimony than that the man who was traveling about with these plans and maps was a German agent?"

This sort of rhetorical question became a common, debilitating element in Bonynge's argument. In lieu of hard evidence, he seemed to be begging the commission to see it his way, to draw the same inferences that he had drawn. But against the strength with which he had delivered his opening statements and the cable evidence, his pleading made the rest of the case come across as undeveloped, full of conjecture and leaps of faith. Other than the cable, he had no paperwork to support his theories, only testimony given years after the fact. He had Kristoff, a voice from the grave, claiming that he had traveled with a man named Graentnor. And he had Herrmann, who had said under oath during their April interview that he remembered Hinsch had often referred to himself as Graentnor. He had an affidavit of Hilken's, in which he recalled paying Hinsch for organizing the Black Tom explosion. But Bonynge had no receipts to prove when the payment had taken place.

The next morning, on September 20, he recounted the scandalous newspaper stories syndicated in 1919 by Paul Altendorf, the former U.S. Secret Service agent, who heard Lothar Witzke confess that he and Kurt Jahnke had helped blow up Black Tom. But Bonynge had no proof that either Witzke or Jahnke had been in New York at the time.

That afternoon, Bonynge described how Paul Koenig had helped von Papen organize the War Intelligence Center in downtown Manhattan by recruiting German agents. He told the commission about Koenig's "D" Cases log and how the names of the men assigned to those cases coincided with the names of men police had arrested for spying in the United States. But Bonynge had no key proving what the "D" actually stood for.

If McCloy had doubts about Bonynge's performance, the *New York Times* didn't. "American investigators came close today to proving the identity of one of the men who blew up Black Tom," the *Times* reported on September 20. "His name is Michael Kristoff." The next day, under the headline SAYS REICH ORDERED THE BLAST, the *Times* reported, "Minute by minute the plot thickened as Mr. Bonynge went on and the names of German spies, incendiaries and agents of sabotage crossed his argument like case characters in a Broadway thriller." Bonynge's last day of arguments, which included accusations that German spies had injected anthrax into horses headed for the Allies, made the biggest news. The story landed on the front page, under the headline GERMANS USED DISEASE GERMS HERE.

Despite the sensational details, Bonynge knew that anthrax injections wouldn't sway the commission. In his closing arguments, he reiterated, "It is not incumbent upon the United States to establish particular agents, or the details of how these particular agents destroyed those plants. The only responsibility resting upon the government of the United States is to establish that Germany was the cause of these losses."

After listening to Bonynge's closing arguments, McCloy cabled the Cravath office in New York. He respected nothing in the law as much as order and clarity, and despite what his colleagues were reading every day in the papers, he predicted the Americans would lose. "They don't have their ducks all lined up in a row," he wrote.

G ERMANY ADMITS USE OF BOMBS AND GERMS HERE IN 1915 AND 1916. The three-line headline landed on page one of the *New York Times* the day after von Lewinski's opening argument. But admitting to one of the trial's most sensational details was an important part of von Lewinski's strategy. He lost nothing by accepting responsibility—diseased horses hadn't blown up Black Tom Island—but he gained the commission's trust. And this case would be won by whomever the judges trusted more.

Five minutes into his opening statement, von Lewinski subtly reminded the commission of the faith the Germans had put in the U.S. government by ceding the power to name the umpire. This faith was something he hoped would be reciprocated. "The American agent expects from me the fullest confidence in the good faith of his government, and I may assure him that I shall never be tempted, even in the heat of argument, to question or doubt this good faith. But I expect most earnestly that the same confidence shall be accorded to the good faith and the good will of my government in the conduct of these proceedings. . . .

"The American agent argues it is not required that he establish how the crime was executed, who did it, and how it was accomplished. These, the American agent says, are mere details. It is not necessary, according to him, to clear them up, as they are not even issues in the present proceedings. . . . What the American agent treats as mere details form the actual, I claim the only, issue in the proceedings. If the American agent proves that Witzke or Jahnke blew up Black Tom, or if he proves that Kristoff blew up Black Tom, and that he was a German agent, then but only then has he discharged the burden of proof. If he is unable to prove this, his case must fail, even if it should be considered as established that there existed an authorization to commit sabotage against ammunition factories and plants in the United States."

Tannenberg had one goal during his portion of the arguments: proving that Herrmann and Hilken were liars. He began by casting doubt on Herrmann's claim that Hinsch and Graentnor were the same man. He reminded the judges of Herrmann's backtracking during his April deposition. Then he went on the attack against Hilken. Tannenberg had a receipt from one of Hilken's accounts at the North German Lloyd for the January 1916 payment of $2,000 to Hinsch, and he had Carl Ahrendt's detailed testimony about taking that money to New York in the winter. The Americans had only Hilken's memory of an August payment. "If anyone perjured himself in this proceeding," Tannenberg proclaimed, "it is Hilken."

Tannenberg spent the rest of the morning establishing an alibi for Jahnke before turning the case back over to von Lewinski. With employment records and eyewitness testimony, he made it seem nearly impossible for the alleged German spy to have been in New York in late July 1916. Then he mocked Bonynge's argument that Koenig's "D" cases were for the destruction of American property. "If Koenig had designated these A cases they would be construed as ammunition cases," von Lewinski argued. "B cases would be bomb cases. C cases criminal cases and so forth. There is no evidence that these cases were, as indicated by the American agent, sabotage cases."

On Friday morning, September 26, von Lewinski began his closing argument.

"In order to understand Fred Herrmann's motive for turning claimants' evidence one must, in the first place, bear in mind some of his general characteristics. He is a man with an inborn, restless, adventurous spirit. When the war broke out he went abroad because, he said, he wanted to get a kick out of it. He made four trips between the U.S. and Europe and risked his life and liberty for the sake of a kick. When the United States entered the war, he fled to Mexico and joined the German secret service there. After the war he became a Chilean citizen for merely practical reasons. He was a man without a country, loyal only to those from whom he may expect the greatest benefits. . . . I submit to the Commission that Herrmann is a proven perjurer, uncorroborated by unimpeached witnesses, contradicted on material points, and his whole life is a fantasy, filled with conflicts and improbabilities at absolute variance with all of the facts established by the evidence."

Then von Lewinski finished with confidence: "We have produced to the Commission all that we know. Nothing has been concealed, nothing has been withheld. My government stands before you with clean hands. The claims should be dismissed."

The commissioners withdrew to their chambers.

Chapter Thirteen

BONYNGE SAILED BACK to the United States as soon as the arguments ended, docking in Hoboken on October 18. He was met there by a reporter, who asked him about his chances with the commission. Bonynge guaranteed that the United States would win.

Martin wasn't so sure. It had been late summer when he had departed for The Hague. He and Bonynge had spent several evenings preparing the cases on the deck of their steamer, the sweet breeze making them forget they were on a business trip. Martin remained in Europe through October, traveling with the commission to Hamburg, where it easily deposed several other lower-profile claims. By the time Martin began his trip back home, the weather had turned cold and frosty. The ocean and the sky merged into a gray haze, and icy spray off the Atlantic pelted the deck of his steamer, keeping him confined to the ship's dining room and his cabin. For the first time since he had joined the MCC eight years earlier, he had no work to do.

When his ship docked on November 14, he was met by the news that the commission had found in favor of the Germans. The judges had ruled just two weeks after the closing statements, barely sifting through the six thousand pages of evidence and briefs filed by both sides. But instead of notifying the lawyers involved, they had opted to release the news through the U.S. State Department and the German Foreign Office. It had taken nearly a month for the diplomats to work out satisfactory language for a statement.

The commission agreed that "there were in the United States certain German agents who were, or at least pretended to be active in sabotage work." And it did not doubt the authenticity of the sabotage cable. But the commission seemed unable to accept that any government would so deliberately try to deceive another, either prior to World War I or during the hearings. "We believe that the present German Government was entirely prepared to bring out the truth and take the consequences whatever they might be," the commission explained. Even when it chastised German witnesses, as it did Nadolny, it was tentative and apologetic. And at times its reasoning was baffling. For instance, although even von Lewinski had easily conceded that Black Tom had been poorly guarded and easily accessible, the judges wrote that it was difficult for them to understand how saboteurs could possibly have "set the fire without being seen or heard." They wondered whether the fire could have started as a result of a spontaneous combustion of the explosives stored there.

Their disbelief was compounded by their take on the American witnesses. They dismissed Kristoff as unstable and described his plaintive cries of "What did I do?" on the night of the explosion as "trivial and that if he was excited it is unlikely he expressed his excitement in the English language." They wondered why, if he was so obviously guilty, the Jersey City police who had questioned him about the fire hadn't pursued him more aggressively.

Nor did the commission accept Hilken's claim that he had paid Hinsch $2,000 in August 1916. And the judges found Herrmann to be one of the most immoral characters they'd ever heard testimony from. "There is nothing about Herrmann of which we feel so sure as that he will lie if he thinks lying worthwhile from his point of view," they wrote.

"We believe Herrmann and Hilken are liars, not just presumptive, but proven."

I t would get more embarrassing for the Americans. Two days after the decision was announced, an insurance agent who had investigated the Black Tom explosion gave an interview to the *New York Times,* saying, "The real story of the explosion is this: the watchmen employed to guard the millions of dollars worth of war materials were bothered by the mosquitoes that infested the swampy land around Black Tom. They had built themselves a smudge fire to drive them off. A spark ignited and set fire to other cars. Finally a car loaded with black powder exploded and everything went up. That is the story of what happened." The "mosquito defense," floated earlier by the Germans, had resurfaced.

Shortly thereafter, Martin asked Bonynge's secretary to find copies of editorials around the country relating to the sabotage claims. There were twenty-six, nearly every one of them teasing the American lawyers for being fooled by a swarm of insects.

W hen Bonynge met with Secretary of State Henry Stimson days after the decision, the secretary told him, "I have no criticism, complaint or fault to find with the Commission." In fact, his only problem with the commission was that it still existed. Stimson and the U.S. government, including President Hoover, wanted to shut down the MCC and, instead of squabbling, support the flailing German democracy. Stimson and the State Department wouldn't stop Bonynge from pursuing a new hearing, but they wouldn't help him either.

Bonynge had options. Peaslee, frustrated by the loss and frightened by the prospect of not recouping his investment, looked for help. He wanted to defray some of the costs of the case and was willing to give up a percentage of his expected windfall for a partner. Knowing Cravath represented the Lehigh Valley Railroad, and having seen one of its lawyers at the Peace Palace, he approached the firm about joining the sabotage cases. "He was desperate," said one former partner.

The firm assigned the case to John McCloy.

Chandler Anderson seemed engaged only when hearing a case that could be settled quickly. The American commissioner was sixty-two years old and thirty-four years into a career specializing in international law. He could be laconic and impatient, traits that, given his soft and friendly features, always startled those who worked with him. His face, round and full, with a bushy gray mustache, resembled that of a walrus. The skin around his eyes was permanently crinkled, as though he had spent too much time smiling or squinting behind his pince-nez glasses.

At times, the American attorneys had been frustrated by his passive stance concerning the sabotage cases, especially compared to how fiercely Wilhelm Kiesselbach, the German commissioner, defended his countrymen in court. The American lawyers had heard that Anderson didn't entirely agree with the commission's ruling, but, as Martin wrote Bonynge, "he was willing to go along rather than go to the trouble of writing an opinion he felt would not be sustained by the umpire."

Thus Martin was surprised when, a few days after the decision was announced, Anderson asked him to come by his office. He wanted to discuss the cases.

"I suppose you're disappointed," Anderson said as Martin sat down.

"Frankly, I'm very disappointed and can't understand how, in the face of the record, the Commission reached this decision," Martin answered.

"Boyden was responsible for the decision," Anderson said. "He wrote it. He was satisfied that Kingsland was not due to German activities." He paused before adding, "But there was some doubt about Black Tom."

Martin was surprised by Anderson's candor.

"I understand you're considering filing a petition for a reargument," Anderson continued. "I suggest you do it soon. The State Department wants to close up the Commission."

"It might take two or three weeks for us finally to decide what to do," Martin said.

"If you do, the umpire will have an open mind."

Martin thanked Anderson and rushed back to his office. He needed to cable Bonynge right away.

A liar—not presumptive, but proven—that's what the com- mission had branded him. The phrase found its way into Paul Hilken's head when he was reading or doing the dishes or just walking around town. The Baltimore papers had followed the case because of him, and their coverage shaped the legacy he was sure he'd leave behind. He did not come across as heroic or patri- otic, as he had hoped, but as shameful. He hurt for his father and for his three children, especially his youngest daughter, a teenager still in school in Baltimore. He desperately wanted vindication.

On Christmas Eve 1930, he found it. He was at his old home in Roland Park, where his ex-wife and daughter still lived. Rum- maging through the attic, looking for a place to hide presents, he found a small door, partially obscured by the eaves. He hadn't lived in the house since his divorce thirteen years earlier, and he had forgotten about this hole in the wall. Behind the door, inside the crawl space, was a square wooden box, about two feet across and two feet deep, packed nearly to the top with old magazines and newspapers. All of them were dated 1916 and 1917, the years he had acted as a sabotage paymaster.

Hilken sat down in the attic and began skimming each one, suddenly remembering the reasons he had saved them. Near the bottom of the pile was the January 1917 issue of a magazine called *Blue Book*. As he flipped through the pages, he noticed a brown imprint that had been branded on several of them. A smile crept across his face as he realized what he was holding.

• • •

Herrmann, Hinsch, Jahnke, Witzke, and dozens of other German spies had scurried for the safety of Mexico City in the weeks before the United States entered World War I, scattering throughout the city, living like nobles in expensive hotels, no longer obligated to maintain their cover stories. They wanted to buy ships, outfit them with guns, and launch them into battle. They considered blowing up Mexican oil fields that were supplying the United States. And they battled one another for control of the Mexican branch of the German secret service.

Herrmann had gone to Mexico with Raoul Gerdts, a German immigrant whom he had met in New York. Gerdts was the gofer of the German secret service, bouncing from one spy to another, carrying envelopes filled with cash and delivering coded messages he couldn't decipher. He was a delicate man with dark features, not handsome but pretty, carrying barely 120 pounds on his five-foot nine-inch frame. He liked to wear tight-fitting black coats and broad-brimmed hats that he pulled low, as if he were hiding his eyes. At times, the hat covered his entire face, revealing only a pencil-thin black mustache and equally thin lips.

In the United States, Gerdts was an eccentric who did little good and no harm, someone tolerated and never taken seriously. But in Mexico, he was invaluable. His mother was Colombian, and Gerdts was fluent in English, German, and Spanish. With his olive skin, he could easily blend in and, even more important, pass back and forth over the U.S. border without raising suspicion. Together, Herrmann and Gerdts had moved into the Juarez Hotel in Mexico City.

Every day, between 4:00 and 6:00 p.m., German agents gathered at Café Europa, the Mexico City version of Martha Held's house in New York. Without the constant presence of high-ranking attachés to fill the leadership void, the man with the hardest reputation emerged as the de facto voice of the group. Adam Siegel was hard, very hard. At just five foot four, the thirty-year-old Siegel was compact and muscular. His close-cropped blond hair, fair complexion, and youthful looks belied the status he held among his colleagues. Fluent in Russian, German, and English, he had escaped from a Russian prisoner of war camp, where he had been beaten so badly that his right eye twitched whenever he spoke.

By April, Herrmann had been in Mexico for two months. Gerdts had helped him settle in, and Siegel had given him a crash course in whom and what to avoid. He finally felt comfortable and was ready to go to work. Before leaving the United States, Herrmann had been told that the Tampico oil fields in northeastern Mexico were a highly prized sabotage target. On April 12, 1917, he approached the German minister, Heinrich von Eckhardt, asked if that were still the case, and told von Eckhardt that he would gladly do the job.

Von Eckhardt looked at the blond-haired boy who was just out of his teens. Herrmann barely spoke German and looked too American to be one of the kaiser's spies. The minister assumed that he was being set up and kicked Herrmann out of his office. Later that day, he cabled the Foreign Office, writing, "This Herrmann professes to have permission from Hilken to set fire to the Tampico oil fields and proposes to carry it out. He asks me whether he is to do it. Would it not be well for me to answer that I am not in communication with Berlin?"

The Germans cabled back, "Herrmann's statements are correct." But the young spy had already decided to set his plan in motion without the minister's approval. Herrmann sought out Siegel and invited him back to his hotel. There he found Gerdts and sent him out to buy several lemons. Upstairs, he and Siegel moved a table from his room out onto the balcony. Together, they began composing a note to Hilken, at first writing it in pencil on a blank sheet of paper.

When Gerdts arrived with the fruit, the men cut several lemons in half and squeezed the juice into a glass until the peels split in their hands and pulp slipped through their fingers. It was late afternoon, the air cooled as the sun went down, and the scent of citrus hung over the balcony. Herrmann pulled out a *Blue Book* magazine dated January 1917, cracked the spine, and opened the magazine to a story titled "The Yukon Trail." He rotated the book counterclockwise a quarter turn, so the text read from bottom to top. He dipped a small, fine-tipped, steel-nibbed pen into the juice as though it were ink and, as Siegel dictated, copied what the two of them had written moments before. The juice dried almost as soon as it soaked into the page, making it impossible for Herrmann to know exactly where one word ended and another began. He wrote the word *told* and accidentally crossed the letter *l* instead of the *t*. The paper was fragile, especially around the margins, and he felt the sharp point rip through the page if he used too much juice. As he finished each line, his hand began to cramp.

They began the message on page 700 and then moved to 698, then 696, then 694. Herrmann then flipped through the magazine and, using the tip of his pen, made small pinpricks in different letters on seemingly random pages. When he was done, he closed the *Blue Book,* handed it to Gerdts, and told him to deliver the message to Paul Hoppenburg, Hilken's agent in New York. Gerdts was to leave in the morning.

Upon arriving in New York, Gerdts discovered that the three-hundred-pound Hoppenburg had recently died. His secretary told Gerdts that all correspondence was to be forwarded to Hilken in Baltimore. Gerdts headed south.

Hilken treated Gerdts like an old friend, even inviting him to stay with the family. After dinner, the two men walked down to the cellar, with Gerdts carrying the *Blue Book*. Hilken needed heat to make the message readable. As his iron warmed up, he slowly flipped through the pages, looking for signs of a secret message. Near the end of the magazine, he saw one. "That is almost yellow enough to read without ironing," he said to Gerdts.

As Hilken applied the iron to each page, a hiss came from beneath its hot surface, followed by a light wisp of smoke. The heel of the iron left behind a brown imprint as the heat scorched the previously invisible lemon juice, revealing Herrmann's message. The sentences that appeared were often interrupted by a four-digit number, such as 1755. Hilken dropped the first number in the sequence, then read the rest of it backward, which led him to a page in the magazine. When he held that page up to the light, he saw small holes over various letters on the page, which spelled out the name he should insert in the lemon juice sentences. After several minutes, Hilken was able to read Herrmann's message:

> Have seen von Eckhardt. He is suspicious of me. Can't convince him I come from Marguerre and Nadolny. Have told him all reference to Hinsch and I, *Deutschland,* Jersey City Terminal, Kingsland, and Tony's Lab. He doubts me on account of my bum German. Confirm to him through your channels all ok and my mission here. I have no funds. Eckhardt claims he is short of money. Send by bearer $25,000. Where are Hinsch and Carl Ahrendt. Tell Hinsch to come here. I expect to go north but he can locate me through von Eckhardt. I don't trust Carl Ahrendt, Kristoff, and that Hoboken bunch. If cornered they might get us in Dutch with the authorities. See that Hinsch brings with him all who might implicate us. What will you do now with America in the war? Are you coming here or going to South America? Advise you drop everything and leave the states. Regards to Hoppenburg. Sei Nicht Dum Mach Doch Wieder Bumm Bumm Bumm.

Hilken laughed at the last line: "Don't be dumb: make it again bumm bumm bumm." It was a verse they had sung together the last time they had been in Hoppenburg's office, in August 1916, to celebrate Black Tom's demise.

Once assigned to Black Tom, John McCloy spent nearly all his time working on the case. His view of the world as a dangerous place, and America's role in policing it, had been shaped by what he saw as Germany's naked aggression during World War I. He had volunteered to fight, had been prepared to kill, and was disappointed when a peace agreement had been reached just as he'd joined the front lines in France. He regretted that the Allied forces had never made a full assault on German soil and was sure that the country would never endure peace until its citizens experienced true war. Time, success, and status hadn't mellowed McCloy's skepticism. He still feared Germany for what it had been and loathed it for what it had done. The allegation of sabotage at Black Tom had only reinforced his views. The Germans had learned nothing; there was no remorse, no regret, only hubris and denial. He had no doubt that they were guilty. What he didn't know was how to prove it.

Into the cold months of early 1931, Ellen McCloy was still struggling to get pregnant. The thought of having a baby consumed her. Traveling with her husband proved the perfect distraction, and John found her to be the ideal spy. She was fluent in German and, with her hazel-brown eyes and soft features, nonthreatening. In fact, Ellen was fearless, and as her husband began to investigate what had happened at Black Tom, he did not hesitate to take advantage of his matrimonial assets. One afternoon at a Berlin hotel, John asked Ellen to watch a potential witness while he used the lobby telephone.

"Whatever you do," he said, "do not take your eyes off of that man."

When he came back, the man and Ellen were gone. He raced around the lobby, toward the bathrooms, and saw Ellen standing outside the men's room, holding her chest, her cheeks flushed, a handkerchief wiping her brow.

"The man began walking away," Ellen said, "so I followed him. He turned towards the bathrooms, and he noticed me, and he started walking faster. I saw him disappear into the men's room. I waited a minute outside hoping he would come out, wondering if someone else would go in. Nothing happened. So I opened the door and I saw his legs dangling from the back window, as he was climbing through it."

During another trip to Germany, the two tracked a Russian count named Alexander Nelidorff, who they believed had information about Black Tom. Ellen and John cornered him at his hotel one afternoon and, playing good cop/bad cop, convinced the count to invite them up to his room. While John was taking notes, his pen ran dry. He noticed two mechanical pencils in the count's lapel pocket, grabbed one, and was practically knocked off his chair as the count sprinted from the room. This time, Ellen wouldn't let him get away. She bolted out of the room, cornering him at the end of a hotel hallway.

"What are you doing?" she asked.

Shaken and embarrassed, Nelidorff reached for the other pencil, slowly lifted the cap, showed her four translucent pellets, and answered, "If your husband had grabbed this pencil and tried to write, these pellets would have released a gas. We'd have been unconscious within a few seconds."

When the McCloys moved back to New York in the spring of 1931, the case became their shared passion. John volunteered to become the partner in charge of human resources at Cravath. It was the least glamorous, least desired job in the office, normally assigned to partners who couldn't bring in clients on their own. Consequently, their impact on the firm was less, their bonuses smaller, and their reputations on Wall Street reduced. But McCloy saw the job's benefits: His new office would have a private conference room attached, necessary for meeting with potential employees and perfect as home base for the sabotage team. Most important, his caseload would be light, and he could devote nearly all his time to Black Tom.

The advertisements, on streetcars around New York and in newspapers in Baltimore, appeared in early January 1931. Sidney Sutherland, a silver-haired writer whose exposés and celebrity interviews made *Liberty* magazine one of the nation's most popular weeklies, was, the ads promised, going to solve the mystery of Black Tom. Sutherland's stories always had a sensational bent, whether it was an interview with silent film star Lillian

Gish or a melodrama about the day in 1892 when John L. Sullivan was knocked out. One of his articles was titled simply "The Most Popular Story Ever Written." Whatever he had found out about Black Tom, it would not be dull.

In February 1931, *Liberty* published the first in Sutherland's thirteen-part series linking the kaiser's government to the sabotage in New York Harbor. Pulling largely from the oral arguments that were public record, Sutherland described Walter Scheele's work making pencil bombs and Anton Dilger's anthrax lab in Chevy Chase, Maryland. He named Kurt Jahnke, Lothar Witzke, and Michael Kristoff as the likely saboteurs and wrote about how they had all gotten together with men such as Franz von Papen and Johann von Bernstorff at Martha Held's house. He dedicated one of the thirteen parts entirely to Paul Hilken's work as paymaster.

Hilken's family thought they had been through the worst of the publicity during the trial. But now, with the Americans trying to reopen the case and the *Liberty* articles, they feared further disruption of their lives. Shortly after the first stories appeared, Hilken's sister Nina wrote to him, "Don't you ever again let the attorneys frighten you or persuade you into talking. They promised no publicity then took no steps to prevent it. You can and must defy every attempt to make you a witness. You lay low and say nothing." A month later, after seeing another Sutherland article in which her brother was prominently featured, Nina wrote to Paul again, worrying about his children:

> I have bought every issue and notice with grief that your name appeared in the last number, and I'm afraid the next numbers will have more. It's too bad. The only course to take now is to act as though we never read *Liberty,* and had no connection with that particular Paul H. Or with those people who know too much. It's too bad for Henry and the girls, because they will worry. If worst comes to worst, they'll just have to move away from Baltimore. In a strange city no one would remember the name.

But Hilken would always remember. In November, the commission had branded him a liar. In February, Sutherland had said he was a traitor. One night in late April, Hilken and Herrmann met at Hilken's apartment on West 183rd Street to share a demijohn of homemade wine and feel sorry for themselves. Hilken still hadn't turned over the *Blue Book* message from Herrmann he'd found in his attic. Once, in February, without telling the American lawyers, he had tried to deliver it personally to Boyden on a trip to Boston, but the umpire had refused to see him or even hear what he wanted to discuss. Hilken had subsequently lost his nerve and decided to keep the evidence hidden. But that night, as the wine took hold, he became more and more upset over the *Liberty* articles. He kept dropping hints that he could change public opinion, that he could prove he and Herrmann had done what they had said. They'd be traitors, but not liars.

Hilken told his friend about the *Blue Book*. "I did not remember the message," Herrmann said. "He would not show it to me at the time and I did not press him about the matter." But Herrmann did press him to go to Peaslee, or at least let him do it. Hilken, drunk and afraid, reminded Herrmann about potential murder charges in Jersey City. Herrmann admitted that he wasn't willing to risk murder charges just to comfort his friend. He'd back him up, but only when he knew that he wouldn't be prosecuted.

The next day, April 23, 1931, Herrmann met with Peaslee in New York. During the meeting, he laid out a series of hypotheticals. If Hilken had evidence about the explosion at Black Tom, how useful would that be to Peaslee? Could Peaslee guarantee that the Jersey City police wouldn't come after them? Two days later, Peaslee called Herrmann back, promising that the Jersey City police were no longer investigating the Black Tom murders. The next day, he got his first look at what would become known as "the Herrmann message."

Not surprisingly, Martin worried that it could be forged. "This message looks like a very important piece of evidence," he wrote to Bonynge on May 2. "I do not see how it could be faked without the connivance of both Hilken and Herrmann. If it should develop that they are parties to faking a matter of this character, it seems to me that we should be in a position to take rather drastic procedure."

Before submitting the Herrmann message to the commission, Martin wanted it verified. His first call was to Albert Osborn, who had been studying handwriting for nearly forty-five years. He had written two books on the subject and designed a microscope, made specifically to study discrepancies in writing samples, which Bausch & Lomb included in its catalog. Unfortunately for the Americans, Osborn had already been hired by the Germans. (A few years after the Black Tom case, Osborn's testimony would help the state of New Jersey convict a German immigrant named Bruno Hauptmann of kidnapping and killing Charles Lindbergh's son.)

Osborn recommended that Martin speak with Eldridge Stein, another forensic analyst. The two experts had started as mentor and protégé nearly thirty years earlier and were now close friends. Their downtown Manhattan offices, Osborn's on Broadway and Stein's on Park Row, were just a few blocks apart. They often consulted together on cases and referred each other for jobs.

Based on Osborn's suggestion, Martin hired Stein. On June 16, Leonard Peto and Henry Arnold, another attorney for the claimants, visited Stein at his office to discuss his initial impressions of the Herrmann message. While staring at the *Blue Book*, Stein began pointing out certain pieces of the letter that made him suspicious of its age. He said the way the page was ripped under certain letters indicated to him that the paper had been old when the message had been written. He also wondered if the fluid used had actually been lemon juice. Arnold and Peto politely cut Stein off. They told him that they weren't interested in having him determine how old the message was or whether it was written in a secret ink. They had hired a military forensics expert named Captain Aloysius McGrail, a Harvard-trained chemist who worked in a government lab analyzing secret writing during World War I, to do that. Arnold and Peto told Stein that all they needed to know was whether the message was written in Herrmann's handwriting. "We felt that Mr. Stein's statements of what he considered to be suspicious circumstances were unfounded," Arnold said years later. "But we also felt that it would be difficult to find a man better qualified than Mr. Stein to pass upon the identities of the handwritings."

Despite Arnold and Peto's concerns, Stein delivered what they needed. He examined the Herrmann message, comparing it to a diary Herrmann had used in 1915 and a written statement he had made in 1930. On June 26, ten days after first meeting the lawyers, Stein submitted a report saying that "there is sufficient individuality, in my judgment, to warrant an opinion that the secret message was written by the same writer who wrote the writings used for comparison." Although he had been asked to refrain from commenting on when the note might have been written, he couldn't resist adding, "I have no opinion whatever regarding the time when the writing in the magazine was written."

The claimants shrugged it off and paid Stein his $350 fee. They were counting on Aloysius McGrail to confirm the message's age. Using a microscope that magnified and then photographed every pinprick made in the *Blue Book*, McGrail studied the integrity of the paper fibers around the edges of the holes. He then compared them to fibers around sample pinpricks he made in a *Blue Book* magazine of the same age. Under the microscope, the fingernail-thin fibers of both magazines looked like large pieces of cotton that had been torn apart. They splayed in several crooked directions, every weave of the paper visible. Those in the original *Blue Book* containing the message were black all the way through, the same color as the ink used on the page. But the fibers from the holes McGrail made were white.

McGrail concluded that the black ink used to print the magazine, still relatively fresh when Herrmann had made his pinpricks, bent with the paper as the needle fractured the surface. By the time McGrail made his holes, the ink had become brittle, and it fractured when punctured, leaving the edges around the holes a lighter, brighter color. To McGrail, the message clearly had been written shortly after the *Blue Book* was originally published in

1917. "It is not a positive test," he wrote, "but one which affords strong evidence."

At the Americans' urging, the commission scheduled a two-day hearing for the end of July to discuss the Herrmann message. Armed with McGrail's affidavit confirming the note's age and Stein's confirming that Herrmann was the author, Bonynge, Martin, Peaslee, McCloy, and the other American lawyers felt confident. They had two more reasons to be hopeful. First, Karl von Lewinski, the German agent who had so skillfully argued the sabotage cases at The Hague, had retired from the MCC in January 1931. Second, as the hardships in Germany continued, the German public had become even angrier and more bitter. The American Embassy in Berlin cabled the State Department that the German chancellor, Heinrich Brüning, might be forced to resign at any moment. With von Lewinski gone, a government potentially in transition, and a new piece of seemingly irrefutable evidence, the Americans were optimistic.

Yet even within the State Department, there were doubts about the Herrmann message. William Castle, the undersecretary for western European affairs, wrote to the U.S. ambassador to Germany, "When I saw the evidence, it did not deeply appeal to me. If it has the value claimed, I shall never again believe the wildest story in a detective novel."

It mattered what Castle, and every other diplomat and bureaucrat in the State Department, thought of the sabotage cases. When not preparing for court, Bonynge and Martin found themselves constantly begging members of Congress to increase funding to fight the Germans. The politicians were wary of supporting something the State Department ridiculed.

Over three days, from July 30 through August 1, 1931, at the Chamber of Commerce Building in Boston, the commission listened to the American and German agents debate the merits of the Herrmann message. Tannenberg, naturally, questioned its authenticity, arguing, "If this document had been found in the archives of the State Department as a document or message intercepted in 1917, there would perhaps hardly be any defense. But this document is now produced by Paul Hilken, and is identified only by Paul Hilken and Fred Herrmann. The Commission found that these two gentlemen . . . had perjured themselves, by giving one affidavit after another repudiating their previous statements. . . . In order to accept this message as authentic, and as meaning what the American agent says, the Commission must rely on the testimony of two witnesses who have been proven to be liars and perjurers."

The umpire agreed. Despite all the expert testimony Bonynge submitted along with the note, Boyden still wanted an expert of his choosing to examine it. The man he wanted was Osborn.

T he Germans were willing to release Osborn on two conditions: he'd never be asked to reveal conversations he had had with his colleagues or the German lawyers, and the Americans would not be in the room when he examined the Herrmann message for the commission. The Americans, hoping to please the commission, agreed.

But Osborn didn't want the job. Normally, he charged his clients an initial fee for preliminary examination and then, rather than take a per diem rate, a percentage of the dollar amount of the case based on the value of his services. If he made his client money, he received a portion of the winnings. If he saved his client money, a similar formula was applied based on what the damages would likely have been without his help. Black Tom, worth tens of millions of dollars, was the largest lawsuit he had ever worked on. It didn't pay to work for the commission, which had no stake in the claims, when Germany—and, therefore, Osborn—had so much to gain by winning. Boyden decided that if he couldn't have Osborn, the commission would base its decision regarding the Herrmann message on the testimony provided by both the American and German experts. He'd get Osborn, but he'd have to take Stein, too.

But Boyden would never hear what either had to say. On Sunday, October 25, 1931, a crisp fall morning in New England, Boyden and his cousin strolled to church near his home in Beverly, Massachusetts. Bright yellow, red, and orange leaves blanketed the sidewalks and lawns. When they arrived at church, the men settled into the family pew. Shortly after the service began, Boyden toppled forward. He was carried to the church vestry and then taken by ambulance to the hospital. Doctors there pronounced him dead on arrival, the victim of a massive heart attack.

It would be five months before President Hoover appointed Supreme Court justice Owen J. Roberts as the commission's new umpire. The *New York Herald Tribune* announced the appointment on March 27, 1932, noting, "The associate justice, who succeeds Roland Boyden, will find little work to do. The Commission has completed its task, except for deciding whether the famous Black Tom sabotage case will be reopened." Unstated was the fact that that case had now outlasted three other umpires.

T hree days after Boyden's heart attack, Arnold and McCloy visited Stein at his Park Row office. Stein had been meeting with attorneys for Black Tom often, discussing different methods of testing the message's authenticity and other experts who might hold sway with the commission. By October, he'd begun to feel like a key part of the legal team and asked probing questions about the investigation. Sometimes, when they felt the answer contained only harmless information, Arnold or McCloy humored him with a response. During this meeting, Stein asked Arnold if he had ever purchased a copy of the January 1917 *Blue Book* similar to the one in which the Herrmann message was written. Stein told Arnold that he wanted one for himself. Arnold answered that yes, someone in his office had bought one. They had picked it up the day after Hilken had showed them the message, from a bookstore called Abraham's.

That afternoon, Albert Osborn called Abraham's Book Store. He asked if the store had recently carried copies of the January 1917 *Blue Book*. Yes, he was told, it had.

Two days later, on October 30, Osborn visited Abraham's. He introduced himself to the clerk, a man named Herman Meyers, as the person who had called earlier in the week looking for a copy of the *Blue Book*. He asked if Meyers could find one. When Meyers returned, he apologetically told Osborn that the store no longer had any in stock. Osborn hid his disappointment and asked how many it had had previously. "Two," Meyers said. Osborn thanked him and before leaving bought a copy of the December 1916 *Blue Book*.

A week later, on November 6, Osborn visited Abraham's again. This time, he brought Wilhelm Tannenberg with him.

The store was on the bottom floor of a two-story brick building on Fourth Avenue in Manhattan. The words ABRAHAM'S BOOK AND MAGAZINE SHOP were painted on the glass storefront. Above the window hung the sign SPECIALIZING IN BACK NUMBERS OF MAGAZINES. Outside the store was a table of merchandise, which people browsed through while waiting at the nearby bus stop.

Osborn introduced Meyers to Tannenberg and explained the Black Tom case and their roles in it. The German agent questioned Meyers for several minutes, searching for specifics about how many copies of the January 1917 *Blue Book* the store had had, when they had been sold, and who bought them. Meyers repeated that they once had two copies in stock. He then described one of the men who had bought a copy as "tall, between thirty and forty years old."

After the interview, Osborn asked Meyers if he would sign an affidavit swearing to what he'd just told Tannenberg. Meyers hesitated. He had never signed an affidavit before, and he wasn't comfortable swearing to the statements he made. They were guesses, he told them, nothing more.

Then Osborn tugged on Meyers's arm, pulling him away from Tannenberg and toward the other side of the store. "Please do this as a favor for Dr. Tannenberg. He just needs it for his records," Osborn said. Then he leaned in closer, adding, "And he is going to buy a lot of magazines." Meyers looked at Tannenberg and, in a raised voice, told him he would think about it overnight. Tannenberg thanked him and then bought all the 1917 *Blue Books* the store had in stock.

The next morning, Tannenberg visited Meyers alone. He pulled out an affidavit, written as if dictated by Meyers, summarizing their conversation from the day before. As they went over it, Meyers made minor changes, which Tannenberg wrote out himself and then initialed with the capital letter *M.* Then the two men walked down Fourth Avenue to a steamship agency, where they had the affidavit notarized.

On the morning of November 16, Stein called Arnold in a panic. He had something to discuss with him, and it needed to be in person. That afternoon, with McCloy present, Stein said that he had heard that a copy of the January 1917 *Blue Book* had been bought at Abraham's by a tall man shortly before the Americans produced the Herrmann message. He wouldn't say who told him this, and he bound them by their word not to mention him as their source. In his opinion, this could be a devastating blow to the case. Herrmann, Stein reminded them, was a tall man, and a story could be concocted that the *Blue Book* in evidence had actually been bought by Herrmann at Abraham's, not discovered by Hilken at home.

Arnold's instincts were to go to Abraham's and investigate. But first, after Stein left the office, Arnold and McCloy called Bonynge and Martin in Washington. They told them what Stein had said, almost laughing out loud at the absurdity of his suggestion. Bonynge and Martin weren't laughing. They had been arguing this case for too long and had been outsmarted too often. They didn't know Stein, who had dealt almost exclusively with Arnold and McCloy, and they couldn't be sure of his intentions. "It was the general consensus," Arnold said, "that this might be a trick, a German plot to induce me to go to the book shop and then, because I had given Stein my word not to mention his name, be unable to say why I had done so. It was argued that the Germans would say that I must have known of a purchase at Abraham's Book Store by Herrmann. Otherwise I would not have gone there to inquire about such a purchase and to find out whether or not the people in the shop could identify Herrmann.

"Unless I could say who had given me the information, it would appear that I had gone there because of my own knowledge of the circumstances."

Instead, Arnold and McCloy focused on changing Stein's mind. They visited him in his office one afternoon several days later and explained that they couldn't possibly pursue this angle unless they had a credible reason. When Stein refused to say anything further, their tone became sharper and more threatening. They told him that if concealing his identity meant harming the case, they wouldn't hesitate to name him. Stein pleaded with them not to do that. "Using my name," he said, "would ruin the closest friendship and business relationship that I have in the world."

It was obvious to both lawyers that he was referring to his friendship with Osborn.

Chapter **Fourteen**

A FTER HILKEN HAD turned over the Herrmann message, Martin had implored him to look for more evidence. But Hilken had remained a reluctant witness, torn between finding more proof and not wanting to see his name in the papers anymore. In December 1931, Martin accompanied Hilken to Baltimore, hoping to force his hand.

The two took a cab from the Hotel Belvedere to Hilken's old house in Roland Park. They spent most of the day looking through Hilken's old papers, boxes, and trunks stored in the attic. Hilken showed Martin where he'd found the *Blue Book*, near the eaves of the house, and the two then pulled up all the floorboards, looking for secret compartments Hilken was sure he had built. They found old letters about official North German Lloyd business and Hilken's checkbook stubs from 1914–1915 and 1917–1919, but nothing for 1916. Frustrated, Martin left Baltimore that night.

Hilken stayed and had dinner with his ex-wife and youngest daughter. They discussed Black Tom and what Martin was searching for, and Hilken asked them both to look through the house one more time. That evening, after Hilken left, his ex-wife and daughter talked about the days when the Hilkens were first divorced, nearly fourteen years earlier. He had left behind a lot of personal files, which had been gathered and piled in the attic. His daughter used the attic as a playroom, and she remembered playing with small notebooks she found among the papers.

Over the next three days, Mrs. Hilken searched her daughter's well-preserved boxes of toys. On the afternoon of the third day, a Saturday, she opened an old trunk. It was full of clothes made for dolls, neatly folded and packed. She unfolded each dress, shaking it out for any loose paper, and then carefully refolded it. Her hands moved quickly and effortlessly, as if the task were as natural as bringing a fork to her mouth, until at last a notebook fell to the floor. The cover read "1916."

The new year rolled around. It was the Depression, and Bonynge needed to convince Congress to fund his work. There were skeptics in the State Department and cynics in the halls of Congress who considered the sabotage cases an obstacle to normal relations with Germany.

Not that far removed from his days as a congressman, Bonynge felt as though he was among friends when he returned to Congress on January 4, 1932. There was no adversary across the way, ready to point out his inadequacies, as there was during his MCC oral arguments. There was no commission, already prejudiced against his primary witnesses. He was arguing in front of a captive audience. And at last he was convincing. Speaking to a congressional committee, he wove a captivating tale of German sabotage and duplicity that inspired those in the room. He finished by saying, "This newly discovered evidence consists of documents which I think are not only persuasive but, in my opinion, absolutely conclusive that the parties charged with setting these fires were German agents and were duly authorized by the German government through their officials, to destroy plants in the United States."

The next day, part of the headline in the *New York Times* read,

WITNESS AT HOUSE HEARING SAYS BLACK TOM BLAME IS PROVED.
Bonynge would get his money.

The euphoria didn't last. Shortly after giving his testimony before Congress, Bonynge received a letter from one of his handwriting experts, Edward Heinrich. Heinrich had just been hired, and while going over the lists of who was going to testify he noticed that Stein was working for the Americans and Osborn for the Germans. He found that odd. "If Mr. Osborn has now rendered an opinion on these exhibits which disagrees with Mr. Stein, I'd be surprised," Heinrich wrote. "Mr. Osborn's son told me several years ago that there was a gentlemen's agreement between Osborn and Stein to avoid appearing against one another. I am curious about this."

So were the Americans. Based on Heinrich's note, Bonynge reexamined both Stein's and Osborn's testimony. Stein's report concluded that Herrmann wrote the message. Then, despite being asked not to, he went out of his way to write that he had no opinion of when the message was written. At first, the Americans had dismissed this as an expert showing off. But then Bonynge remembered that it had been Osborn who had recommended Stein. He remembered it had been Stein who had tipped off Arnold and McCloy about the "tall man" who'd bought a *Blue Book* from Abraham's. Bonynge turned to Osborn's thirty-five-page report. It never confirmed who wrote the message. Instead, Osborn focused entirely on experiments that proved, in his opinion, the message couldn't possibly have been written by anyone in 1917. Just as Stein had suggested in his first conversation with Arnold and Peto, Osborn declared that the way certain letters in the message punctured the edges of the paper proved that the pages were old and brittle when the note was written. He said that certain microscopic strands of paper left behind by the pinpricks were lighter than others because of the way they fell against the page. He also concluded that the message couldn't have been written in lemon juice because the note did not have the traits of something written by a "blind man." Words did not frequently overlap, nor were there extraneous spaces between letters. The ink, he concluded, must have been sepia-toned, something that was bright enough to see when wet but that became invisible after drying.

Suddenly, conspiracy theories raced through Bonynge's head as he realized that Heinrich was right: the two experts wouldn't oppose each other. All the things Stein wouldn't say, Osborn did, and vice versa. Bonynge's heart sank as he concluded that the two were working together.

The first part of the German defense against the Herrmann message relied on the testimony of experts, especially Osborn, who refuted that the message had been written in 1917. The second part hinged on proving that Herrmann had bought the *Blue Book* early in 1931 and then fabricated the message before turning it over to Martin. The final piece depended on the two men who had been so convincing in 1930: Ahrendt and Hinsch. They were both mentioned in the message. "I don't trust Carl Ahrendt," Herrmann wrote. "See that Hinsch brings with him all who might implicate us." Now Tannenberg needed their elaboration.

Tannenberg interviewed Ahrendt in Detroit in February. As an American testifying on behalf of Germany, he had been the most credible German witness during the first oral arguments. From Ahrendt, Tannenberg simply needed to hear that he had no knowledge of a wartime message sent by Herrmann to Hilken. Whereas Ahrendt was nothing more than a midlevel administrator, Hinsch had been accused of being intimately involved. Denials wouldn't be enough for him. In early March, a few weeks after taking Ahrendt's statement, Tannenberg traveled to Berlin. He met with Hinsch at the Foreign Office, handed him the Herrmann message and Ahrendt's affidavit, and told him to get his story straight.

The Americans knew that their opponents would go after Herrmann. As they had with the first trial, the Germans would make this about the credibility of witnesses, as much as about the evidence. For every expert the Americans hired to authenticate the Herrmann message, the Germans would have someone saying the exact opposite. "I fear," Peaslee wrote to Hall in March 1932, "if the Commission has before it simply an array of conflicting highly technical evidence, it is very likely to succumb to the arguments of the German commissioner and throw us out of court again."

But unlike in 1930, the Americans now had an ally on the commission, Chandler Anderson. Since Boyden's death, the once uninterested American commissioner had taken on a more active role, as his frustration with the 1930 decision had grown into full-blown animosity toward the German agents and commissioner. He felt responsible for not doing more at The Hague. He had disagreed with Boyden and Kiesselbach, but in the interest of expediency, he had gone along with their decision. Yet the case remained unsettled. And because he believed that the Herrmann message was real, he now felt he had been duped. In March 1932, after a visit from Anderson, Martin wrote to Bonynge that Anderson "told me frankly he thought he was in a position to write an opinion reviewing the prior decision of the Commission. . . . He would point out that, if there is no question of the authenticity of these documents, the Commission would be justified in changing the ruling of 1930."

Anderson was convinced, but now the Americans had to persuade someone else: the new umpire, Owen Roberts.

The fifty-seven-year-old Roberts had been a member of the Supreme Court for two years when Hoover named him the MCC's umpire. His lips, long and flat, nearly stretched from one side of his face to the other, making it seem as if he was perpetually on the verge of smiling — or scowling (no one was ever sure). He had been in private practice, had taught law at Penn, and had been a Philadelphia prosecutor.

He was also well versed in the shadow world. After World War I, Wilson had asked Roberts to prosecute espionage cases on behalf of the U.S. government. Roberts had discovered how Americans had turned against their country, how enemies had plotted to destroy it, and how vulnerable the United States had been to attacks from within. The sabotage cases felt familiar to him, like an old book he'd read before.

It wasn't just the subject that made Roberts comfortable. In private practice, he had often used Osborn to authenticate documents. Through Osborn, Roberts had met Stein, who kept an office near his in Philadelphia. The umpire respected their opinions, and Osborn knew Roberts believed in them.

At the end of February, the Americans had turned in additional reports regarding the authenticity of the Herrmann message. In a brief, Bonynge summarized the work of "an eminent handwriting expert" who had confirmed that Herrmann had written the message. It was obvious he was referring to Stein, although he didn't include any reports from Stein along with this brief.

Osborn thought this was odd, and he wrote Tannenberg a letter that feigned alarm and hinted at an American cover-up. "There is a veiled reference to an eminent handwriting expert, Mr. Stein, but there is no explanation as to why he was not asked to make a case outside of the handwriting, or, if he did make a report, no reference is made to what became of it," Osborn wrote. For emphasis, he underlined the last part of the sentence in blue.

Tannenberg forwarded Osborn's letter to Kiesselbach, and Kiesselbach told Roberts that he thought the Americans were withholding information. He followed up with a letter to the umpire, to which he attached a copy of Bonynge's February brief. He highlighted a passage that referred to an opinion of Stein's that the Germans claimed had never been in any reports. "It corroborates rather strongly the information I communicated to you," Kiesselbach wrote. "Mr. Stein made a further report outside of the handwriting but not produced by the claimants."

Roberts agreed. The Americans didn't know it yet, but they had already lost the new umpire.

•   •   •

In June 1932, with the Weimar government entering what would be its final year, Franz von Papen was named the new German chancellor. He was a transitional figurehead, between the end of one failed experiment in democracy and the beginning of a horrific dictatorship. He wasn't chosen because he could save Weimar, but because he was a weak, right-leaning, little-known member of the Reichstag whose appointment mollified the Nazis. They would accept no one else in the position, and their power within the government and over the people had become too great to ignore. A year later, sensing he'd be forced out, von Papen would cede the chancellorship to Adolf Hitler, in exchange for the job of vice chancellor.

While von Papen's appointment strengthened Germany's resolve to win the sabotage cases, the American lawyers were soon confronted with an even bigger obstacle: Hinsch had finally given testimony regarding the Herrmann message.

When Hilken testified, he had described in great detail his relationship with Gerdts, saying that they'd met several times in 1916 and 1917. But Gerdts had been vague in his testimony, never specifying when the two had met or how well they knew each other. Hinsch seized on the differences, hoping it would appear as though Hilken were lying. Hinsch testified, "Hilken told me that this book had been brought to him by a man named Gerdts, who had been unknown to him up until then. He then showed me the page of the message containing developed writing, which read, 'The bearer of this message is Raoul Gerdts who carries a personal message to you. You can trust him in full.'"

While Herrmann had testified that the message had been written with lemon juice, Hinsch borrowed from Osborn's expert opinion and disagreed. By 1917, Hinsch declared, the Germans had abandoned using lemon juice in favor of a new formula, brought to the United States by Herrmann and Hilken, that did not require heat to expose it. "Invisible writing fluids that could be made visible with heat were no longer used by this time for important communications of this kind. . . . This was such a primitive and generally known method that the preparation of a communication with a fluid of this kind afforded no assurance of its remaining secret."

Herrmann's other Mexican confidant, Adam Siegel, had testified that the message had been long and dictated by him into a magazine. But Gerdts had said that the message came in a book of poetry. Hinsch took advantage of the discrepancy, claiming that the message was written in a hardbound book and had been no more than one or two sentences. "I distinctly remember, since I carefully read the message several times at Hilken's home and discussed it with Hilken in detail, that the text of the message was very short and that the page with the writing developed by Hilken contained only an identification of Gerdts, the request for $25,000 and the advice that Gerdts would report verbally about all other matters."

The Americans countered with experts, six in all, not including the now suspected Stein. Each bought their own *Blue Books* from 1917 and 1932. They wrote on them with lemon juice to see how the paper — from the old issues and the new — reacted. They wrote on them with sepia-toned ink to see how quickly it disappeared. They pierced the middle of the pages in both the old and the new magazines with pins and then examined the penetrations under a microscope to see if the ink on the pages cracked. They built elaborate models that evenly distributed pressure from the pen across the entire page, from the middle to the edges. Using steel-nibbed pens, they gauged how brittle the paper in the 1917 magazines was compared to that in the 1932 issues. They applied irons, heated to 200 degrees Celsius, to the pages to determine how much heat developed lemon juice as well as other secret inks.

Their experiments were exhaustive and detailed, and McCloy mirrored them. During weekends at his in-laws' house in Hastings-on-Hudson, he would sit in a high-backed, hardwood chair at a desk that overlooked the property. He'd dip a steel-nibbed pen into a glass of lemon juice and try rewriting the Herrmann message. (He'd already memorized it from reading it so often.) McCloy's nieces and nephews would gather around the chair asking him what he was doing. His attention remained focused.

When done, he'd study the pages: Did the juice soak through to the back? To other pages? Was it visible when he first wrote with it? How long did it take to disappear? Just as in college, when he read multiple books on a subject to make certain he took all arguments seriously and fairly, he tried again and again to prove Osborn right. He never could.

All six experts working for the Americans concluded that the message had been written when the paper was still relatively fresh. The language in their reports wasn't just authoritative; it was brash, aggressive, and challenging. "Not only is there no evidence to substantiate Mr. Osborn's claims," wrote one of the analysts, "it seems entirely logical to draw the conclusion that at the time the Herrmann message was written, the paper was not more than six or seven months old. It is quite fair to say that Mr. Osborn's opinion is without any proper basis of fact."

In October, Kiesselbach arrived in the United States. He immediately met with Tannenberg at the MCC office in the Investment Building on K Street in Washington, D.C. It was late. The office was quiet and dark. A slight chill filled the hallways, trapped inside whenever the front door of the building opened. Cold weather was coming.

Kiesselbach wanted to hear more about Osborn, about his accusations that Stein had submitted a report detrimental to the Americans' case and that Bonynge and Martin had ignored it.

By October 1932, Roberts had spent seven months reviewing thousands of pages of briefs, hundreds of affidavits, and countless reports concerning handwriting analysis. He felt he knew the sabotage cases as well as if he had been presiding over them from the beginning. It was time to settle them. Roberts announced that he'd hear the attorneys on November 21–25, in a conference room in the Investment Building.

Shortly after Roberts announced the dates for the arguments, his secretary received a phone call in his Capitol Hill office. The man introduced himself as Eldridge Stein, the handwriting expert, calling from New York. He said he had an urgent matter to discuss with the umpire of the Mixed Claims Commission. Roberts refused the call, instructing his secretary to tell Stein that he wouldn't see or speak to him while the case was pending.

But Stein would not be so easily dismissed. On Friday, November 4, he sent a letter by courier to Bonynge's law office on Broadway. That morning, he mailed a copy of the letter to Arnold. Although Arnold wouldn't receive it until Monday, he didn't have to wait that long to learn what it said. Bonynge called him, screaming, as soon as he read it.

Stein accused Arnold of suppressing a report he had filed on June 10, 1931. He claimed that the report concluded that the Herrmann message and another piece of evidence relating to the Kingsland case were forged; that the claimants had submitted a manipulated supplemental report at the Boston oral arguments to make it look like he believed the Herrmann message was authentic; that he had handed the report to Arnold personally; and that he was sending this letter "so that some voluntary action may be taken immediately to correct this unfairness. Such conduct would be especially repulsive to me since now this case comes before Mr. Justice Roberts, for whom I gave service on many varied and important matters and whose confidences I prize highly."

Arnold's hand shook as it cradled the phone, his brow ridged in anger. The letter came more than a year after the Boston arguments and just two weeks before the hearings scheduled in Washington. He called Stein and demanded that they meet that afternoon. Stein balked; he didn't want to meet at Arnold's office. Instead, he proposed a meeting at his office at eleven o'clock the next morning. Arnold then called Bonynge, Peaslee, and McCloy; they'd confront Stein together.

At 10:00 a.m. on Saturday, Arnold, Bonynge, McCloy, and Peaslee met at Bonynge's Broadway office. The day before, each man had attacked different parts of Stein's letter, looking for holes, as though they were preparing to cross-examine a witness. They had found several. For example, McCloy, who had been at Martin's office in Washington on Friday, arrived with letters from Stein to Martin indicating that Stein had sent his reports directly to Martin, bypassing Arnold. Meanwhile, Arnold had searched his files for the June 10 report and found nothing.

They all considered the possibility that Stein was colluding with Osborn. Osborn had recommended Stein. Several handwriting experts had told one or more of the lawyers that it was common knowledge the two had an understanding never to disagree with each other. Arnold even remembered Stein casually mentioning that he had never disagreed with Osborn in court. Stein's source about a "tall man" buying a *Blue Book* around the same time Herrmann first mentioned its existence was now obviously Osborn. The language of the alleged June 10 report practically mirrored what Osborn had written in several of his reports for the Germans.

The four men arrived at Stein's two-room office promptly at eleven. His secretary was there, and she led them into the back room, where Stein was waiting. He was surprised to see all four attorneys and unprepared for their anger. They were no longer employers visiting an employee. The relaxed relationship that Arnold had shared with Stein was replaced by Bonynge's cold formality. He saw Stein as an opposing witness and treated him with hostility. He asked Stein if he kept a notebook of his appointments, and if so, whether he had recorded the first time he'd met Arnold. Stein produced the notebook. The entry for his first meeting with Arnold was dated June 16. Stein tried to explain away the discrepancy by claiming that he had met informally with Peto, as a favor to Osborn, several days before that.

Bonynge then asked for a copy of the June 10 report. Stein offered a bound black volume containing dozens of reports for several different cases. The name, address, and date of each report was typed at the top. There was no heading for the June 10 report. Instead, the date and the address of Peto's office, not Arnold's, where Stein claimed he had sent the report, appeared in pencil in the bottom left corner.

Arnold looked at Stein and, for the first time, accused him of lying. Then McCloy did the same. When Bonynge asked how the report had been delivered—had Stein done it? had his secretary? had he sent a messenger? had someone dropped it in the mail?— Stein said he could not remember. He told Stein to ask his secretary to find a copy of the cover letter that accompanied it, but she could not. Bonynge asked Stein's secretary if she remembered mailing or delivering the report directly to Arnold. His tone was accusatory, stunning her for a moment. She said that she could not recall, then settled on a story that she had personally delivered it on her way to Grand Central one afternoon.

Then Bonynge read a letter, dated June 1931, that had been written by Arnold to Stein. In it, Arnold specifically requested that all of Stein's reports bypass him and be sent directly to Martin for filing as evidence. McCloy produced copies of the reports and letters from Stein to Martin acknowledging Arnold's request. Bonynge and McCloy threw the material onto Stein's desk, as Bonynge asked, "How can you reconcile the receipt of Arnold's letter and your sending of the reports directly to Washington with what you claim today?"

Stein didn't answer directly. Instead, he kept repeating that he was certain he had sent the June 10 report.

Bonynge asked if he had ever discussed the sabotage cases with Osborn. Stein denied that he had. Then Arnold wanted to know how Stein had found out about someone buying *Blue Book* magazines at Abraham's. How had he known that the Germans would try to claim that the person who had bought it was Herrmann?

Stein admitted that he and Osborn had talked about the cases "in a very general way." Arnold asked if he had ever opposed Osborn in any cases. Stein said that he had. Arnold asked if Stein had ever disagreed with Osborn, even when they were on opposing sides. Stein said that he did not think he had, that he had been "very friendly with Osborn for a number of years."

The lawyers then demanded that Stein show them the statements in the Boston argument where he had been misrepresented. When he couldn't, they pointed out that the language of his alleged June 10 report was nearly identical to Osborn's for the Germans. McCloy induced Stein to admit that he had never expressed doubt about the authenticity of the Herrmann message in any of their meetings. Bonynge asked how, in light of everything Stein had been told and admitted, he could take the position that the documents were not genuine. Why would he try to destroy the case and attack Arnold's integrity?

Stein said nothing. He picked up some papers McCloy had thrown on his desk, the proof Arnold had asked him to send the reports directly to Washington and the proof from Martin's office that he had done so. Stein looked up, stared at Arnold, and apologized. With the lawyers standing across from him, he asked his secretary to draft a letter formally apologizing to the American contingent and withdrawing his accusatory letter. Then Arnold asked Stein whether Osborn or anyone else affiliated with the commission was under the impression that the Americans were suppressing a report. "Stein gave us his solemn, unequivocal assurance that no one knew of these documents except himself, his secretary and ourselves," Arnold later said.

After two hours, the Americans left, vindicated but unsatisfied.

That afternoon, back at his office, Bonynge contemplated the perilous position Stein had put the case in. Telling Roberts about Stein and Osborn's collusion would reduce the power of the Herrmann message and raise the question of whether the Americans actually were suppressing a June 10 report and had merely bullied a terrified Stein to change his story.

By Monday morning, forty-eight hours after meeting with Stein, Bonynge couldn't contain his dread. When he hadn't received a copy of Stein's letter apologizing and withdrawing his accusations by midday, he wrote Martin his third nervous letter in three days:

I have not this morning received that letter that Mr. Stein agreed to write. I do not like this situation at all. I am satisfied in my own mind that Stein has been working in collusion with Osborn and other German experts and I do not want the situation to be developed so that we may not be able to establish that fact before the Commission.

If you get the slightest intimation that the Commission or any member thereof, has been informed regarding the letter that Stein wrote to Arnold, I wish you would promptly advise me by phone so that we may be prepared to meet it. My personal opinion is that the letter was inspired by Osborn.

With just two weeks until the Washington arguments, Bonynge had neither the time nor the resources to discredit it.

By the time the oral arguments in Washington began on November 21, the United States had a new president-elect, Franklin Roosevelt. Like Hoover, FDR wanted the commission to end its business as soon as possible. Roosevelt, a Democrat, had been elected with 57 percent of the vote, and his party had a majority of twenty-three seats in the Senate. If Bonynge and the Americans couldn't prove their case, FDR wouldn't have any opposition if he decided not to finance another American appeal.

Roberts also wanted the commission to wrap things up. Before the arguments began, he put a three-day limit on the hearings. In case the lawyers didn't understand that he wanted this to go smoothly and end quickly, and that he wouldn't be open to appeals, he sent the same message through reporters. The *Washington Star,* when previewing what it dubbed a case of "spies and coded messages," reported that "when the case is decided — which is expected soon after the final argument — the Commission will close its doors for the last time."

•   •   •

But the entire American contingent had even greater worries than
the end of the commission. The lawyers still didn't know whether
the panel was prejudiced against them or, as Stein had assured
them, was unaware of his accusations. As Bonynge stood to make
his opening statements, he studied the eyes of the judges to gauge
whether they viewed him as guilty or innocent. Throughout the
case, the Germans had been masterful at outsmarting the Americans. He didn't know if Osborn and Stein were acting alone, if the
Germans had put them up to it, or even if they were colluding at
all. But the Germans were in his head, and his argument reflected
his insecurities.

Instead of building up the validity of the Herrmann message
with analysis, he felt compelled to compare his experts to Osborn.
Bonynge sounded as though he were on the defensive, pleading
with the judges to believe in his experts because of their intentions,
not their reports. "You will find," he argued, "numerous instances
in which Mr. Osborn has gone out of his way to question the hon-
esty and integrity of the American experts in the experiments they
made, again demonstrating his partisanship, his absolute partisanship, in this matter because of the fee that he expects to obtain as a
result of his examination. In making his criticisms of these witnesses, he shows a spirit of hostility. . . . He has put himself in the
position where his opinion is prejudiced by the fact that he is apparently constantly thinking of the size of the fee, which was to be
dependent upon whether he was successful.

"On the other side, we have a large number of experts. None
of them has any interest in the result of the litigation, and three
have no interest in any fee whatsoever because they received
no fee."

But the judges had little interest in the experts' intentions or
attitudes. They had been given nearly a thousand pages of material detailing their experiments and opinions. What they wanted
were summaries of the opinions, explanations of why the tests per-
formed were accurate.

Bonynge, however, was blinded by his fears. He felt compelled to restore the credibility of his witnesses, Herrmann and

Hilken, and he was convinced that he needed to preempt German accusations that the message was a fabrication before proving it was real. He became disoriented, several times referring to the time between when the message was introduced and when the experts examined it as years, not months. He corrected himself only once, after Roberts interrupted and sarcastically commented on the mistake.

His confidence eroding, Bonynge stumbled through the end of his argument, offering at long last a convoluted explanation for the Herrmann message's authenticity: "I do not know how it appeals to others or to the experts, but it has always appealed to me as a non-expert, simply as a layman, that if the message had been fabricated within a few months of the time when it was first presented, the experts would have found unmistakable evidence of that fact. It seems to me that if it was within a few months after the time, that even the odor of the lemon would not have entirely disappeared."

It was almost pathetic. With all the experts, their analysis, and the testimony of witnesses (such as Siegel, Gerdts, Herrmann, and Hilken) to the writing of the letter, a centerpiece of Bonynge's defense was the smell, or lack thereof, of lemon on the paper.

After two days, Tannenberg stood up to make his case. He had listened to Bonynge rail against Osborn—a man, he recalled, who was so respected by the commission that it had wanted him to act as its handwriting analyst. Nothing Bonynge had said made Tannenberg think the commission thought any less of Osborn or believed Herrmann. So rather than rebut Bonynge, he attacked:

"There is no doubt from all the evidence on record that all that Herrmann desired to get was money from Hilken or Hoppenburg. And this man writes a message containing not only references to Black Tom, but containing a direct and positive reference to Kingsland and also giving the names of the alleged perpetrators, and his alleged co-workers, and his alleged superiors in the scheme, and then sends Gerdts with this message, written in lemon juice, from Mexico to the United States at a time when the border was more carefully watched.

"All this was for the purpose of getting $25,000 from Hilken. . . . Was it necessary to make this long statement and put in a reference to all these matters, the Black Tom disaster, the Kingsland plant, and the alleged perpetrators, when here was a man who could have carried everything that Herrmann desired Hilken to know in his head?"

Tannenberg hoped the judges would wonder the same thing.

On December 3, Roberts released his decision. In his forty-page opinion, he wrote that any reasonable man, looking at the translation of the message, would conclude that Herrmann and Hilken knew that the Kingsland fire and the Black Tom explosion had been the work of German agents. Such a man would conclude that Hinsch, Hilken, and Herrmann, undoubted agents, were involved, as was Kristoff. "I may disregard all the other evidence," Roberts wrote, "and if I deem this message genuine, hold Germany responsible in both cases."

But he was teasing the Americans. A reasonable man might think one way, but this case was cluttered with complexities. The thousand pages of expert analysis from both sides didn't enlighten Roberts; they confused him. For every scientist the Americans presented saying the message was authentic, the Germans had one saying it wasn't. "It remains to consider whether these doubts can be resolved by the expert testimony," Roberts wrote. "The experts themselves had to resort to experiments with lemon-juice writing on new and old paper to reach their conclusions. On the expert evidence alone my judgment would be left in balance as to the authenticity of the document."

He also believed that Hilken and Herrmann were capable of fabricating evidence. But most of all, Roberts agreed with Tannenberg's logic that no spy would send a message that long when all he needed was money. "The document comprises 254 words. Those that have to do with the request for money amount to only 20. All the remainder are wholly irrelevant to the purpose at hand. . . . But enough has been said to show how extraordinary a manner this document dovetails with all the important and disputed points of the claimants case and how pat all these references are, not to the request for funds but to the claimants points of proof. . . .

"I find myself unable to overcome the natural doubts and misgivings which cluster about this document. I am not, therefore, prepared to make a finding that this is the missive which Herrmann dispatched to Hilken in 1917.

"The supplemental petition for rehearing is dismissed."

It was another devastating blow for the Americans—another defeat, another humiliation. Yet there was an opening. Unlike in 1930, when Anderson had disagreed with the umpire but hadn't wanted to bother writing a dissent, he made his objections known. In an opinion he wrote to Roberts, he beseeched the umpire not to be fooled by any of Germany's arguments. The agents had been deceitful throughout the process, and the country was not entitled to the benefit of the doubt because of its stance on American munitions during World War I. His argument was passionate and partial. Although Roberts ignored it, the Americans clung to it. Someone was listening to them, but it seemed time was running out.

Chapter **Fifteen**

I N JANUARY 1933, Hitler, as the head of the most popular
political party in Germany and the largest faction of the
German parliament, was appointed the country's chancellor. It
was a temporary appointment, meant to last only until a nationwide election scheduled for early March. Hitler promised that he
wouldn't interfere with the nation's democratic process.

O n January 14, 1933, John McCloy met with Henry Stimson
to plead for the secretary's continued support. A year earlier,
it had been Bonynge who had gone before Congress and guaranteed success. Now he had no credibility. Martin was too low on the
totem pole, and Peaslee didn't have McCloy's levelheaded demeanor.

For McCloy, it was a humiliating appointment. Before the
1932 decision had gone against them, he, Bonynge, Martin, and
Peaslee were seen as nuisances and their sabotage cases considered
impediments to the State Department's diplomatic efforts with
Germany. But after losing, they were considered worse: incompetent and irrelevant, legal community punch lines. Stimson thought

so little of McCloy that before they met for the first time, he spelled McCloy's name wrong in his daily calendar.

The secretary of state wasn't interested in perceived slights by the commission or outright lies by the Germans. He told McCloy, "You've had your day in court." He suggested that they accept defeat and move on. But McCloy couldn't do it. At this moment, he wasn't a partner at a Wall Street law firm but a man who needed a favor. "Mr. Secretary," McCloy said, "I can prove this case if you'll let me." But his pleas were wasted on the lame duck Stimson. In March, Cordell Hull, the new president's choice for secretary of state, would take over.

On February 27, just a week before the German elections, a mysterious fire destroyed the Reichstag building. Almost immediately, a Dutchman named Marinus van der Lubbe, a communist protester often seen marching in front of the building, was arrested. Hitler told the public that van der Lubbe had been caught within blocks of the Reichstag, with a book of matches in his pocket and smelling of gasoline, and had admitted to setting the building on fire.

Hitler, playing off his nation's fear of communism, used van der Lubbe's arrest as an excuse to declare emergency rule. He banned Communists and Socialists from taking part in the election, arrested their party leaders, shut down their newspapers, and dispatched his supporters to intimidate and beat vocal and recognizable protesters. The elections would still be held in early March, but Hitler's victory was already ensured.

During Hull's first few days in office, one of the State Department bureaucrats wrote him a memo that read, "Little, if anything, can be said in favor of these sabotage claimants, for the reason that the Commission composed of two Americans and one German has twice ruled adversely on these claims." Given

Roosevelt's desire to close the sabotage cases, Hull was inclined to agree.

FDR's disposition came as somewhat of a surprise to the American lawyers. Before and during World War I, he had been assistant secretary of the navy. He'd seen every report concerning pre-war German espionage, from the moment von Papen had started producing false passports to the day Wilson had declared war on the Central powers. In letters he wrote during the war, Roosevelt's espoused feelings for the Germans and their tactics escalated from annoyance to fear to near hatred. But as president, he saw Germany as an important partner in a new world order. The work of the commission was just a problem he'd inherited, one he wanted to do away with as quickly as possible.

While Hull agreed with Roosevelt, Chandler Anderson lobbied the president. He wrote to Roosevelt that if the United States closed the commission without one more hearing to prove that Germany had lied, the sabotage cases would "be the subject of discussion for many years to come, a constant source of irritation."

But there was another factor. Soon after Hitler's rise, stories about his private army, known as the Brownshirts, marching through Berlin's streets armed with gas masks and grenades, began appearing in the American press. Pictures of bonfires, plumes of smoke rising from huge piles of books, were becoming more and more common. Roosevelt sensed his nation's distaste for Hitler, writing early in 1933 that he believed "90% of the American people felt more hostile towards Germany now than at any time since October, 1914." As a result, he decided to give the American lawyers time to file an appeal against the commission's decision and the commission time to review the appeal, but he wanted the cases wrapped up by the end of 1933.

More than ever, the Americans felt as though the Germans had duped the commission. The false testimony from Hinsch, expert reports that defied science but still cast doubt on the Herrmann message, and collusion between Osborn and Stein had all conspired against them. While the Americans had argued the evidence, the Germans had manipulated Roberts. Bonynge finally realized that he needed a new strategy.

Boynge had been arguing the case based on its merits, naively counting on the goodwill of the MCC and the power of his evidence. Whenever he accused the Germans of misleading the commission, he did so in the most diplomatic language, as if the Germans weren't guilty of lying so much as miscommunicating the truth. But when Bonynge filed the petition for a rehearing in May 1933, proof of Germany's guilt was no longer a focal point. Polishing the images of Herrmann and Hilken didn't matter. His priority, the first point he argued, was the deceitfulness of the German government. "Certain important witnesses," he wrote, "furnished fraudulent, incomplete, collusive and false evidence which misled the Commission. . . . Such a situation in any international arbitration of such vital importance is intolerable and unthinkable." For the first time while presenting the cases, Bonynge used language that showed he was not afraid of offending the panel.

For seven months, the lawyers heard nothing. Not even Anderson knew which way Roberts was leaning. The lawyers didn't know whether they had insulted Roberts or made him think, but they continued to file evidence in support of the petition. The most incendiary testimony came from Paul Hilken's distinguished, pro-German father, Henry, confirming that his son had worked as the saboteurs' paymaster. The senior Hilken, who had avoided testifying for several years and did so only after being threatened with jail time, even supplied more North German Lloyd records confirming that Hinsch and Herrmann had been on his payroll.

The Germans, meanwhile, responded as though it was beneath them to defend themselves against new evidence. Debating the Americans again only gave credence to the allegations. Instead, they tried to define the jurisdiction of the commission, arguing that it didn't have the right to reopen the case. This was the first tactical mistake they made.

On December 15, Roberts released his decision. The first few paragraphs were a neutral summary of the American claims, giving no indication which way he would rule. He categorized the allegations as serious but admitted that he hadn't reviewed any of the evidence and had no opinion as to whether they were true.

Then his tone changed. Roberts was put off by Tannenberg's challenge to his authority, especially when the German had been accused of lying and falsifying evidence. Rather than feel angered by Bonynge's comments that the commission was pitiful, Roberts took offense that Tannenberg chose to act as if he were a peer of the judges, not someone who needed to defend himself. "Every tribunal has inherent power to reopen and to revise a decision induced by fraud," Roberts announced. For the first time, an umpire of the commission had written an opinion that chastised the Germans.

Days after Roberts's decision, the State Department informed Bonynge and Martin that it would no longer pay their lease for a private office, that their files had to be transferred to a government building, and that they wouldn't be paid for at least a month — penance, the lawyers felt, for keeping the case alive.

Late one night in early December, McCloy was in the conference room adjacent to his Cravath office, going over the latest batch of Black Tom documents. They came in almost daily: briefs from Martin summarizing affidavits, missives from Peaslee about German conspiracies, even letters from the American commissioner, Anderson, about new strategies the Americans should try.

One of the most recent reports had come from Blinker Hall in London. He had found an old set of notes containing post-arrest interviews with the World War I spy Franz von Rintelen. Von Rintelen had bragged about causing strikes along the docks in New York Harbor and using cash he had smuggled overseas to influence the Irish immigrant laborers. He mentioned an Irish labor leader, James Larkin, whom he had desperately tried to bribe.

Hall's notes recalled that von Rintelen had approached Larkin about doing sabotage work on behalf of Germany, but he had been rebuffed. They also detailed attempts by Wolf von Igel, von Papen's replacement as Germany's military attaché, to convince Larkin that strikes weren't enough to stop the flow of munitions, that Larkin should help organize sabotage plots in the harbor if he truly wanted Germany to beat Britain in the war. Again Larkin had refused.

McCloy had heard the labor leader's name before. His office had become the New York clearinghouse for Black Tom files, and McCloy had cataloged every name and fact about the case on thousands of note cards. Each one had a title in the upper left-hand corner. A tight, finely written cursive filled the card with relevant information about the case. To McCloy, the case was no different than a puzzle, and he needed to turn every piece over before he could put it together.

McCloy maneuvered around the files, piled high on the conference room table and packed tightly in cabinets, to find other references to Larkin. He fingered the cards, some of whose edges were soft and rounded from being handled so often. An entry for Larkin led him to an entry for Witzke, who had named Larkin as a potential saboteur. Another line on the Larkin card mentioned C. P. Palmer, a U.S.-based British agent who had followed Larkin after the night of the Black Tom explosion. McCloy then dug through his files and recovered a report from Palmer. The agent wrote about working undercover and forming a relationship with Kurt Jahnke. During a meeting one afternoon, Palmer had mentioned Larkin's name, and Jahnke had walked out. Palmer never saw him again. "The belief was created," McCloy wrote, "that Larkin must have known much concerning the German sabotage activities, if indeed he had not been actually implicated in the destruction work."

Late in the morning on December 15, 1933, McCloy boarded the steamship *Washington,* which would leave New York Harbor at noon, bound for Ireland.

• • •

After the McCloys had left Paris in 1931, they had settled in an apartment on Sutton Place along the East River, one of Manhattan's most exclusive addresses. There they had frequently entertained Ellen's sister, Peggy; her brother, Jack; and all of their kids. While Ellen happily prepared dinner, John would throw water balloons off the balcony with his nieces and nephews. The two of them pretended that the sound of other people's children wasn't heartbreaking. By the end of 1933, after nearly four years of marriage, they were no closer to starting a family than they had been on their wedding day. They filled their lives with what was available to them: They spent weekends at Ellen's parents' estate in Hastings-on-Hudson and attended the opera. Ellen was committed to charity work with Lenox Hill Hospital. John was committed to Black Tom. McCloy had become what Peaslee called "the laboring oar" of the investigation. He took pleasure in the most arduous, time-consuming tasks, from indexing every name and fact relevant to the case to preparing the first drafts of most briefs. He loved the process of building a case, sketching out every possible scenario on a yellow legal pad, turning a messy pile of evidence into a neat, orderly, and persuasive argument.

McCloy was neither flashy nor elegant. He still preferred acceptance gained through effort. He never desired the attention of a room, only the respect of the people who made the decisions. With as many as six lawyers—from three different law firms and a government agency—often debating the best strategy for the Black Tom case, McCloy strived to be the person everyone depended on, the one whose counsel they followed, the sage in the crowd. Before any discussion regarding the case, McCloy would sit alone in his Sutton Place study and practice what he called "yellow padding." He'd outline what he ultimately hoped to accomplish, carefully plotting what he expected each person to say and what his, or someone else's, reaction would be. If the conversation ever became contentious or veered dangerously far from what he deemed important, he gently nudged it back. For years, during his days in boarding school, at Amherst, and at Harvard, he had always been the quiet kid paying his own way, keeping his head down, while all the privileged students preened and vied for one another's attention. He had learned how to listen, how to read the personalities in the room. That served him well now, helping him hone diplomatic skills that he had already relied on to win over friends, clients, contacts, and even his wife.

Those skills also helped him keep anxious law partners at bay when support from his firm was waning. After the 1932 defeat, most of the senior partners had urged McCloy to drop Black Tom. He had worked on almost nothing else for two years. While he saw progress in every new brief he filed or witness he interviewed, he was working in a vacuum, and his commitment threatened to undermine his career. The dogged lawyer once known around Wall Street as "the guy who outplayed Bill Tilden" was now ridiculed and, behind his back, referred to as "Black Tom Man." Years later, a former Cravath attorney would say that at one point, the only person who believed in him was Ellen.

Almost twenty years removed from running the most powerful union in Ireland, Larkin had taken on the persona of a rebel in winter. He worked within the law instead of flouting it. He was still an inspirational speaker—he had been elected to the Irish parliament and was an elder statesman in the Workers Union of Ireland—but he no longer tried to incite riots with his tongue. Earlier in his life, he had courted opportunities to go to jail for his cause; now he surrounded himself with a protective layer of lawyers and advisers. He was wary of speaking with strangers.

McCloy arrived in Dublin on the night of December 21, and early the next morning, he visited Larkin's office at the Workers Union headquarters, known as Unity Hall. Shortly after leaving New York, McCloy had learned that Roberts decided he'd rehear the case if shown compelling evidence. Larkin, McCloy believed, could be the Americans' most important witness.

McCloy had barely walked through the door when he was told that Larkin wasn't available. McCloy went back the next morning. This time he was told that Larkin wouldn't be back in Dublin for several days.

McCloy had hoped to appeal directly to Larkin. But now, after two wasted days, he needed help. It was Christmas Eve when he finally reached Charles Boyle, one of Larkin's lawyers, at home in the Dublin suburbs. McCloy explained who he was, the circumstances surrounding Black Tom, and that he felt Larkin had information that could help him prove his case. Boyle, who could barely rise up from his bed because of a bad back, told McCloy he'd relay the message to Larkin, "but I won't urge him to give any information." Either way, whether Larkin agreed to the interview or not, Boyle offered to call McCloy at his hotel as soon as he heard.

Three days later, on the afternoon of December 27, McCloy received a call from Boyle. Larkin would meet him at Boyle's house if he could come over right away.

McCloy arrived by taxi and was shown upstairs to Boyle's bedroom, where Boyle was still recuperating. At his bedside was Larkin, his cheeks still ruddy from the cold, his coat draped over his shoulders. McCloy thought that Larkin hadn't been there very long.

Boyle introduced the two men, but Larkin didn't want to waste McCloy's time. He apologized that McCloy had come all the way to Dublin and then said there was no way he would take any steps that might help "moneyed groups."

McCloy said that he didn't know what Larkin knew or whether he could be helpful. But if he refused to testify, McCloy couldn't force him.

Then he lingered, listening to Boyle and Larkin talk about Boyle's bad back and where Larkin had traveled. They asked McCloy if he was enjoying his stay in Dublin. He stopped being the lawyer in the room and became nothing more intrusive than an American guest. Larkin talked about his days in New York, how he was always being tailed and how the police were always harassing him. He recalled that in 1919, he had been sentenced to five years in Sing Sing prison for anarchy after one of his incendiary speeches, only to be pardoned by Governor Al Smith. There was no bitterness in his voice. Instead, he told his stories with an impish grin, as though he were remembering childhood high jinks.

When McCloy rose to leave, Larkin offered him a ride back to Dublin. Along the way, he acted as a gracious host, telling McCloy about Dublin's history. He suggested that McCloy spend that evening at the Abbey Theatre, where an early play of George Bernard Shaw's was in production. Neither of them brought up Black Tom.

As they pulled up to the Shelbourne Hotel, where McCloy was staying, Larkin urged him to stay in Dublin for a few days. He suggested that they spend the next day together, so he could show him around the city. McCloy didn't hesitate to accept his offer.

McCloy knew that Larkin had been trying to gauge his intentions and perhaps deciding whether he'd tell McCloy what he knew. McCloy was encouraged the next morning when he called Larkin at Unity Hall and was asked to come over for a meeting.

As soon as McCloy arrived, Larkin's son, James Jr., escorted him to his father's office. The two sat down inside, and the elder Larkin began telling them both about Irish politics, his role in it, and why it had taken him to America so many years before. McCloy listened patiently, avoiding questions, ignoring any impulses to ask about Black Tom. The door to Larkin's office swung open constantly and without notice, often startling McCloy. Workers, men thick around their arms and chests and backs from lives spent as laborers, needed Larkin's advice and counsel. Their problems sounded urgent, and each time Larkin stopped talking, McCloy worried that he wouldn't start again, that he'd reconsider and usher McCloy out the door.

But that didn't happen. After a long while, McCloy was comfortable enough to say, "If you have information, I cannot understand why you would not give it to me, even though it might assist moneyed people. To not give it might equally help other moneyed groups. The German government, and the German Lloyd in particular would benefit by the defeat of the claims I represent."

"If that happened," Larkin answered, "it would be unfair. The German Lloyd and its officers were important instruments of sabotage."

"If that's how you feel, then purely in the interests of justice, you should tell me what you know."

For a brief moment, the room fell silent. Larkin turned to his son, a grown man who had been sitting quietly in the corner as his father had conducted his business, and asked him why he shouldn't tell McCloy what he wanted to know. "The Germans have denied responsibility," Larkin said, sounding outraged. "Unless you can think of some good reason why I should not do it, I am disposed to give a statement about how they tried to use me."

James Jr. said nothing. Voices again filled the room. Finally, Larkin agreed to give a brief statement, but it would have to be later, when he wasn't so busy. He promised to call McCloy as soon as he was available.

McCloy didn't hear from Larkin that night or the next two days. He began to worry. Then, on Sunday, December 31, he walked back to Unity Hall. Larkin was in his office and treated McCloy like an old friend. Again Larkin did most of the talking, giving his opinion on the current state of Ireland, its politics, and the church. The room soon became too crowded for a private conversation, and McCloy, growing frustrated, got up to leave. He told Larkin that if he intended to give McCloy anything, he'd have to do it soon, because McCloy was leaving for the United States late the next night. Larkin promised he'd be ready the following morning.

McCloy left the Shelbourne Hotel early on January 1, 1934. His route to Unity Hall was littered with debris from the New Year's Eve celebrations the night before. When he arrived, the building was quiet and empty, devoid of the chaos he had experienced every other time he'd been there. Larkin was in his office, alone. He greeted McCloy happily, then led him through a door to an anteroom, which looked as though it had been set up for an interrogation. There was a small table, three small chairs, and a typewriter. Another man walked into the room. Larkin introduced him to McCloy as Mr. Carney. He sat down in front of the typewriter, and McCloy and Larkin sat across from him.

Suddenly, the familiarity the two had developed over the previous few days was gone. As he had when they'd first met, Larkin didn't wait for McCloy to ask him a question. He began speaking, quickly, as Carney's fingers pounded the typewriter.

During their two extended conversations, McCloy had purposely avoided the subject of Black Tom, preferring to let Larkin dictate when, or if, it came up. Now he was stunned by what he heard.

Larkin mentioned relationships with Franz von Papen and Karl Boy-Ed, the German military attachés plotting sabotage in the United States. He told of Wolf von Igel asking him to interfere with the shipment of munitions, and about going to Hoboken for a demonstration of the exploding tubes. "Specific plans had been discussed for destroying the munitions at the Jersey City Terminal," Larkin said.

The affidavit began shortly before noon. Several hours later, Larkin was still speaking from memory, without any prodding from McCloy. He spoke with conviction and authority, about subjects he had never discussed in McCloy's presence. "In the afternoon," McCloy remembered, "I became impressed with the importance of obtaining some indication of Larkin's reputation as a truthful person." As Larkin continued in a trancelike state and Carney continued typing, McCloy scurried out of Unity Hall. He called on a lawyer named Albert Wood, who was at his home in Dublin. Wood explained that he had once represented Larkin's union but was now "appearing in court against his interests." Then he told McCloy what he needed to hear. "Larkin is a man backed by a character of a most exceptional quality, unselfish motives, and the deepest convictions. I am convinced that he is incapable of stating a deliberate untruth." McCloy tracked down another high-profile Dublin attorney named James Geoghegan. Geoghegan had previously served as justice minister and been a member of the Irish legislature. He swore in a written statement that Larkin was "incapable of telling a lie." Armed with these testimonials, McCloy stopped at the U.S. Consulate to alert the diplomat on duty he'd be back later that evening to have Larkin swear to his statement. He then made his way back to Unity Hall.

It was late in the evening, but Larkin was still going. The halls of the building echoed with the sound of Carney's furious typing. Larkin spoke of leaving for Mexico once the United States had entered the war and hearing German agents there brag about "the Jersey City Terminal explosion, which had been brought about by liquid fire." He remembered staying at the Juarez Hotel in Mexico City, where Herrmann had written his message, and hearing about plans to blow up the Tampico oil fields. McCloy returned to his seat, listened, and waited. He didn't say a word.

Around midnight on January 2, twelve hours after Larkin had begun his affidavit, he finished. McCloy rushed him to the U.S. Consulate, where the consul general was waiting to notarize Larkin's statement. Afterward, McCloy drove Larkin back to his house. Later that morning, he finally sailed home.

Larkin's testimony, naturally leaked, drew the attention of newspapers. Both the *New York Times* and the *New York Herald Tribune* printed some of his sensational accusations and brought McCloy unwanted publicity. His name was at the top of the stories, credited as the man who had found Larkin and potentially saved the Americans' case. In a small way, "Black Tom Man" was vindicated. But while Bonynge (who may have encouraged his staff to leak Larkin's story) happily chatted up reporters and commented on the record, McCloy refused their calls. When the *Times* printed his middle initial as *D* rather than the *J* that honored his father, he didn't even bother to correct the paper of record.

Whether the new evidence had any impact or was even true didn't matter at all to the Nazis. It was the Weimar politicians who, after Versailles, had felt responsible for preserving Germany's honor. Hitler didn't concern himself with such intangibles.

He was consolidating power, naming himself both chancellor and president in August 1934, thus officially ending Germany's experiment with democracy. He considered the United States to be hopelessly weak, a mongrel society, and it held little strategic interest to him. In Black Tom, he saw a case that his country had already won twice and was now being heard by a commission the American president was anxious to shut down. Whether the Larkin evidence was damaging or not, whether the case was reheard or dropped, whether Germany was once again found innocent or eventually proven guilty would have no impact on his rule. Any negative decision could be blamed on the regimes he had replaced. As one representative of his government wrote in 1934, "The sabotage trial no longer appears very important politically."

In May 1934, Wilhelm Kiesselbach, frustrated at the prospect of more oral arguments, resigned as the German commissioner. His replacement was a less capable German named Victor Huecking. That same month, a member of the Foreign Office, Richard Paulig, took over as the new German agent. Huecking and Paulig were caretakers more than advocates, not invested emotionally and, unlike their predecessors, under no mandate to protect Germany's reputation. After Roberts ruled in November 1934 that Germany had to respond to the Larkin affidavit and several other new pieces of evidence, Paulig waited a year before finally submitting a brief to contradict it. Roberts waited three months after that, until February 1936, to announce what both sides expected: the Larkin affidavit compelled him to rehear the case. New oral arguments were scheduled for May.

Even with the Larkin affidavit, the Americans weren't anxious to endure another round of oral arguments. Twice before, they'd expected to win, and twice they'd been outmaneuvered by the Germans. McCloy especially felt that the Americans were in a position of power and should take advantage of it by pushing for a settlement. In a perfect world, the Americans would get all the money owed to them, now calculated to be in excess of $50 million. But the American attorneys knew there was no chance of that happening. Even $25 million would have been wonderful. But that, too, seemed an unrealistic request of a country that was financially strapped and knew that the MCC was always unpredictable. During the fall of 1935, while waiting for German briefs to be filed and Roberts to reschedule the hearings, McCloy, Bonynge, Martin, and Peaslee came up with an offer: the Germans would pay $12.5 million, half of what the United States wanted; McCloy and Bonynge would lobby Congress to repeal certain trade restrictions between the United States and Germany; and Germany would not be asked to admit guilt for committing acts of sabotage. The American lawyers were wary of going through their own diplomats, whose interest in the commission was limited to shutting it down. Instead, they wanted to take the deal directly to Hitler.

Peaslee knew a man named Frederico Stallforth, a banker who had worked with Germany while living in Mexico during World War I. Tall and lanky, and as slick as hair oil, Stallforth used his contacts to con his way into a meeting with the führer, where he mentioned the proposed settlement. Several months earlier, in March 1935, Hitler had announced that Germany would defy the Treaty of Versailles by rearming the military. He had then begun rebuilding his armed forces at a rapid pace — within a year after making his announcement, Hitler's army had remilitarized the Rhineland, the previously neutral buffer between France and Germany — and at tremendous cost, which required financial and natural resources he didn't have. The settlement Stallforth suggested would repeal trade restrictions and give Hitler access to raw materials he desperately needed. In the spring of 1936, Hitler asked Hermann Goering, his top aide, to handle the settlement talks.

Goering, a decorated German pilot during World War I, had joined the National Socialist, or Nazi, Party shortly after the war. He was the embodiment of the nation Hitler was trying to build, a blond-haired, blue-eyed son of an aristocrat. When he had been wounded in 1923 while fighting by Hitler's side during the Beer Hall Putsch (Hitler's attempt to rally his Munich supporters and overthrow the German government), he had endeared himself even more to the future dictator. When Hitler had been named chancellor in 1933, he made Goering the commander in chief of the police and gestapo, which meant that Goering was responsible for setting up the earliest concentration camps. And when Hitler wanted to rebuild the air force, he assigned Goering the task. In 1936, Hitler announced his four-year plan to make Germany's economy war-ready, and he charged Goering with implementing it. Goering enjoyed the perks that came with his power: he lived in a palace in Berlin, changed between his various uniforms and finely tailored suits five times a day, flaunted his medals and jewelry, and called himself "the last Renaissance man."

Goering understood how important new trade agreements with the United States could be, and he made settling Black Tom a priority. On the afternoon of May 5, 1936, he telephoned Ferdinand Mayer, the American chargé d'affaires in Berlin, and asked if they could meet at Mayer's home. The next morning, when Goering arrived, he expressed remorse that German-American relations were not as they once had been or should be. He asked, "Did the United States wish to improve its relations with Germany? If the answer is in the negative, then that is that. If, however, the answer is in the affirmative, then we should thresh it out."

Mayer cabled Goering's question to Cordell Hull. The answer was yes, Hull cabled back, and settling Black Tom would be a start.

Oral arguments before the MCC began as scheduled on May 12 in Washington, D.C., while Goering and Mayer worked toward scheduling face-to-face negotiations. The German lawyers moved slowly and deliberately, partially because they wanted to pull back if it looked as though the hearings would go in their favor.

This time, however, that was unlikely. The Americans had learned from their recent success. This wasn't a panel that responded to nuanced evidence; it required bold arguments, easily and succinctly summarized in black-and-white terms. The American arguments connecting Germany to Black Tom had thus far been linked by minute details that were not easily verified: the Herrmann message; a $2,000 payment from Hilken to Hinsch; the accusation by Kristoff, now dead, that Hinsch was Graentnor. But now the Americans had a simple argument to make—that Germany had built its entire case on a foundation of lies—and they were making it at a time when becoming friends with Germany was less and less of a priority.

Larkin, unlike Herrmann and Hilken, had never lied about Black Tom to benefit himself. He had not reviewed the case before giving his affidavit and did not know which names and facts would help the Americans. His statement was irrefutable, his character verifiable. But the Americans weren't taking any risks. Bonynge, still the ranking, government-appointed attorney to the MCC, would no longer be arguing the cases. Instead, William Mitchell, three years removed from serving as U.S. attorney general, had been asked to orate. At sixty-two, Mitchell was a legendary orator. He was plainspoken and even in tone, traits he'd brought with him to Washington from his boyhood home in Winona, Minnesota, along the banks of the Mississippi River. His father had been a Minnesota Supreme Court justice and had passed down to his only son a respect for the law. Even while serving as a cabinet member, he had remained a man who, one of his boyhood friends recalled, was "not a politician but someone who confined himself to his profession."

By mid-May, the weather in Washington had already turned muggy, transforming the inside of the Supreme Court Building into a massive oven. For days on end, the temperature settled in the low eighties, and even with the windows open, the light wind did little more than rearrange the air.

Before arguments began on May 12, the Germans protested that Mitchell, now in private practice, shouldn't appear before the court. Roberts upheld Paulig's objection for twenty-four hours, enough time for Cordell Hull to give the former attorney general a special appointment to the MCC. When Paulig complained afterward that there was no precedent for such a shotgun appointment and that it violated the spirit of the claims, Roberts laughed away the notion. "I should personally like to hear Mr. Mitchell," he said derisively. Paulig's objection was overruled; Mitchell would argue the cases.

He did so with an eloquence and lyricism that Bonynge had never captured. There was no pleading in his voice or yearning for acceptance in his body language. Mitchell was clear and authoritative, and most of all, he made the case simply and efficiently. Only one point mattered: Germany had lied and lied and lied.

"There is one thing to be said," Mitchell argued, "and this is difficult to say. There is very conclusive evidence in this case that certain persons high in official life in Germany suppressed evidence and told falsehoods in this case. Whatever their standards may have been in private life, and however good their word may have been in private affairs, when it comes to matters of defense of their government, these men feel justified in making statements and taking action which they could not possibly be willing to undertake in a private situation."

Paulig's stature was clearly diminished against Mitchell's gravitas. Nor did Paulig compare to his German predecessors. He didn't have the wits and calm of von Lewinski or the deceptive brilliance of Tannenberg. He was a bureaucrat, assigned a case that his country wanted to go away as much as it wanted to win.

By the end of the oral arguments, it was apparent which way Roberts was leaning. As Bonynge stood up to make the closing argument for the Americans, Roberts interrupted him: "Before you go Mr. Bonynge, I have just prepared a little memorandum here so that the German agent and you shall have on record what is on my mind about the Stein matter."

Roberts then read from his prepared statement: "I have

known Mr. Albert S. Osborn for many years. When I was in practice I retained him in connection with several problems arising with respect to documents whose authority was contested. At some point he referred me to Mr. Eldridge W. Stein as a competent expert in similar matters. Mr. Stein, at that time, had an office in the Bulletin Building, Philadelphia. On one or more occasions, I consulted him.

"Just before the date set for hearing in the sabotage claims, probably some time in November of 1932, Mr. Stein attempted to get into communication with me by telephone. He wished an interview with me concerning the sabotage cases in which I knew he was a witness for the claimants. I refused to allow him to communicate with me.

"During the meetings of the Commission preliminary to the hearing, Dr. Kiesselbach advised Mr. Anderson and me that the claimants had suppressed an expert report adverse to the authenticity of the Herrmann message. I cannot say that Dr. Kiesselbach specifically stated the source of his information.

"The communication naturally disturbed me. . . . My impression that there had been such suppression was strengthened by Mr. Osborn's statement, in one of his affidavits, that it was remarkable that no opinion by Mr. Stein, a competent expert in such matters, had been submitted as to the age of the documents.

"In the oral arguments the German agent made no reference to this matter and as the American agent did not refer to it the impression remained that there had been a withholding of a report which might have shed light on the question argued before the Commission. The umpire and the American commissioner hold that claimants have shown there was not sufficient ground for suspicion and for that reason the claimants are entitled to a reconsideration."

Roberts's admission of prejudice during the 1932 hearings was embarrassing and humbling, both for him and the lawyers who had to listen to it. It humanized him and emboldened the Americans, as if the umpire's fallibility excused any mistakes they had made up to that point.

•   •   •

The arguments to rehear lasted for two weeks, but the commission needed just four days to reach its decision. On June 3, 1936, it set aside the ruling of 1932, in which it had decided that the Herrmann message was a fake, and agreed to rehear the sabotage cases as if the commission had never seen the message before. "The claimants have shown," Roberts wrote, "that there was no sufficient ground for suspicion [that they had suppressed a Stein report], and for this reason they are entitled to a reconsideration." What Roberts didn't write thrilled the American lawyers even more: For the first time, there was no chiding of American witnesses. From now on, it would be the Germans' lack of credibility, not the Americans', that would stain every brief they wrote and cling like static to every argument Paulig made.

The Germans knew it, too. The day after the commission announced its decision, a German diplomat named Hauptmann von Pfeffer informed the U.S. Embassy in Berlin that Goering's schedule had opened up: "He would be pleased to receive the American representatives in Germany." The Germans were ready to begin talks immediately.

Chapter Sixteen

THE AMERICAN CONTINGENT set out for Germany on June 19, 1936, sailing for eight days and arriving in Bremerhaven, in northern Germany, on June 27. The Americans had been told by the Germans that from Bremerhaven, they'd take a train 240 miles east to Berlin, where they'd arrive in the evening. But when the SS *Europa* docked, a German representative met them at the port and told them that plans had been changed. The Germans feared the publicity that might result from a meeting with the Americans in the capital city. Without warning, the settlement talks had been moved to Munich. The Americans boarded a train, which sped south through the night, hidden by darkness, and arrived in Munich the next morning.

The McCloys checked into Munich's Reginaplast Hotel. They had two days to enjoy the city before the talks officially began. One evening, they went to the opera with some of their Nazi hosts. The following day, John was invited to join a baron for an afternoon of fly-fishing in the countryside. Ellen remembered her husband being picked up in the hotel lobby by one of the handsomest men she had ever seen. His good looks didn't allay her fears. Before she and John had left their room that day, she warned him that the Nazis were only trying to ingratiate themselves with him. They knew he was getting close, and they would just as soon fool him as deal with him.

Early in the negotiations, McCloy worried that his wife might be right. Goering had designated von Pfeffer as the German face of the settlement talks. A former leader of Hitler's feared storm troopers, von Pfeffer was, as McCloy remembered, "a Nazi from Naziville and a great friend of Hitler." When the Americans, including Bonynge, Martin, Peaslee, and McCloy, and the Germans sat down at the table, Bonynge made it clear that his authority from the State Department did not extend beyond the Mixed Claims Commission settlements. Any other agreements, especially trade agreements Germany was hoping to establish with the United States, would not be discussed. Von Pfeffer bristled, and he pushed the Americans on the issue. McCloy, usually so detached and calm during negotiations, began to lose his patience. The entire group had been unnerved by the unannounced change of venue and the dash through the night to Munich. In the previous two days, they had all seen elements of German society that frightened them. "It was terrifying," McCloy would say years later. "All those goose-stepping soldiers. I could feel war in the air."

The more von Pfeffer bullied Bonynge to expand the scope of the talks, the angrier McCloy became. At one point, an aide brought von Pfeffer a note, which he began to read while McCloy was trying to make a point. Raising his voice, McCloy said, "Sir, you apparently are more interested in what is handed to you under the table than what I say to you above it."

With that, the tenor of the meeting quickly changed, as if von Pfeffer finally accepted the fact that they were negotiating a settlement of the sabotage cases and nothing else. The two groups worked late into the night, with von Pfeffer often taking breaks to telephone Goering or Hitler and confer with them directly.

The Germans and Americans calculated that the sabotage claims were worth nearly $52 million, including damages and interest. Both parties knew that Germany couldn't afford that kind of payoff. Von Pfeffer needed a proposal to take to Hitler that wouldn't be a blatant reminder of how poor the Germans were. If the Weimar government hadn't been willing to look guilty, Hitler was not willing to look weak. They all agreed that they would spend the next few days drafting a settlement that included realistic terms.

Von Pfeffer submitted his proposal to Bonynge on July 6, making it clear what the Germans expected: "The settlement is intended to be the first step on the part of Germany for an energetic effort to improve the mutual relations between our countries . . . but in no case should there be any appearance that the German government might concede any liability with respect to the claims."

He offered the Americans $20 million, but he didn't want the money to come directly from Germany's reserves. The U.S. Treasury had been holding $20 million worth of German marks, seized during World War I and scheduled to be given back to the Germans once all the MCC cases had been settled. Von Pfeffer wanted to use that money to pay off the settlement.

Even at less than 50 percent of what the claims were now worth, the Americans saw the merits of von Pfeffer's proposal. Everyone walked away with something: The claimants got what they cared about most, the money. Germany could pay out with money it, and perhaps the German public, didn't really count as its own, receive a promise of improved relations, and not have to accept responsibility for sabotage.

That afternoon, Bonynge formally responded to von Pfeffer in a letter. "I have the honor to acknowledge receipt of your letter," Bonynge wrote, "and beg to advise you that the proposal as contained for the settlement of the sabotage claims before the Mixed Claims Commission is hereby accepted on behalf of my government." They called it the Munich agreement. It was worth only $3 million more than the settlement the two countries had momentarily agreed to nearly a decade earlier.

They spent the next three days negotiating the finer points of the agreement. Then Bonynge, Martin, von Pfeffer, and two other

German representatives met to review the final documents. Bonynge felt compelled to reiterate how little authority he had beyond the scope of the sabotage cases. While he agreed in theory that relations should improve, he couldn't guarantee it. He even read aloud a letter he had received from the State Department on June 19, the day he had left for Germany. "You will make it clear you are not privileged to discuss any other matter pertaining to the general relations between the two countries," Bonynge said. "Settlement of the sabotage claims cannot be conditioned upon discussion or settlement of any such matters."

Von Pfeffer and his colleagues acted as if they understood what Bonynge was saying.

That night, led by von Pfeffer, the Germans hosted a dinner for their American counterparts. They ate at a restaurant in Munich, where the staff fluttered around the Nazis with a reverence that bordered on fear. Those in power had grown accustomed to such treatment, no longer acting as though they had earned it but rather that they deserved it.

As the meal ended, one of the Germans rose from his chair and requested that the waiter bring a phonograph to the table. He then put a record on the turntable as those around him, including John and Ellen McCloy, began thinking he was going to play music. But as the record turned, voices came from the speaker—voices speaking English. It took just a moment for McCloy to realize that he was listening to himself, talking on the phone with lawyers from Cravath's New York office. The Nazis had recorded the calls from his hotel room. As he shifted angrily in his seat—confused, embarrassed, uncomfortable—his hosts laughed at the prank they had pulled.

The next morning, Bonynge cabled Cordell Hull that the "settlement of the sabotage cases is now agreed upon." Both the Americans and the Germans also agreed that neither group would publicize the settlement until it had been officially ratified by the Germans and accepted by the commission. That didn't stop the

news from leaking out. On July 17, the *New York Times* correspondent based in Munich wired to his office in New York a story
"that Bonynge, who had been conferring in Munich as secretly as
possible for two weeks, had reached a tentative agreement on the
Black Tom explosion case. Bonynge sailed for New York today to
report to Secretary of State Cordell Hull."

The next day at a press conference, when asked about the ac-
cords, Hull was coy with reporters. He said that he had "scattered
and partial reports but it would be misleading to make an announcement." He wasn't lying. While the two countries had
agreed on a deal and most of the American contingent was on its
way home, Martin and McCloy were still in Germany, awaiting
ratification.

In fact, almost as soon as the deal was made, it started to fall
apart. Several U.S. claimants that had won cases and had received
partial payments were awaiting more money in interest from the
German Special Deposit Account in the U.S. Treasury. If the Munich agreement was accepted and the fund totally depleted, they'd
receive nothing more. This group included companies such as
Chase Bank, Standard Oil, and Singer Manufacturing, and they
had powerful advocates. At first, they pressured the State Department to void the deal, even if it did signify an American victory.
But then they went even further. Chase sent a lawyer to Germany
to meet with Hitler's treasurer, Hjalmar Schacht. He carried a letter from a Chase vice president insisting that Schacht convince
Hitler to back out of the agreement because "numerous institu-
tions in America" would use "every means at their command" to
make sure it didn't happen. The Americans had finally beaten the
Germans, but now their own countrymen were trying to undermine them.

The Germans didn't need pressure from American companies
to want out of the deal. Despite what von Pfeffer had said during
the negotiations, any settlement that didn't guarantee good relations between the two countries was unacceptable. At first, von
Pfeffer had thought that he could persuade Bonynge to include
such a pledge as they spoke face-to-face. But when it became

apparent that he couldn't, the Germans stalled. Weeks passed as Martin and McCloy waited for the agreement to be ratified. The Germans lavishly entertained the Americans, hoping their warmth would persuade them. When that didn't work, the Germans opted for a display of might over merriment, fear over friendship.

The Berlin Olympics started on August 1, in a stadium ringed by more flags adorned with swastikas than those with Olympic rings. The Nazis envisioned these two weeks as their introduction to the world. They hosted more athletes from more countries than had participated in any Olympics before, and they spent more on propaganda promoting the Nazi agenda than any country had spent on the entire event. The streets of Berlin seemed perpetually lined with Germans waving the Nazi flag. The Nazis built 150 buildings for the games, including the 110,000-seat Olympic Stadium, which they proudly bragged could empty in a little less than fourteen minutes. Nearly four million fans, the most in Olympic history, attended the games. Those who couldn't be there had only to flip on their radios to feel as though they were: more than twenty transmitters and three hundred microphones were stationed in front of the stadium. Once the games began, they were broadcast in at least twenty-eight languages around the world, making them the most widely listened to sporting event in history up to that time, and creating an impression of Berlin as a modern, efficient, and powerful capital.

For most of the Olympics, the McCloys stayed close to Munich. But as the games concluded, Goering invited them to watch the events with him from Hitler's private box at the stadium. He wanted them to see what they'd been missing.

Even within the massive, oval-shaped, open-air stadium, Hitler's box felt confining. It jutted out from the middle of the stands, a concrete platform surrounded by low-slung concrete walls and metal railings. Huge platters of food were brought to Goering and his aides, while the rest of the guests in the box were ignored. At one point, Ellen got up to leave but was stopped by a Nazi guard standing at the door. "I have to use the ladies' room," she said in German. "Let me out or it will be embarrassing."

When she returned, she brought sausages for everyone who was still hungry.

The McCloys hadn't been brought to Berlin for the spectacle of sport. And although Goering hadn't brought up the Munich agreement during the evening, by the end of the night it was clear why they were there. For two weeks, the stadium's oval track had been the world's centerpiece, featuring runners, high jumpers, and shot-putters. But nothing had inspired an ovation like the one McCloy was hearing now. It echoed through the building, 110,000 voices becoming a single, static, unsettling cheer.

Hitler had achieved what he'd wanted through the Olympics. Germany had won more medals than any other country, outpacing the United States, its nearest rival, by more than thirty. But athletic might also invoke civic pride. Hitler and the Nazi Party had vowed to break the constraints of Versailles. Their first task had been rebuilding the military. Their second had been showing it off to the world.

McCloy watched as more than 200 drummers, 1,750 brass musicians, and 1,400 German soldiers, sailors, and members of the air force goose-stepped atop the cinder track where so many world records had been set, saluting German leaders as they marched by Hitler's box. The musicians played patriotic German songs and the overture of Wagner's opera *Rienzi*. The bowl-shaped stadium darkened, and four beams of light cut the black sky into quarters. One landed on the Nazi swastika posted high atop one end of the stadium. Two others shone on the Nazi and Olympic flags flying above Hitler's box. And the last framed the Olympic flame, burning above the gate where the marathoners would enter.

It was spooky, not elegant; frightening, not joyous. The McCloys were enveloped by the darkness, their faces lit up only briefly under the crisscrossing beams. To John, standing and watching Goering applaud, listening to the crowd roaring its approval, and seeing the light focused on the flag hanging high above the stadium, it felt more like a pep rally for the Nazi way of life than a celebration of sport. McCloy had been invited to be intimidated.

The military band rounded the first turn of the track, and the sound of their instruments became muffled, drowned out by escalating cheers. A tunnel leading into the darkened stadium was glowing, as though it were in flames. A slow rumble echoed over the stadium's empty infield. A column of soldiers emerged, carrying torches. They split into two lines, rivers of fire flowing slowly along the two sides of the stadium, until the inner circle of the arena was bordered by a ring of fire. McCloy looked at his wife and saw the flames dancing off her eyes, looking as though they might burn her lashes.

He realized then that he'd be leaving Germany without an agreement.

Shortly after the May oral arguments, Chandler Anderson had left Washington, D.C., for his summer home in York Harbor, Maine. At last, he felt satisfied with the direction of the Americans' case. He was sixty-three years old and looked forward to a season near the ocean, falling asleep to the sound of the waves crashing on the shore and echoing through his open windows.

Those were the last sounds he heard before he died in his sleep in early August. The Americans had lost their most powerful advocate.

By late fall 1936, the Munich agreement had not been ratified, and the American lawyers had little hope that it would be. The U.S. companies still waiting to be paid from the German Special Deposit Account, including several manufacturers the Germans hoped to do business with, had spent most of September and October threatening Goering that they wouldn't trade with Germany if the Munich agreement was carried out. Meanwhile, Hitler's own Foreign Office, which had been cut out of the negotiations by Goering, continued to fight the agreement, as-

serting that the Americans had no intention of linking future relations to it.

In late November, the Germans signaled their intention not to
ratify the agreement via a series of slights against the American
lawyers. On November 23, the Foreign Office sent its embassy in
Washington a list of U.S. citizens who were barred from entering
Germany. It included John McCloy and Amos Peaslee. A week
later, it forwarded the list to its representatives in London, Rome,
Brussels, The Hague, and Bern. That same day, in a meeting with
his ministers, Hitler said he no longer wanted to be bothered with
the Munich agreement. The next morning, December 1, von
Pfeffer sent Cordell Hull a letter saying that "the evil sabotage case
is not a matter of great concern in Europe." He added that he had
agreed to the settlement only as a step toward redeeming German-
American relations. Von Pfeffer accused the United States of lacking the same goodwill. While he stopped short of officially pulling
out of the agreement, he made it clear that it would never be
honored.

Harold Martin's frustration with the Germans was tempered
by a happy occasion: his daughter Francesca's wedding. After
Alcie Martin died, it had been Francesca who had buoyed her father's spirits and watched after her younger sister. Eight years earlier, Francesca had encouraged her father to make his first trip to
Europe for the Black Tom case, just a few weeks after his wife's
death. She had promised her "Daddykins" that his daughters
would be fine and had urged him to try to be happy.

Seeing Francesca walk down the aisle at St. Alban's Episco-
pal Church in Washington, he didn't have to try very hard. She
was wearing her mother's long-sleeved, satin and lace wedding
gown. After the ceremony in which she wed a navy lieutenant,
Martin hosted a small reception at his home, which was decorated with poinsettias and large white chrysanthemums. When
the cake was wheeled out, Francesca cut it with her new husband's navy-issued sword. At that moment, Black Tom mattered
little to Martin.

• • •

On January 4, 1937, Bonynge submitted a motion to the MCC demanding that the settlement be recognized and that the Germans pay their debt. But he was only exhausting his options; he didn't expect the commission to rule in his favor. Instead, the lawyers focused on preparing their brief for a rehearing, reminding themselves that the Nazis were only delaying the inevitable.

As usual, the Cravath office served as the Black Tom depository. Yet again, McCloy sifted through all the material, pulled it apart, and then rebuilt the case from scratch. He connected the vast networks set up by the Germans to infiltrate munitions depots and plants all over the country, then wrote vividly about the explosions that had followed. He retraced the steps taken by the German lawyers, von Lewinski and Tannenberg, to establish a duplicitous defense, which led back to an August night in 1930 when Hinsch and Marguerre had given their first, oddly similar, dovetailing affidavits. McCloy had material to cast doubt on the testimony of nearly every German witness or expert. Larkin's affidavit, still unchallenged, connected von Papen, von Igel, and Boy-Ed to sabotage. Herrmann and Hilken, suddenly as credible as any German witness, linked Nadolny and Marguerre to the distribution of the exploding glasses. While reviewing the reams of evidence, McCloy realized that more than a dozen people testifying for both the Germans and the Americans had told similar accounts of two different events: Hilken's $2,000 payment to Hinsch after Black Tom and the writing of the lengthy Herrmann message in a 1917 issue of *Blue Book*. Only Hinsch, who had denied getting paid and insisted that the message had been one line written in a hardcover book, contradicted this second bit of testimony. McCloy made a note: "Hinsch has maintained that at least 14 witnesses have not told the truth in these cases, but supplied no evidence other than his denials." The only German witness whom the Americans hadn't been able to discredit was Carl Ahrendt, who had proven to be unbreakably loyal.

Every day, the Americans grew so confident that bad news no longer haunted them. In April 1937, when Cordell Hull officially received notice from the Foreign Office that Germany would not honor the Munich agreement, the American lawyers treated it as just another German brief. In July, the MCC, which now included Anderson's replacement as American commissioner, Christopher Garnett, ruled against Bonynge's January motion to force Germany to pay the settlement. But even that denial was coupled with a small triumph. Roberts was still so angry that Osborn and Stein had tried to deceive him that the next day he took the unusual step of calling a special session so that he could depose Osborn himself.

In a dank conference room in the Supreme Court Building, Roberts sat at a table opposite Osborn, his anger unabated. He was a Supreme Court justice who had been made to look like a fool, his trust betrayed by two men who had worked with him before and who knew he'd believe in them.

"Do you confine yourself to the examination of disputed documents or do you do investigative work?" Roberts asked.

"I do no investigative work," Osborn answered, raising his voice as if he were offended.

"How did you come to take an affidavit from Mr. Meyers at Abraham's Book Shop? Is that part of the examination—"

"I did not take any affidavit from him," Osborn interrupted.

"Were you present when one was taken?"

"No."

"I find an entry in your book, 'Wrote Dr. Tannenberg and prepared affidavit for Mr. Meyers at Abraham's.' What does prepared mean?"

"I included in my letter to Dr. Tannenberg the statement that I thought information I had obtained should be put in the form of an affidavit."

"And you prepared one."

"Yes, I think so, a suggested one. What I prepared was not used."

"Well now, I would like to know again whether the English language is accurately used in your diary? Does 'prepared' mean 'prepared' or 'suggested'?"

"That was put in the form of a suggestion. That was sent to Dr. Tannenberg. My affidavit was not used."

"Mr. Osborn, you have been to the witness stand many, many times?"

"Many times."

"And it will do you no good to fence with this Commission."

"I am not going to try to do it."

"You are trying to do it, in my opinion."

"I am sorry."

"I am sorry, too."

"I did not mean to do that."

"I think you are competent enough to give me categorical answers and you are certainly competent enough to understand my questions."

"I will try to do it exactly."

It didn't matter. For Osborn, it was too late to make amends. Roberts had no more questions.

Meanwhile, the case lingered, existing in an unfinished yet unquestioned state. As Hitler pined for war in Europe, Roosevelt preached isolationism for the United States. They were on different paths; a relationship would be impossible. There was no longer a sense of urgency on the part of either government. Roosevelt, resigned to the notion that the American claimants would never recede and knowing that the case was all but decided, no longer pressured the State Department to shut down the MCC. Hitler focused on German expansion, announcing in November 1937 his plans to annex Austria and Czechoslovakia. Roberts waited until December to set the deadlines for filing new briefs, giving both nations until the end of 1938, a full year, to put their arguments in writing. He scheduled the final oral arguments for January 1939, more than two decades after the Black Tom explosion had occurred.

• • •

As the wife of a partner at Cravath, Ellen McCloy had become a fixture on the social circuit, always a member of whatever committee was organizing a lavish ball for a hospital, a museum, or some other charitable cause. She endured the conversations other women had about their children, never letting on how much it pained her that she didn't have her own. Instead, she bragged about her nieces and nephews, sounding as passionate about their first smiles, first teeth, and first steps as if they were her own children.

Throughout their marriage, the McCloys' efforts to conceive had mirrored their struggles with Black Tom, evoking frustration then disbelief, anger then doubt, and finally hope. Through her charity work with hospitals, Ellen had met a pioneering gynecologist named Isidor Rubin. By pumping oxygen into the cervix, Dr. Rubin could test whether a patient's fallopian tubes were open. Ellen's were entirely blocked. Using small amounts of oxygen pumped into the tubes, Dr. Rubin helped them expand and open. It was an invasive procedure, with the gas in her abdomen sending waves of pain up her back and into her shoulder blades. Dr. Rubin timed his tests to occur when she was ovulating, and there was no way of knowing how long her tubes would stay inflated. On the days she returned home from a doctor's appointment, John was often interrupted in the middle of a meeting by an urgent phone call from his wife, telling him he had to meet her at the apartment right away. He didn't need to ask why.

By April 1937, Ellen had endured several months of treatments with Dr. Rubin. After every trip to the hospital, she'd simply say, "I'm having the most wonderful pain in my shoulders." One afternoon, as Easter neared, Ellen and her sister, Peggy, were having lunch in Manhattan. It was an unusually mild early-spring day. Shoppers browsed through the stores along Madison Avenue. Crowds gathered around the window at Saks Fifth Avenue enjoying the holiday display. As they strolled along the sidewalk after lunch, Ellen and Peggy stopped in a fortune-teller's small storefront shop. They were offered steaming cups of tea, with black leaves floating on top. Slowly, they sipped their drinks, being careful not to swallow any of the leaves. When they finished, they handed their cups to the fortune-teller, who examined the leaves in the bottom. She looked up at Ellen and said, "Something will happen, I think seven months from now, that will change your life."

Ellen, two months pregnant at the time, knew she was right.

John J. McCloy II was born on November 5, 1937. In August 1938, the McCloys and their son traveled to the Ausable Club in the Adirondacks, a favorite vacation spot of well-to-do professionals from Washington, New York, and Philadelphia. Each family rented a cabin hidden in the woods or perched on the waterfront. Hiking trails crisscrossed the grounds, each one disappearing into the mountains, where some followed streams that led into a river abounding with salmon and dangerous rapids. Occasionally, the river would fall over a steep decline, the echo of the rushing water floating back up to the trail.

The sense of pride McCloy felt bringing his family to these mountains ran as deep as the valleys. He remembered being dragged to the Adirondacks by his mother when he was a boy, carrying ice up the hills to the rich families' cabins, giving sailing and tennis lessons to their privileged children. Those summers were for meeting the right people, seeing how Anna McCloy wanted him to live, learning what she expected him to become. He had done everything she had demanded he do.

But this summer, he had little time to enjoy himself. While Ellen spent lazy afternoons strolling with the baby around Upper Ausable Lake, John spent most of his time holed up in their cabin, preparing the final Black Tom brief, due that September.

By now, nearly every witness for both sides was tainted. Some had given false testimony. Others had no credibility because of their work as spies during World War I. Only two men, James Larkin for the Americans and Carl Ahrendt for the Germans, impressed the commission as truthful—impressions neither side, despite their greatest efforts, had been able to change.

In June 1938, while digging through a box of North German Lloyd files at Hilken's old office in Baltimore, a young commission lawyer named Simon Sobeloff had come across a letter from Carl Ahrendt to his former boss Paul Hilken. Neatly typed and coated with dust, it was dated January 19, 1917, and introduced a packet of business memos. At the bottom of the page, handwritten in pencil, was a personal message from Ahrendt: "Yours of the 18th just received and am delighted to learn the von Hindenburg of Roland Park won another victory. Had a note from March who is still at McAlpin. Asks me to advise his brother that he is in urgent need of another set of glasses. He would like to see his brother as soon as possible."

Ahrendt had underlined the word *glasses*.

When Sobeloff gave Ahrendt's note to Martin, the lawyer quickly realized what had been found. It was studded with code. Ahrendt had referred to Hilken by his nickname, "von Hindenburg," and Herrmann by one of his aliases, "March." He hadn't bothered disguising the Hotel McAlpin, where Herrmann often stayed. Most damning was Ahrendt's allusion to glasses. The timing of the note piqued the Americans' interest as well. It had been written eight days after the Kingsland fire. Putting all the clues together, Ahrendt's postscript read suspiciously like a congratulatory note on the occasion of the Kingsland plant's explosion.

Ahrendt's denials that he knew anything about German sabotage had been the centerpiece of the German case. In 1930, the German agent, Tannenberg, had asked him, "Did Captain Hinsch show you at any time during the years 1915, 1916 or 1917 any explosive tubes, little glass tubes?"

"No," Ahrendt had answered.

Tannenberg also asked, "Did Herrmann tell you at any time about those explosive tubes or pencils?"

"No."

Sitting in his cabin at the Ausable Club, McCloy scanned the note. He flipped through the pages of Ahrendt's testimony. Then he wrote a memo to himself that he'd eventually incorporate into his brief: "We have no idea what explanation Germany will have for this evidence. . . . But it is straining human patience as well as credulity to suggest that this postscript is not of the most significant guilty import. . . . It destroys forever all credibility of Ahrendt."

It also lifted the Americans' hopes.

Chapter Seventeen

ROBERT BONYNGE SAT in his Washington hotel room alone, late in the evening on Sunday, January 15, 1939. All day, a freezing rain had fallen, and Bonynge had stayed inside, reviewing his notes, only partially able to concentrate. The next morning, the final round of oral arguments would begin. After fifteen years, Bonynge's victory was almost assured. He felt light-headed and dizzy, the words on the pages he studied drifting in and out of focus—symptoms of his excitement, he thought. Only when the pain gripped his chest did he realize he was wrong.

As they had three years earlier, the Americans asked William Mitchell to make their case. The former attorney general and McCloy spent almost all of November together in Washington, reviewing McCloy's several-hundred-page Black Tom brief as though it were scripture. They wanted to answer every last question about who had blown up Black Tom, to make the judges on the commission wonder how they or their predecessors could ever have doubted the Americans. They wanted to make the Germans recognize that they hadn't been outmaneuvered by smarter lawyers, that they'd actually been caught.

Mitchell spent the first few days of oral arguments rehashing the entire history of the case, beginning with the January 26, 1915, cable from Germany authorizing sabotage in the United States. McCloy beamed as he listened to Mitchell eloquently recite the arguments he had constructed. At times, Mitchell spoke so softly that the judges had to perch on the edges of their seats just to hear him. As they did so, he knew that he had their attention.

At the end of his third straight five-hour day framing the Americans' case, Mitchell finally addressed the Ahrendt postscript. "It was written in New London," Mitchell said in a pleasing voice, as if beginning to tell a bedtime story, "and addressed to Hilken in Baltimore on January 19th, 1917, just eight days after the explosion at the Kingsland plant. The body of it is a business letter, of no particular importance really. Then there is a postscript, added in Ahrendt's handwriting."

Mitchell then read it aloud: "Yours of the 18th just received and am delighted to learn that the von Hindenburg of Roland Park won another victory. Had a note from March"—at this point, Mitchell stopped reading and reminded the panel that March was one of Herrmann's many aliases—"who is still at the McAlpin. Asks me to advise his brother that he is in urgent need of another set of glasses."

Mitchell again interjected, telling the judges that the word *glasses* was underlined, before beginning again. "He would like to see his brother as soon as possible."

Mitchell then continued his argument. "Now there is a great deal to be said about that document. We have got to bear in mind that Ahrendt was close to these men, was their errand boy and that he carried money and bills to pay these people. His story is that he denies categorically that he had ever heard of this thing, he did not know anything about these glass tubes, he had never heard a word of incendiary devices. He was one of the men who, under the leadership of the former German agent, Dr. Tannenberg, denied that there had been any sabotage operations during neutrality."

From a pile of papers stacked on a table, Mitchell lifted one sheet and began to read. "In 1933, he was examined by the American agent, who asked: Do you insist on your oath that you knew nothing of Hinsch's and Herrmann's admitted sabotage activities and that they were never discussed by either Hinsch or other parties with you or in your presence?

"'I do,' Ahrendt answered.

"In the face of the record are you willing to submit your testimony to the Commission that you deny knowing anything about the activities of Herrmann and Hinsch and that they were not discussed or revealed to you at any time? Are you willing to ask the Commission to believe your denial in the face of your record?

"'Yes.'"

Even Roberts couldn't help but giggle at the charade. The game was up.

Years later, when Martin was writing his final report about Black Tom, he called Bonynge's sudden illness a "minor heart attack." It didn't kill the American agent, but it did hospitalize him. Yet on Friday, January 20, he arrived at the Supreme Court Building and announced he was ready to argue his part of the case. He looked ashen and weak. The attorneys were usually required to stand during their presentations, but Roberts offered Bonynge a chair. He readily accepted.

Bonynge picked up where Mitchell had left off, arguing intensely for an hour in the morning and two hours in the afternoon about the validity of the Herrmann message. He began by telling the commission that in a "last desperate effort" to avoid responsibility, Germany had succeeded only in proving that its "whole defense was fraudulent." He said that through "false and perjured" testimony, Germany had sought to "poison the mind" of the commission. He reiterated the charges of collusion between Stein and Osborn, reminding Roberts that their successful scheming had been the primary reason Roberts had decided against the Americans in 1932. He then emphasized that their collusion was part of the reason the umpire, after humbly admitting that he had been fooled, had decided for the Americans four years later. Of course,

Roberts hadn't forgotten. He wouldn't be made to look like a fool again.

Over the last two weeks of February 1939, the three commission judges met to decide the final outcome of Kingsland and Black Tom. By March 1, it was clear to Victor Huecking, the German commissioner, that he wouldn't persuade his colleagues. Rather than file a certificate of disagreement, he resigned, writing to Roberts, "The grave situation with which I felt myself confronted made it my duty to consider whether I could still cooperate. . . . My conviction that you no longer had an open mind has deepened. . .˙. As you told the American commissioner and me, this case has been a disillusion to you and has left a strong emotional feeling with you. I cannot be but afraid that this emotional feeling carries you away."

Huecking hoped that his resignation would render any decision the commission made illegitimate. But Garnett and Roberts, insulted by Huecking's accusations, were more determined than ever to bring the case to a conclusion. Over the next few months, they worked on crafting their opinions, writing several drafts, sifting their thoughts for weeks at a time. Roberts especially tried to temper his anger with every new version. Huecking was right: Roberts had been emotional about the case. By now, he felt as aggrieved as the American claimants. But precisely because of this, he understood that his final decision needed to be a document that withstood challenge from the Germans and set a standard for international tribunals. He couldn't let his personal feelings make this case vulnerable to any more litigation. His word had to be infallible, the decision passionless.

That June, when the Germans learned that Roberts was finally ready to reconvene the commission, they immediately protested. The German chargé d'affaires wrote to Cordell Hull, "Since the withdrawal of Dr. Victor Huecking on March 1st, the Commission has been incompetent to make decisions and consequently there is no legal basis for a meeting of the Commission.

The Government of the Reich will ignore the decision to call the meeting, as well as any other act of the Commission that might take place."

Roberts wasn't concerned about the Germans' threat, and on June 15 he called the commission to order in a Supreme Court Building conference room. Bonynge and Martin took their seats on one side of a felt-topped, horseshoe-shaped table. Neatly laid out in front of them were notepads, pencils, pens, and ink blotters. Facing them, on the other side of the table, were matching pads, pencils, pens, and blotters, put there for the absent German agent.

Garnett announced that he'd been notified that neither the German agent nor the German commissioner would participate in any MCC proceedings. He then read from a portion of his opinion. "The retirement of the German commissioner did not deprive the Commission of the power to decide the questions at issue. . . . The pleadings filed on behalf of Germany were false, and were known to be false. . . . Ahrendt and Hinsch, German witnesses produced to disprove the confessions of Herrmann and Hilken, are shown to have been perjurers. . . . We have therefore decided that the decision reached October 16th, 1930 at Hamburg must be set aside. . . . Since the authenticity of the Herrmann message has been established, the liability of Germany in both the Black Tom and Kingsland case has been clearly established and the cases are in position for awards."

Roberts followed Garnett's summary with his own. "I concur with the American commissioner," he began. "The withdrawal of the German commissioner did not oust the jurisdiction of the Commission." He then read from a prepared statement for five minutes, summarizing the history of the decisions, the commission's negative opinion of the Herrmann message in 1932, and the specific evidence that had made the judges rethink their position in the intervening years. "Further argument and extended study of the contents of the Herrmann message tends to negate the adverse conclusions drawn prior. I agree with the American commissioner that on the evidence now before the Commission the decisions must be in favor of the authenticity of the message."

Roberts then scheduled an October hearing to announce the amount of the rewards.

The German reaction the next day made it clear that the Nazis had no intention of making any payments. The Reich's official news agency issued a statement calling the decision "devoid of all legality" and "the opening gun of a new anti-German campaign in America. We see in this entire affair proof that the United States and its official representatives are trying to injure the reputation of Germany in the eyes of the entire world."

For several weeks after the arguments, the seventy-seven-year-old Bonynge continued to feel weak and tired. He knew that his heart was failing.

When he had appeared before the commission in June, his wan face, nearly translucent skin, and smooth head made it appear as though his bones were visible. He'd looked less than alive. In early September, he checked into New York's Presbyterian Hospital. He died on September 22.

McCloy wrote to Cordell Hull that the State Department had never truly appreciated Bonynge, that his work had set the standard for international arbitration. At a special meeting of the commission on September 25, called to honor Bonynge, Martin spoke eloquently about the man he had so selflessly served. "He never spared himself in the great task of doing everything humanly possible to bring to a successful conclusion the truly monumental work of settling the questions arising out of the war between this country and Germany. His tact, fairness, industry, legal ability and good fellowship are to a great extent responsible for the successful conclusion of this great work.

"I may truly say that he has earned in departing this life the farewell, 'Well done, thou good and faithful servant.'"

When Martin finished, Roberts promised that his statement would be made part of the commission's official files. Then the umpire asked for the record to show that, according to the State Department, Bonynge's loyal aide had been promoted. Harold

Martin was the new American agent to the Mixed Claims Commission.

There was still the matter of the reward. Peaslee sent Martin a memo declaring that the cases were worth $74 million, making his contingency payment a little less than $7 million. This so outraged Martin's sense of fairness that he forwarded the note to McCloy and attached his own estimate of no more than $35 million.

The commission split the difference. At the hearing on October 30, Roberts announced that the Americans had won a $50 million judgment. Less than half of that, $21 million, was for damages. The remaining $29 million included interest payments from the day New York Harbor had been attacked in 1916 to the day the suits had been closed in June 1939.

It was the largest award ever given by an international tribunal, but the money wasn't what captured the public's imagination. As Hitler expanded his empire, Germany became an ominous threat. War was imminent. The American lawyers' victory represented more than a legal triumph. They had beaten the Germans. They had cracked their codes written in lemon juice and traced their anthrax labs to the outskirts of Washington, D.C. "The procession of choice scoundrels, dashing dare-devils, and bulldog sleuths which marches through the case out-points an Oppenheim thriller," *Harper's* magazine wrote of the case in December 1939. "It is doubtful if a score of Hollywood films could use up its plot material."

Harold Martin retired from the commission on June 30, 1941, eighteen and a half years after he began what he thought would be a "temporary" job. He was the only man who worked on the cases from beginning to end, having a hand in the distribution of nearly $353 million in awards, including the $50 million Black Tom decision.

But his work was always that of the government, and upon his retirement he was neither rich nor poor. The end of his service to the commission was recognized with a story in one of the local papers. In the middle of the page was a picture of Martin seated at his desk, rows of heavy-looking books behind him, a pile of documents placed neatly in front of him. His coat was off, but his tie was still knotted at his throat, his Adam's apple bulging just above his collar. A pipe dangled from his mouth, and a silvery wisp of hair curled just above his eyes. The caption read, "Checking figures on World War I Claims."

He continued working up until the final day of the commission. "After tomorrow, he plans to take things easy at his home," the paper reported. "The U.S. and Germany will send its records over to the Archives Building and move out of the cubbyhole office on the top floor of the State Department. H. H. Martin's work will be over."

Black Tom was Martin's last job. He was sixty-two when he retired, and he spent the rest of his life living comfortably off the Civil Service and Disability Retirement Fund he had dutifully contributed to for nearly forty years. When he died of cancer in 1955, he was survived by his two daughters and their husbands and his five grandchildren.

Amos Peaslee eventually earned more than $4 million for his work on the sabotage cases. He would be as gracious with his riches as he had been committed to the cases. He bought a stately farm in his hometown of Clarksboro, New Jersey, and moved into a large house there with his family. He bought an unused school in Clarksboro and turned it into a neighborhood recreation center. He donated land for the building of community tennis and basketball courts. Years later, he would endow the debate society at Swarthmore College, his alma mater.

Even after Black Tom, Peaslee remained active in law and politics. He served as a delegate to two Republican conventions and maintained offices in Washington, New York, and in Clarksboro. His interest in international law was especially acute, and he compiled a volume of work called *Constitutions of Nations,* the first book to translate every nation's constitution into English. "When he'd go to church, he wasn't thinking about God," his son Dick Peaslee said. "He was thinking about his next project. He was not a philosophical guy; he just acted."

His work, not just on Black Tom but also with the Republican Party, didn't go unnoticed. In 1953, President Dwight Eisenhower named Peaslee his ambassador to Australia.

Late in the fall of 1939, after the Black Tom awards had been announced, John and Ellen McCloy took their two-year-old son to the Ausable Club for a brief retreat. Unlike the previous summer, McCloy was able to enjoy the time away. He had won the biggest case of his career, he was making nearly six figures as a partner, and the bonus he'd get for Black Tom would be $50,000. It was the level of comfort, professionally and financially, that he—and his mother—had always hoped he'd attain.

One afternoon, while strolling with Ellen along a footpath at the base of the Adirondacks, McCloy heard a deep voice from behind bellowing his name. When he turned to see who it was, he recognized Henry Stimson. It had been six years since they had last seen each other, when Stimson had hastily ushered McCloy out of his office after McCloy had come begging for help to keep Black Tom alive. McCloy was stunned that Stimson had any idea who he was. The conversation quickly turned to Black Tom, at which point Stimson congratulated McCloy, telling him, "As a lawyer, I know how tough it is to win a case when your own government is against you."

It wouldn't become apparent to McCloy how impressed Stimson was until late the next year. Stimson, then Roosevelt's secretary of war, was unnerved by Germany's intelligence operation. In the fall of 1940, it seemed as though every morning began with headlines about a munitions plant exploding in New Jersey or a ship mysteriously sinking in New York Harbor. On

November 12, three arms factories—two in Pennsylvania, one in New Jersey—exploded within fifty minutes of one another, killing thirty-two people. To some, at least, it seemed that history was repeating itself. Stimson needed an aide who had expertise in dealing with espionage, one who looked for it in every scenario. He thought, "McCloy knows more about subversive German agents in this country I believe than any other man."

That belief indicted U.S. intelligence as much as it complimented McCloy. Since World War I, the United States had only flirted with building a large-scale spy network. In 1919, the nation was enduring bouts of high inflation, high unemployment, strikes, and race riots. A revolution in Russia and radicals within the American workforce stoked fears that communists would, at any minute, attempt to overthrow the government. That spring, high-profile Americans such as J. P. Morgan, John Rockefeller, and Oliver Wendell Holmes received bombs in the mail, none of which detonated. In June, a radical blew himself up on the steps of Attorney General A. Mitchell Palmer's home in Washington, D.C. The house was across the street from where Assistant Secretary of the Navy Franklin Roosevelt lived. The Roosevelts found pieces of the dead man's body on their front steps.

After the explosion, Palmer's Justice Department was given $500,000 to form an antiradical intelligence division within the Bureau of Investigation. A young acolyte of Palmer's named J. Edgar Hoover was put in charge of ferreting out the unpatriotic. Sensing a need to keep pace with Hoover's squad to stay relevant, both the MID (Military Intelligence Division) and the ONI (Office of Naval Intelligence) expanded their staffs to focus on investigating subversives. The head of the MID created a plan to go to war against revolutionaries within the United States. Meanwhile, his counterpart at the ONI declared that German and Russian Jews, Mexican bandits, and labor union radicals had combined to plot "terror that will surpass anything that ever happened in this country." America found itself in the midst of what became known as the Red Scare.

Compared to Hoover's group, the leaders at the MID and

ONI appeared to be amateurs. Hoover quickly established an elaborate card catalog that contained the names of sixty thousand people deemed un-American, and his division was given free rein by Congress to break down the doors of any organization it suspected was spreading communism. More than ten thousand people were arrested in the last months of 1919, many of them shipped overseas without ever being tried. The fear of radicalism compelled ordinary citizens to act out—in Washington, a mob castrated and hanged a man arrested for subversion—comfortable that their government cared more about stemming civil disobedience than violating civil rights. One night in January 1920, anti-radical agents coordinated a cross-country sweep, arresting thousands. The series of raids conducted during these months were called the Palmer Raids, and the attorney general was hailed as America's savior. Shortly after the January crackdown, Palmer announced that a communist revolution would take place in the United States on May 1, 1920.

But when May 1 came and went without incident, Palmer's credibility vanished. As more and more of the people arrested in the January raids were released from prison for lack of evidence, Americans' enthusiasm for domestic intelligence and unchecked police action waned. Civil liberties suddenly garnered political and public attention. Republicans attacked President Wilson and the Democrats for blatantly violating the Bill of Rights. A three-year-old group called the National Civil Liberties Bureau renamed itself the American Civil Liberties Union in January 1920 and was vigorously supported by Helen Keller and prominent lawyers such as Clarence Darrow and future Supreme Court justice Felix Frankfurter.

By the summer of 1920, the staffs and budgets of the MID, the ONI, and Hoover's antiradical division were slashed. Palmer, who had hoped that his vigilance against communists would help him win the 1920 presidential election, was under constant criticism. The spy game had left an unseemly impression on the American public.

Despite the backlash, one espionage unit continued to work

in anonymity. It was called the Black Chamber. Established during World War I, the Black Chamber broke the codes of enemies and allies alike. After the war, its top analyst, Herbert Yardley, refused to relinquish his role. Yardley was a persuasive man with a gift for using the secrets he knew to frighten his less well-informed superiors. He easily convinced them that a postwar code-breaking unit was vital to American interests. Armed with a $100,000 budget, split between secret State Department and MID funds, Yardley moved the Black Chamber from Washington, D.C., to a nondescript brownstone in Manhattan. He was a mad genius. Living above his office, Yardley often stayed up all night, delirious with fear that America's security was at dire risk with every code left unbroken. He deciphered messages that led to the arrests of Russian spies; he broke English and French codes detailing new warships that far surpassed American models; he intercepted messages that helped the United States negotiate more favorable disarmament terms with the Japanese. For his efforts during the 1920s, Yardley was awarded the Distinguished Service Medal.

By the end of the decade, however, Yardley's efforts had earned him little more than his ribbon. In 1928, Herbert Hoover appointed Henry Stimson secretary of state. When Stimson learned that the State Department had funded a clandestine code-breaking unit, he ordered it shut down immediately. He was appalled by the idea, saying years later that he believed "gentlemen do not read each other's mail." Yardley was given just three months' severance. Two years later, embittered and unemployed, he published his secrets in a sensational book called *The American Black Chamber.* In it, he shocked readers with tales of international intrigue and intelligence secrets, and included the codes used by Japan and Germany. The book became an international best seller, and one of those most fascinated by it was John McCloy. Yardley's book included deciphered messages from Germany showing that it had helped blow up munitions depots in the United States in 1916. McCloy knew that this was hardly usable evidence in the Black Tom case, but at the time it encouraged him to keep digging and convinced him that a strong intelligence bureau was vital to U.S. security.

U.S. intelligence hadn't improved by the time Stimson, now Roosevelt's secretary of war, hired McCloy as a consultant in September 1940. By December, McCloy joined the staff full-time as a special assistant to Stimson, at a salary of $8,000. There was much catching up to do. Three years earlier, in 1937, the United States had spent just 10 percent of what Russia and Japan had on espionage. Since then, it had raised its budgets, but it was still woefully lagging. According to General George Marshall, before World War II military intelligence was "little more than what a military attaché could learn at a dinner, more or less, over coffee cups."

During the 1930s, the FBI had established itself as the nation's police force. Agents arrested the gangster George "Machine Gun" Kelly in 1933 and killed John Dillinger outside Chicago's Biograph Theater in July 1934. Both gave the FBI an aura of invincibility previously reserved for heroes in dime-store magazines. Then, in 1936, Roosevelt asked J. Edgar Hoover to investigate the rising number of Nazi and communist groups in the United States. By the end of the decade, the president had given the FBI responsibility for investigating espionage, sabotage, and other subversive activities. The three intelligence bureaus—the ONI, MID, and FBI—let territorial rivalries and personality conflicts interfere with the sharing of vital information, however. The military chiefs were especially jealous of Hoover. The head of the MID bristled at what he called Hoover's "dictatorial attitude," and both the MID and the ONI were wary of handing over deciphered enemy codes to FBI agents.

Soon after his arrival in Washington in 1940, McCloy began devising a plan to change that attitude. His initial report reflected a lifetime of idiosyncrasies. It was thorough, detailed, and organized, but it was also peppered with paranoia, however realistic, that was heightened by his Black Tom experiences. He was convinced that Hitler was using propaganda aimed at German-Americans to help soften the United States' defenses before a major German attack. "Only a well organized and well financed bureau or department could counteract this new weapon of war," he wrote. He called this hypothetical, centralized intelligence agency "Department X" and included a chart in his report that detailed how information would flow between a director and his representatives at the MID, the ONI, the FBI, and ten other counterintelligence departments. Roosevelt never acted on the proposal, but when the CIA was formed in 1947, its hierarchy bore a striking resemblance to McCloy's Department X.

During McCloy's days in the War Department, Black Tom was never far from his mind. That was especially true after Japan attacked Pearl Harbor in December 1941. Fear of the Japanese and what their next attack might entail gripped the United States. Fueled by newspaper stories about Japanese spies scattered up and down the West Coast who communicated via transistors with submarines, Americans lived with a growing concern for their safety. In January 1942, the *Los Angeles Times* editorialized that "the rigors of war demand proper detention of Japanese and their immediate removal from all danger spots." California congressman Leland Ford demanded that "all Japanese, whether citizens or not, be placed in inland concentration camps." It was hyphenism all over again as the FBI soon began arresting Japanese-American men considered to be threats to national security. Meanwhile, Roosevelt and his advisers, including McCloy, discussed how to thwart more attacks within the United States. By February 1942, it was agreed that internment was the only option to ensure safety. Roosevelt made McCloy responsible for the relocation of 120,000 Japanese living on the West Coast. As he handed down the order, the president gave McCloy a knowing glance and said, "We don't want another Black Tom."

At the highest levels of government, internment was seen as a logical safeguard against the dangers of war, no less practical than building more warplanes and manufacturing more bullets. McCloy concerned himself less with the morality of imprisoning American citizens than with the legality of it. As Americans confronted the shame of internment over the next forty-five years, culminating in an official apology to Japanese-Americans in 1988, McCloy would be demonized. At the time, though, he earned the confidence of those in power.

McCloy worked the halls of Congress as smoothly as he had the white-shoe firms on Wall Street. Stimson trusted him to handle tasks that no one else could or would—grunt work that came with little glory. He even set up a cot in the offices of the Senate Foreign Relations Committee so that he would be available at a moment's notice to defend one of Roosevelt and Stimson's proposals. That kind of fervent dedication led Stimson to write that he didn't think anyone in Washington did anything before "having a word with McCloy."

McCloy's reputation grew over the next fifty years. Following World War II, Harry Truman named him the first civilian high commissioner in Germany, making McCloy responsible for rebuilding the battle-scarred country. He was a confidant of Dwight Eisenhower's, and John Kennedy called on him to help negotiate the Cuban missile crisis. Lyndon Johnson made him a member of his informal Board of Advisors and appointed him to the Warren Commission to investigate Kennedy's assassination. It was rumored that McCloy was offered, and turned down, more cabinet posts than any man in history. The kid who had to leave Philly because of his poor bloodlines became the chairman of the World Bank, Chase Bank, and the Council on Foreign Relations. In fact, he earned the nickname "the Chairman" while becoming synonymous with the establishment culture that ruled the power corridor between Washington and New York. Even when he was in his eighties, one magazine called him "the most influential private citizen in America."

When McCloy died in March 1989, he was ninety-three years old and had outlived Ellen by three years. His Manhattan funeral was attended by heads of state, diplomats, and high-powered lawyers and bankers. From the pulpit of an Upper East Side church, Helmut Schmidt, the former German chancellor, called McCloy the "architect" of modern Germany. Richard Nixon sat listening intently from the front row. Secretary of State James Baker read a letter from President George H. W. Bush, calling

McCloy "one of the giants . . . in the history of this country. He was a trusted advisor of American Presidents from Franklin Roosevelt to Ronald Reagan."

No one mentioned Black Tom. It had been forgotten.

Acknowledgments

I BEGAN RESEARCHING this book the month before my wife, Stacy, and I found out she was pregnant with our first child. By the time it was written, edited, and mercilessly critiqued by friends, our son, Zachary, was two years old. And I am grateful for my lovely bride, who cheerfully prodded me on, even if it meant I was an absentee husband and father. I am also indebted to my mother-in-law, Marilyn Kronland, grandma extraordinaire, who took over when Stacy worked and I felt deadlines looming.

The National Archives in College Park, Maryland, are a wondrous place. I was fortunate to have archivists Tim Nenninger and Milton Gustafson help me navigate the Black Tom files in the early days. Paul McKissick, an archive specialist, always honored my requests and ensured my trips from New York were never wasted. Meg Lovell, a brilliant researcher, committed her senior year at the University of Maryland to helping me complete my research. Her keen eye for detail was a gift. In New York, Ross Schneiderman, a dogged reporter, uncovered facts I didn't know I needed. And at Amherst College, Daria D'Arienzo's meticulously organized collection of John McCloy's papers was a pleasure to use.

So much of this book entailed writing about topics that were new to me. Luckily I have friends with some expertise. Mark Helm provided sage counsel regarding my legal queries. Dr. Paul Yonover took time out of his practice to research infertility treatments from the 1930s, and even more time to explain them to me. Professor Tom Schwartz, one of Vanderbilt's finest historians, graciously met with me in the early stages of my research and made wise notes on the manuscript. Guergoi Milkov and Mile Verovic helped me translate several documents written in German and gave assistance with calls to Berlin.

I'm also fortunate to have incredibly understanding friends at my day job. The editor in chief of *ESPN The Magazine*, Gary Hoenig, was kind enough not to fire me. And those who worked most closely with me during this project—David Cummings, Luke Cyphers, David Fleming, and Seth Wickersham—were infinitely patient. As was Gary Belsky, who gave me time off, improved the manuscript, and provided huge doses of encouragement.

My agent, Richard Abate, gave the proposal the good scrubbing it needed and kept me from embarrassing myself. His enthusiasm was invaluable. And Geoff Shandler—my editor, neighbor, and good buddy—has the sharpest red pencil of anyone I know. Lucky for me.

Source Notes

The bulk of the material for this book was found in the affidavits, briefs, memos, and letters of the principal subjects involved. All of those are filed in Record Group 76, under the heading "Records of the Mixed Claims Commission, United States and Germany," at the National Archives (NA) in College Park, Maryland. They provide richly detailed accounts of conversations between judges and lawyers, as well as the efforts investigators took to track down potential witnesses. John McCloy's children, John McCloy II and Ellen McCloy Hall, were both generous with their time on the phone and in person relating anecdotes about their parents, as was Dick Peaslee, who gave me access to his father Amos Peaslee's Black Tom files.

I read all or most of dozens of books about German-American relations between 1914 and 1939, German spies living in the United States prior to World War I, and the destruction of Black Tom. The following books were especially valuable: Christopher Andrew's *Her Majesty's Secret Service;* Reinhard Doerries's biography of Johann von Bernstorff, *Imperial Challenge;* Jules Witcover's *Sabotage at Black Tom;* Kai Bird's biography of John McCloy, *The Chairman;* and Henry Landau's *The Enemy Within.*

There are several places in the book where I delve into detail about well-known policies and events, such as Wilson's neutrality policy and Hitler's rise to power. The generally accepted facts surrounding these events are not cited.

Chapter One
3 Heinrich Albert was: Johannes Reiling, *Deutschland: Safe for Democracy* (Stuttgart: Franz Steiner Verlag, 1997), p. 15.
3 He watched as: Henry Landau, *The Enemy Within* (New York: G. P. Putnam's Sons, 1937), p. 5; Interview with Norman Brouwer, Curator, South Street Seaport Museum, New York, March 3, 2003.
3 By 1914, more: Interview with Norman Brouwer, March 3, 2003.

4 He had come: Reiling, *Deutschland,* p. 16.

4 As a result: Jules Witcover, *Sabotage at Black Tom: Imperial Germany's Secret War in America, 1914–1917* (Chapel Hill, N.C.: Algonquin Books, 1989), p. 5.

5 "I'm going to": Interview with Norman Brouwer, March 3, 2003.

5 "In districts where": Thomas J. Tunney, *Throttled! The Detection of the German and Anarchist Bomb Plotters* (Boston: Small, Maynard, 1919), pp. 126–27.

6 From 1914 through 1916: Christopher Andrew, *For the President's Eyes Only: Secret Intelligence and the American Presidency from Washington to Bush* (New York: HarperCollins, 1995), p. 31.

6 On the surface: Landau, *The Enemy Within,* pp. 4–5.

6 German-American banks: Amos Peaslee, brief (draft), Black Tom, August 15, 1924, NA (College Park).

6 In Chicago: Reinhard R. Doerries, *Imperial Challenge: Ambassador Count Bernstorff and German-American Relations, 1908–1917* (Chapel Hill: University of North Carolina Press, 1989), p. 69.

7 Nativism was rampant: Kenneth T. Jackson, *The Encyclopedia of New York City* (New Haven: Yale University Press, 1995), p. 583.

7 Among the earliest: Ibid., p. 582.

7 In New York: Ibid., p. 584.

7 They hadn't come: Ibid., p. 582; Eric Homberger, *The Historical Atlas of New York* (New York: Henry Holt, 1994), p. 98.

7 Ten years later: Kay Saunders and Roger Daniels, eds., *Alien Justice: Wartime Internment in Australia and North America* (Queensland: University of Queensland Press, 2000), p. 67.

8 One study done: Frederick C. Luebke, *Bonds of Loyalty: German-Americans and World War I* (DeKalb: Northern Illinois University Press, 1974), p. 66.

8 A typical political cartoon: Ibid., p. 87.

9 Many in the United States: Ibid., pp. 77–78.

9 The son of: Doerries, *Imperial Challenge,* p. 5.

9 When he was named: Ibid., p. 14.

9 As he said: Ibid., p. 15.

9 He summered in: Ibid., p. 23.

9 When the German-American: Ibid., pp. 53–54.

10 One bank showed: Peaslee, brief, August 15, 1924.

10 When Martha Held: Sidney Sutherland, "German Spies in America, Part IV," *Liberty,* March 14, 1931.

10 At street level: Landau, *The Enemy Within,* p. 146.

10 Held claimed: Ibid., p. 145.

11 During the summer: Witcover, *Sabotage at Black Tom,* p. 3.

11 Occasionally, that included: Sutherland, "German Spies, Part IV."

11 The Germans thought: Landau, *The Enemy Within,* p. 5.

11 He lorded over: Sutherland, "German Spies, Part IV."

12 When the war: Landau, *The Enemy Within,* p. 8.

12 Bankrolled by Albert: Ibid., p. 11.

12 He hired: Ibid.

13 For twenty dollars: Ibid., p. 13.

13 "I know that": Ibid., p. 12.

13 Several days later: Ibid., pp. 14–15.

14 In November 1914: Official General Orders of the Imperial German Government, NA (College Park).

14 Two months later: Final Decisions and Opinions—Sabotage Claims (Superintendent of Documents, 1939), pp. 22–23.

15 James Larkin was: Emmet Larkin, *James Larkin: Irish Labour Leader, 1876–1947* (Great Britain: Routledge and Kegan Paul, 1965), p. 3.

15 As an adult: Ibid., pp. 8–9.

15 Larkin never drank: Ibid., pp. 6–7.

15 In 1914, just: Ibid., p. 146.

16 In November 1914: Ibid., p. 166.

16 In one of: Ibid., p. 169.

16 In Philadelphia, he: Ibid., p. 171.

17 Meeting at 60: Ibid., p. 182.

Chapter Two

18 The boundaries were: Homberger, *The Historical Atlas of New York*, pp. 136–37.

18 In one New York: Frederick M. Binder and David M. Reimers, *All the Nations under Heaven: An Ethnic and Racial History of New York City* (New York: Columbia University Press, 1995), p. 104.

19 As shoppers moved: Museum of the City of New York, exhibit.

19 This was a place: Phillip Lopate, *Waterfront: A Journey around Manhattan* (New York: Crown Publishers, 2004), pp. 52–53.

19 During three months: Michael Duffy, "Battles: The First Battle of Champagne, 1914," Firstworldwar.com, http://firstworldwar.com/battles/champagne1.htm.

20 "Something must be done": Franz von Rintelen, *The Dark Invader: War-Time Reminiscences of a German Naval Intelligence Officer* (New York: Penguin Books, 1939), p. 39.

20 In an autobiography: Ibid., p. 39.

20 Von Rintelen was: Harold Martin, memorandum, Franz von Rintelen, December 20, 1930, NA (College Park).

20 He ended each: von Rintelen, *The Dark Invader*, p. 44.

20 He was given: von Rintelen, *The Dark Invader*, p. 45; Martin, memorandum, Franz von Rintelen.

21 Von Rintelen arrived: Martin, memorandum, Franz von Rintelen.

21 During his first: von Rintelen, *The Dark Invader*, pp. 50–51.

21 Scheele had been: Landau, *The Enemy Within*, p. 44; Sidney Sutherland, "German Spies in America, Part V," *Liberty*, March 21, 1931.

22 In August 1914: Landau, *The Enemy Within*, p. 50.

22 Scheele moved to: Final Decisions and Opinions, p. 92.

22 Scheele met with: von Rintelen, *The Dark Invader*, p. 57.

22 Musing about undetectable: Ibid., p. 58.

23 Scheele said that: Sutherland, "German Spies, Part V."

23 Laughing, he suggested: von Rintelen, *The Dark Invader*, p. 64.

23 Scheele had the German: Final Decisions and Opinions, p. 92.

23 One afternoon: von Rintelen, *The Dark Invader*, p. 58.

23 On May 3: Landau, *The Enemy Within*, pp. 305–6.

24 From early 1915: German Sabotage Evidence Prior to Black Tom, NA (College Park).

24 The Swedish chemist: *The World Book Encyclopedia* (Chicago: World Book, 1998), s.v. "Nobel, Alfred Bernhard."

24 He had then: G. I. Brown, *The Big Bang: A History of Explosives* (Gloucestershire: Stroud, 1998), p. 105.

24 In the early: Ibid., p. 88.

24 The fear in: "The History of the New York City Bomb Squad," New York City Police Museum.

25 On July 4: Tunney, *Throttled,* p. 42.

25 On October 12: Ibid., p. 44.

25 Tunney had just: Ibid., p. 3.

25 But Tunney was: Ibid., p. 129.

25 Only once had: Ibid.

26 But even he: Ibid.

26 "It would be": Arthur S. Link, *Wilson: The New Freedom* (Princeton: Princeton University Press, 1956), p. 277.

26 "Americans must have": Arthur S. Link, *The Papers of Woodrow Wilson,* vol. 33 (Princeton: Princeton University Press, 1980), pp. 147–50.

27 The ONI, established: Michael Lee Lanning, *Senseless Secrets: The Failures of U.S. Military Intelligence from George Washington to the Present* (Secaucus, N.J.: Carol Publishing Group, 1996), pp. 115–17.

27 To ensure security: Ibid., p. 136.

27 Meanwhile, the MID: Ibid., p. 116.

27 By 1903, it: Ibid., p. 135.

27 The general in: John Patrick Finnegan, *Military Intelligence* (Washington, D.C.: Center for Military History, U.S. Army, 1998), p. 15.

27 Shortly before Wilson's: Lanning, *Senseless Secrets,* p. 137.

28 Early in 1915: Finnegan, *Military Intelligence,* p. 17.

28 One high-ranking: Nathan Miller, *Spying for America* (New York: Paragon House, 1989), p. 185.

28 After he left: Andrew, *For the President's Eyes Only,* p. 31.

28 Formed in 1865: Philip H. Melanson with Peter F. Stevens, *The Secret Service: The Hidden History of an Enigmatic Agency* (New York: Carroll & Graf Publishers, 2002), p. 20.

28 While skimpy budgets: Ibid., p. 28.

29 After America's victory: Ibid., p. 29.

29 The Secret Service: Miller, *Spying for America,* p. 186.

29 After he found: Andrew, *For the President's Eyes Only,* p. 32.

30 House had built: Doerries, *Imperial Challenge,* p. 143.

30 Former president Theodore Roosevelt: Luebke, *Bonds of Loyalty,* p. 145.

30 Several newspaper reports: Ibid., p. 135.

30 Fears intensified on: *The World Book Encyclopedia,* s.v. "Lusitania."

30 Still, Wilson resisted: Kai Bird, *The Chairman: John J. McCloy—The Making of the American Establishment* (New York: Simon & Schuster, 1992), p. 41.

30 Wilson also resisted: Andrew, *For the President's Eyes Only,* p. 33.

31 On July 23: The Weather, *New York Times,* July 23, 1915.

31 He woke up: Landau, *The Enemy Within,* p. 100; Andrew, *For the President's Eyes Only,* p. 32.

31 In the agent's report: Andrew, *For the President's Eyes Only,* p. 32.

31 In the briefcase: Ibid., pp. 32–33; "How Germany Has Worked in U.S. to Shape Opinion, Block the Allies and Get Munitions for Herself, Told in Secret Agents' Letters," *New York World,* August 15, 1915.

32 One political cartoon: Luebke, *Bonds of Loyalty,* p. 147.

32 The California Board: Jackson, *The Encyclopedia of New York City,* p. 464; Richard C. Leone and Greg Anrig Jr., *The War on Our Freedoms: Civil Liberties in an Age of Terrorism* (New York: PublicAffairs, 2003), pp. 28–29.

32 Amid this wave: Andrew, *For the President's Eyes Only,* p. 34.

33 Paul Hilken lived: Harold Martin Affidavit, May 29, 1932, NA (College Park).

33 Hilken had been: "German Spies in Baltimore," *Baltimore Post,* October 9, 1933.

34 In December 1913: Ibid.

34 "I felt that": Ibid.

34 When Franz von Rintelen: Paul Hilken Affidavit, August 26, 1930, NA (College Park).

35 "That was his": "German Spies in Baltimore," *Baltimore Post,* October 10, 1933.

Chapter Three

36 He constantly gossiped: Interview with Kathleen Dalton, Harvard University, March 12, 2003.

36 Some college newspapers: Bird, *The Chairman,* p. 40.

37 "I was a supporter": John McCloy with Shepard Stone, "Autobiography" (draft, courtesy of Rockefeller Archive Center, Sleepy Hollow, N.Y.), p. 14.

37 The camp in: Bird, *The Chairman,* p. 41.

37 One of the campers: Ibid., p. 42.

37 At the time: Max Holland, "Citizen McCloy," *Wilson Quarterly,* Autumn 1991, p. 27.

37 McCloy's father: Bird, *The Chairman,* p. 25; McCloy, "Autobiography," p. 5.

38 He worked his way: Bird, *The Chairman,* p. 25; McCloy, "Autobiography," p. 5; Holland, "Citizen McCloy," p. 26.

38 In 1900, the McCloys: Bird, *The Chairman,* pp. 25–26.

38 John Sr. had taught: McCloy, "Autobiography," p. 5; Bird, *The Chairman,* p. 26.

38 One day in: McCloy, "Autobiography," p. 6; Bird, *The Chairman,* pp. 25, 27.

38 He wouldn't make: McCloy, "Autobiography," p. 6.

38 "I'd read them": Ibid., p. 7.

38 Despite being a respected: Bird, *The Chairman,* p. 27.

38 But $3,000 was not: Holland, "Citizen McCloy," p. 29.

39 But she also: McCloy, "Autobiography," p. 7.

39 She styled the hair: Bird, *The Chairman,* p. 28.

39 During the summer: McCloy, "Autobiography," p. 9; Walter Isaacson and Evan Thomas, *The Wise Men: Six Friends and the World They Made* (New York: Simon & Schuster, 1986), p. 67.

39 The school was: Interview with Susan James, Director of Communications, Peddie School, October 1, 2004.

39 "You've got one": Interview with John McCloy II, November 8, 2003.

40 He recited: McCloy, "Autobiography," p. 6.

40 His mentor was: Ibid., p. 12.

40 After Peddie, McCloy: Bird, *The Chairman,* p. 40.

40 Whereas Douglas was: Bird, *The Chairman,* p. 40; Isaacson and Thomas, *The Wise Men,* p. 68.

40 While McCloy was: Alan Brinkley, "Minister without Portfolio," *Harper's,* February 1983; Interview with Ellen McCloy Hall, May 14, 2003.

40 McCloy attended: Bird, *The Chairman,* p. 45.

41 Early on the morning: Ibid., p. 43.

41 "Justice never was": Ibid., p. 45.

41 Wilson was so: Lanning, *Senseless Secrets,* p. 37.

42 Tunney wrote in: Tunney, *Throttled,* p. 9.

42 Before the war: Landau, *The Enemy Within,* p. 61.

42 One of his key: Ibid., pp. 67–68.

42 Koenig nicknamed Scheindl: Ibid., p. 68; Evidence re Paul Koenig, NA (College Park).

43 The operation Koenig: Evidence re Paul Koenig.

43 Two of the names: Ibid.

44 One night, before: Witcover, *Sabotage at Black Tom,* p. 154.

44 At dusk one: von Rintelen, *The Dark Invader,* p. 70.

45 Larkin lived in: Larkin, *Larkin,* p. 180.

45 An ad for: Ibid., p. 179.

46 By April, he: Ibid., p. 180.

46 Larkin's shame at: Ibid., pp. 185–86.

46 In July alone: "Bayonne Oil Works Closed by Labor Strike," *Wall Street Journal,* July 21, 1915; "New Snarls Delay Bridgeport Peace," *New York Times,* July 27, 1915; "Buying and Selling Strikes," *Wall Street Journal,* July 27, 1915.

46 In the fall: Larkin, *Larkin,* p. 187.

47 The two men: Ibid.

47 In May 1915: Hilken Affidavit, August 26, 1930.

Chapter Four

49 Mingling with: von Rintelen, *The Dark Invader,* p. 52.

49 The German government: Ibid., p. 55.

49 He closed up: Ibid., pp. 118–19.

50 On the morning: Ibid., p. 119.

50 Before World War I: Christopher Andrew, *Her Majesty's Secret Service: The Making of the British Intelligence Community* (New York: Penguin Books, 1986), p. 86.

50 In early August: Ibid., p. 87; Landau, *The Enemy Within,* p. 152.

50 British cable companies: Interview with Ralph Erskine, *Journal of Intelligence History,* June 2, 2004.

50 As a consequence: Andrew, *Her Majesty's Secret Service,* p. 87.

51 At first, lacking: Ibid., p. 88.

51 An Australian crew: Ibid., pp. 88–90.

51 In November 1914: Ibid., p. 91.

52 "I felt like": Ibid.

52 They formed: Ibid., p. 93.

52 Within a month: Ibid., pp. 99–100.

53 The U.S. ambassador: Landau, *The Enemy Within,* p. 154.

53 In the spring: Andrew, *Her Majesty's Secret Service,* p. 108.

54 Von Rintelen slowly: von Rintelen, *The Dark Invader,* p. 119.

54 There was no one: Landau, *The Enemy Within,* pp. 52–53; Doerries, *Imperial Challenge,* p. 143.

55 Again hoping to: "Seize Embassy Notes," *Washington Post,* September 2, 1915; "Austrian Envoy Offered to Tie Up U.S. Arms Plants," *Chicago Tribune,* September 5, 1915; "German Attaché Gave Papers to Archibald to Convey to Berlin, von Bernstorff Admits," *Washington Post,* September 5, 1915.

55 Thomas Tunney had: Tunney, *Throttled,* p. 12.

56 In the fall: Ibid., p. 13.

56 Shortly thereafter: Ibid.

56 After von Papen's letters: Landau, *The Enemy Within,* p. 57.

57 In late November: Andrew, *For the President's Eyes Only,* p. 35.

57 On November 29: Ibid.

58 December 13 broke: The Weather, *New York Times,* December 13, 1915.

58 Before departing, he: Evidence in Sabotage Cases, NA (College Park).

58 The two met: Landau, *The Enemy Within,* p. 67.

58 Five days after: "Conspiracy Started Here," *New York Times,* December 18, 1915.

58 Bail was set: "Koenig Held in $50,000," *New York Times,* December 19, 1915.

59 He considered himself: "Von Papen, Sailing, Thanks His Friends," *New York Times,* December 23, 1915.

59 His confidence was: "German Official Disavows Plot Here," *New York Times,* December 19, 1915.

59 One of them: Landau, *The Enemy Within,* pp. 54–55.

Chapter Five

60 Twenty-seven-year-old: Final Decisions and Opinions, 1939, p. 79.

60 As a result: Ibid.

60 Almost instantly: Ibid., pp. 80–81.

61 In early January: Official General Orders of the Imperial German Government, NA (College Park).

61 Meanwhile, with some: Wolf von Igel Affidavit, May 4, 1925, NA (College Park).

61 Between January 10: Landau, *The Enemy Within,* pp. 308–9.

62 The German Lloyd's: Final Decisions and Opinions, 1939, p. 187.

62 Modeled on: Lorraine Diehl, *The Late Great Pennsylvania Station* (New York: American Heritage, 1985), pp. 98–99.

63 Among them was: Landau, *The Enemy Within,* p. 82; "U.S. Suit Bares Atrocities of German Spies," *New York Post,* June 26, 1928.

63 In January 1916: "Cousin Pointed Out Black Tom Suspect," *New York Times,* September 4, 1916.

64 Frederick Hinsch asked: Landau, *The Enemy Within,* p. 82.

64 He introduced himself: "Cousin Pointed Out Black Tom Suspect."

64 The men began: Ibid.

65 During that time: Landau, *The Enemy Within,* p. 309.

65 Then they moved: Witcover, *Sabotage at Black Tom,* p. 166.

65 One night in: "Cousin Pointed Out Black Tom Suspect."

65 When the men: Brief, The Immediate Circumstances in Connection with the Black Tom and Kingsland Explosions, NA (College Park).

65 The instructions: Landau, *The Enemy Within,* p. 75.

66 In addition: "Zeppelin Kills 6 Parisians," *New York Times,* January 30, 1916.

66 Most able-bodied farmers: Belinda Davis, *Home Fires Burning: Food, Politics, and Everyday Life in World War I Berlin* (Chapel Hill: University of North Carolina Press, 2000), p. 23; Martin Gilbert, *The First World War: A Complete History* (New York: Henry Holt, 1994), p. 256.

66 Hilken's first meeting: Final Decisions and Opinions, 1939, p. 151.

66 The Germans wanted: Hilken Affidavit, August 26, 1930.

67 As they spoke: Ibid.

67 In the Section III-B: Ibid.

67 The first, Hans Marguerre: Hans Marguerre Affidavit, July 30, 1930, NA (College Park).

67 As Hilken said: Hilken Affidavit, August 26, 1930.

67 Fred Herrmann and: Hilken Affidavit, August 26, 1930; Final Decisions and Opinions, 1939, p. 160.

68 He was just: Ibid., p. 159.

69 Herrmann boarded a ship: Landau, *The Enemy Within,* p. 73.

69 The son of: Final Report of the American Agent, 1941, NA (College Park), pp. 58–59.

70 He told his parents: Hilken Affidavit, August 26, 1930; "New Plots, Fresh Fears, Old Germs," *Baltimore Sun,* October 28, 2001.

70 It was all: "New Plots, Fresh Fears, Old Germs."

70 In his trunk: Final Report of the American Agent, 1941, pp. 58–59; "Chevy Chase Germ Factory Depicted as German War Plot," *Washington Star,* June 29, 1930.

70 Dilger cultivated: Frederick Herrmann Affidavit, April 17, 1930, NA (College Park).

70 Marguerre told Hilken: Marguerre Affidavit, July 30, 1930.

70 It would be: Final Report of the American Agent, 1941, p. 76; Hilken Affidavit, August 26, 1930.

70 Marguerre instructed him: Marguerre Affidavit, July 30, 1930.

71 "I told him": Ibid.

71 Marguerre reached underneath: Ibid.

71 Herrmann remembered them: Frederick Herrmann Affidavit, April 3, 1930, NA (College Park).

71 The outer shell: Marguerre Affidavit, July 30, 1930.

72 Marguerre gave: Frederick Herrmann Affidavit, August 28, 1930, NA (College Park).

72 The German Lloyd offices: Witcover, *Sabotage at Black Tom,* p. 9.

72 "I took my car": Frederick Hinsch Affidavit, August 4, 1930, NA (College Park).

72 Hilken told Hinsch: Ibid.

73 "During these next": Ibid.

73 "an innocent looking": "Chevy Chase Germ Factory Depicted as German War Plot."

74 The shelves were: Herrmann Affidavit, April 17, 1930.

74 "He thought": Ibid.

74 While awaiting Hilken's: Herrmann Affidavit, August 28, 1930.

75 "Let's go upstairs": Ibid.

75 Then Herrmann put: Ibid.

75 Black Tom Island: Ibid.

76 Herrmann handed: Ibid.

Chapter Six

78 Hinsch's initial purchase: Hinsch Affidavit, August 4, 1930.

78 On the piers: Ibid.

78 One afternoon in: Michael Kristoff to Alexander Kassman, Lehigh Valley Railroad detective, November 29, 1916, NA (College Park).

79 In February 1916: American Rebuttal of Jahnke Alibi, January 31, 1930, NA (College Park).

79 He was five foot eleven: Landau, *The Enemy Within,* p. 34.

79 Although he had: Sidney Sutherland, "German Spies in America, Part III," *Liberty,* March 7, 1931.

79 A coworker at: American Rebuttal, January 31, 1930.

79 As proof of: Sutherland, "German Spies, Part III."

80 The agents listened: American Rebuttal, January 31, 1930.

80 A British intelligence: Ibid.

80 One of Jahnke's: Sidney Sutherland, "German Spies in America, Part XI," *Liberty,* May 2, 1931.

81 Witzke, boyishly handsome: Lothar Witzke Affidavit, German Exhibit Q, NA (College Park).

81 He worked for: Maria Jesse Affidavit, German Exhibit LXXXVII, NA (College Park).

81 At 6:00 a.m.: Hinsch Affidavit, August 4, 1930.

81 A storm was: Weather, *Washington Post,* June 23, 1916.

81 Unbeknownst to most: Hinsch Affidavit, August 4, 1930.

81 At 315 feet long: "Unarmed German Submarine with Merchandise Cargo Now Lies Near Baltimore," *Baltimore Sun,* July 10, 1916.

81 Hinsch joined the *Timmins:* Hinsch Affidavit, August 4, 1930.

82 At noon on: Ibid.

82 The *Timmins* patrolled: Ibid.

82 At 1:00 a.m.: Ibid.

82 Hinsch steered the *Timmins:* Ibid.

82 He explained that: "Unarmed German Submarine with Merchandise Cargo Now Lies Near Baltimore."

83 Hinsch congratulated him: Hinsch Affidavit, August 4, 1930.

83 At Old Point Comfort: Ibid.

83 At 3:45 p.m.: "Unarmed German Submarine with Merchandise Cargo Now Lies Near Baltimore."

83 As the *Deutschland:* Ibid.

84 An Associated Press reporter: Ibid.

84 They traveled north: Sutherland, "German Spies, Part XI."

84 After spending the night: "Unarmed German Submarine with Merchandise Cargo Now Lies Near Baltimore"; Witcover, *Sabotage at Black Tom,* p. 8.

85 On one side: Hinsch Affidavit, August 4, 1930.

85 That morning: "Unarmed German Submarine with Merchandise Cargo Now Lies Near Baltimore"; Witcover, *Sabotage at Black Tom,* p. 8.

85 For three weeks: Hinsch Affidavit, August 4, 1930.

86 President Wilson was: "President Is Off Capes," *New York Times,* July 31, 1916.

86 Early on the morning: Hinsch Affidavit, August 4, 1930; Witcover, *Sabotage at Black Tom,* p. 9.

86 The captain responded: "Ask a Navy Guard for Dash of U-Boat," *New York Times,* July 31, 1916; Witcover, *Sabotage at Black Tom,* p. 10.

86 "Captain": Ibid.

86 "No, no": Ibid.

87 Three days later: "Deutschland Off on Dash to Ocean as Warships Wait," *New York Times,* August 2, 1916.

Chapter Seven

88 Suitcases filled with: Witcover, *Sabotage at Black Tom,* p. 157.

88 Mena Reiss, a model: Ibid., p. 159; Sutherland, "German Spies, Part IV."

88 At Held's, she: Witcover, *Sabotage at Black Tom,* p. 157; Sutherland, "German Spies, Part IV."

88 At the end: Witcover, *Sabotage at Black Tom,* p. 158; Sutherland, "German Spies, Part IV."

89 Reiss became so: Sutherland, "German Spies, Part IV."

89 By 5:00 p.m.: U.S. Exhibit O, NA (College Park); Witcover, *Sabotage at Black Tom,* p. 160.

89 During the previous: American Brief, March 30, 1930, NA (College Park).

89 Two of them: Ibid.

89 Black Tom was: Witcover, *Sabotage at Black Tom,* p. 160.

89 Kristoff left his: "Cousin Pointed Out Black Tom Suspect."

89 One night, Rushnak: Ibid.; Harland Manchester, "The Black Tom Case," *Harper's,* December 1939.

90 As Jahnke and: American Brief, March 30, 1930.

90 Within half an hour: Ibid.

90 Jahnke and Witzke: Ibid.; Witcover, *Sabotage at Black Tom,* p. 161.

90 At around 12:45 a.m.: American Brief, March 30, 1930.

91 "It was burning": Ibid.

91 One of the firemen: Ibid.

91 At 2:08 a.m.: Ibid.

91 "It was like": "Munitions Explosions Shake New York," *New York Times,* July 31, 1916; Witcover, *Sabotage at Black Tom,* p. 12.

91 A doctor, who: Carl Ramus Affidavit, August 21, 1916, NA (College Park); "Tell of Black Tom Blasts," *New York Times,* August 22, 1916.

92 City Hall lost: "Millions of Persons Heard and Felt Shock," *New York Times,* July 31, 1916.

92 The Jersey City: "N.Y. Firemen Work in Rain of Bullets," *New York Times,* July 31, 1916.

92 Across the harbor: "Munitions Explosions Shake New York"; Witcover, *Sabotage at Black Tom,* p. 13.

93 Shortly after the second: "Tell of Black Tom Blasts."

93 The Brooklyn Bridge: "Munitions Explosions Shake New York"; Witcover, *Sabotage at Black Tom,* p. 13.

93 Shrapnel tore into: "Ellis Island Like War Swept Town," *New York Times,* July 31, 1916.

93 People as far: "First Explosion Terrific," *New York Times,* July 31, 1916; Witcover, *Sabotage at Black Tom,* p. 12.

93 At 3:00 a.m.: "Ellis Island Like War Swept Town."

93 People in Manhattan: "Munitions Explosions Shake New York."

94 Not everyone stood: Manchester, "The Black Tom Case"; "Cousin Pointed Out Black Tom Suspect."

94 Once the sun: "Known Dead Now Six," *New York Times,* August 2, 1916.

94 Three months later: Sidney Sutherland, "German Spies in America, Part VII," *Liberty,* April 4, 1931.

94 Miraculously, the official: "Millions of Persons Heard and Felt Shock"; "First Explosion Terrific"; "Known Dead Now Six."

94 By 6:00 a.m.: Witcover, *Sabotage at Black Tom,* p. 20.

95 Thousands of people: "Glass Damage Exceeds a Million," *New York Times,* July 31, 1916.

95 At one point: "Ruins Disclose Disaster's Cause," *New York Times,* August 1, 1916.

95 At the north: Ibid.

95 The area south: "Thousands View Damage," *New York Times,* July 31, 1916.

95 Nearly the entire: "Glass Damage Exceeds a Million."

96 From the shattered: "First Explosion Terrific"; American Institute for Economic Research, "AIER Cost-of-Living Calculator," http://www.aier.org/calc.html.

96 By midnight Sunday: "Railroad Heads to Be Arrested," *New York Times,* August 1, 1916.

97 The *New York Times:* "Many Explosions Since War Began," *New York Times,* July 31, 1916.

97 Instead, the *Times:* "First Explosion Terrific."

97 "There is nothing": "Washington Starts Explosion Inquiry," *New York Times,* July 31, 1916.

97 The British government: Witcover, *Sabotage at Black Tom,* p. 170.

97 August 4, 1916: The Weather, *New York Times,* August 4, 1916.

97 At the corner: Emporis Buildings, "Astor Hotel," Emporis, http://www.emporis.com/en/wm/bu/?id=136663.

97 Before they sat: Hilken Affidavit, August 26, 1930.

98 With their backs: Frederick Herrmann Affidavit, August 26, 1930, NA (College Park).

98 "It's better": Hilken Affidavit, August 26, 1930; Witcover, *Sabotage at Black Tom,* p. 163.

Chapter Eight

101 McCloy was a year: Andrew, *Her Majesty's Secret Service,* pp. 108–13.

101 McCloy dropped out: Holland, "Citizen McCloy," p. 31.

102 By then, the war: Bird, *The Chairman,* p. 52.

102 The day after: Holland, "Citizen McCloy," p. 32.

102 After the war: Interview with John McCloy II, November 8, 2003.

103 McCloy's first job: McCloy, "Autobiography," p. 17.

103 A longtime law: Pepper Hamilton LLP, "The History of Pepper Hamilton from 1890–1955," http://www.pepperlaw.com/about_history_1890–1955.cfm.

103 While John McCloy: Bird, *The Chairman,* p. 26.

103 It was Pepper: Ibid., p. 41.

103 "John," Pepper said: Ibid., p. 57.

104 The *New York Times:* "Scott Fitzgerald, Author, Dies at 44," obituary, *New York Times,* December 23, 1940.

104 Five million square feet: David von Drehle, "The Soaring 20s," *Washington Post,* September 26, 1999.

104 With the help: Bird, *The Chairman,* p. 59.

105 Revenues at one: Bird, *The Chairman,* p. 59; American Institute for Economic Research, "AIER Cost-of-Living Calculator," http://www.aier.org/calculate.html.

105 Shortly after arriving: Bird, *The Chairman,* p. 58.

105 Along the way: Ibid., p. 59.

105 She wrote: Anna McCloy to John McCloy, ca.1926, John J. McCloy Papers, Amherst College Archives and Special Collections.

106 McCloy did just: Robert Swaine, *The Cravath Firm and Its Predecessors, 1819–1948,* vol. 2 (privately published), p. 469.

106 Cravath refused to hire: Bird, *The Chairman,* p. 61.

106 While other firms: Swaine, *The Cravath Firm,* p. 4.

106 At six foot four: Ibid., p. 573.

106 Even into his: Ibid., p. 576.

106 A *New Yorker:* Ibid., p. 574.

106 As he grew: Interview with John McCloy II, November 8, 2003.

106 He was a handwringer: Interview with Nancy Walworth, former McCloy secretary, June 9, 2003.

107 He stayed at: Bird, *The Chairman,* p. 64.

107 "It didn't require": Ibid., p. 65.

107 He kept a white: Ibid., pp. 72–73; Interview with John McCloy II, November 8, 2003.

107 One afternoon, he: Bird, *The Chairman,* p. 59.

107 Trubee Davison, the son: Ibid., p. 69.

107 It usually took: Ibid., p. 73.

108 It was the summer: Interview with John McCloy II, November 8, 2003.

108 When his train: Ibid.

108 He didn't need: Ibid.; Bird, *The Chairman,* p. 74.

109 Ellen Zinsser waited: Bird, *The Chairman,* p. 74.

109 Even in the moist: Interview with Ellen McCloy Hall, May 14, 2003.

109 At thirty-one years old: Ibid.

109 She was a college: Ibid.; Interview with John Zinsser, April 14, 2003.

109 Their father: Interview with John Zinsser, April 14, 2003.

110 Within the family: Ibid.

110 Ellen earned the nickname: Interview with Ellen McCloy Hall, May 14, 2003.

110 One year for: Interview with John Zinsser, April 14, 2003.

110 Douglas was now: Ibid.

111 The doctor drove: Bird, *The Chairman,* p. 75.

111 One afternoon, McCloy: Ibid.

111 Frederick Zinsser leaned: Interview with John McCloy II, April 15, 2002.

111 Most of his: Bird, *The Chairman,* p. 74.

111 When they announced: Ibid., p. 75.

111 "All you had": Interview with John McCloy II, April 15, 2002.

111 They planned: Bird, *The Chairman,* p. 75.

111 Their engagement was: Interview with John McCloy II, April 15, 2002.

112 Anna McCloy was: Interview with Ellen McCloy Hall, May 14, 2003; Interview with John McCloy II, November 8, 2003.

112 A freezing wind: Other Weddings, *New York Times,* April 26, 1930.

112 While the staff: Interview with John Zinsser, April 14, 2003.

112 She knew that: Interview with Ellen McCloy Hall, May 14, 2003.

112 That morning, Ellen: Interview with John Zinsser, April 14, 2003.

112 John spent the day: Ibid.; "Travels by Airplane for Zinsser Wedding," *New York Times,* April 25, 1930.

112 But by 8:00 p.m.: Interview with John Zinsser, April 14, 2003.

113 One afternoon, she: Bird, *The Chairman,* p. 76; Interview with John McCloy II, April 15, 2002.

113 All through the summer: Bird, *The Chairman,* pp. 76–77.

113 In early September: Ibid.

114 In 1929, they: Final Commission Report, 1941, NA (College Park).

114 The German military: Treaty of Versailles, Article 163.

114 The importing of: Ibid., Articles 170, 181.

114 Germany's territory: Ibid., Articles 27–30.

114 Despite a national: Ibid., Article 244, Annex IV, Part 6.

115 Most devastating to: Ibid., Article 231.

115 Many German citizens: Margaret Macmillan, *Paris 1919: Six Months That Changed the World* (New York: Random House, 2001), pp. 157–58.

115 Many Americans on: Ibid., p. 467.

115 Secretary of State: Ibid.

115 American politicians: Ibid., p. 478.

116 After the war, vagrants: Joseph Roth, *What I Saw: Reports from Berlin, 1920–1933* (New York: W. W. Norton, 1996), pp. 66–67, 77.

116 The shelters closed: Ibid., pp. 69–71.

117 On July 2: Final Decisions and Opinions, 1939, pp. 6–7.

117 The German strategy: Landau, *The Enemy Within,* pp. 131–32; Russell Van Wyk, "German-American Relations in the Aftermath of the Great War: Diplomacy, Law, and the Mixed Claims Commission, 1922–1939" (dissertation, University of North Carolina, 1989), p. 60.

117 The Americans took: Van Wyk, "German-American Relations," pp. 81–82.

117 The new Weimar: Ibid., p. 77.

118 He sent a note: Ibid., p. 63.

118 The rules of: Landau, *The Enemy Within,* pp. 131–32; Treaty of Berlin, Final Decisions and Opinions, 1939, pp. 6–9.

118 In May 1923: "Parker Succeeds Day as Umpire of Vast War Claims," *Washington Evening Star,* May 21, 1923; "Anderson Placed upon Claims Body," *Washington Evening Star,* June 15, 1923.

118 For the first: Van Wyk, "German-American Relations," p. 117.

119 But there was: Witcover, *Sabotage at Black Tom,* p. 363; Van Wyk, "German-American Relations," p. 124.

119 A former Republican: "Robert Bonynge, Lawyer 54 Years," obituary, *New York Times,* September 23, 1939.

120 A native of: memorandum, Martin's Promotion on MCC, November 6, 1923, NA (College Park).

120 Martin had spent: Harold Martin, Letter of Resignation from Navy Solicitor's Office, October 16, 1922, NA (College Park).

120 During World War I: memorandum, Martin's Promotion on MCC.

120 When the navy: Harold Martin to Robert Morris, September 27, 1922, NA (College Park).

120 He was married: Harold Martin to Gilbert Guthrie, May 28, 1924, NA (College Park); Josephus Daniels to Thomas S. Butler, February 18, 1921, NA (College Park); Harold Martin to E. R. Preston, October 18, 1922, NA (College Park).

120 The fact that: Harold Martin to Robert Morris, September 27, 1922, NA (College Park).

120 It was a testament: Martin to Guthrie, May 28, 1924, NA (College Park); Daniels to Butler, February 18, 1921, NA (College Park); Martin to Preston, October 18, 1922, NA (College Park).

121 When Martin was: F. H. Cooke to Harold Martin, October 20, 1922, NA (College Park).

121 Within a year: memorandum, Martin's Promotion on MCC.

121 He'd do things: Martin to Bonynge, November 1, 1929, NA (College Park).

121 "It will probably": Harold Martin to E. R. Preston, October 18, 1922.

Chapter Nine

122 In March 1924: Van Wyk, "German-American Relations," p. 124.

122 Von Lewinski had: "Lawyer for Germany in Big War Claims," *New York Times,* January 11, 1931.

123 Some were as small: Compilation of Awards, NA (College Park).

123 "It is indeed": Van Wyk, "German-American Relations," p. 125.

123 The city was: Roth, *What I Saw,* p. 113.

124 When antiquated, mostly: Ibid., pp. 97–99.

124 The day of: "Cousin Pointed Out Black Tom Suspect."

125 The police interviewed: Ibid.; Witcover, *Sabotage at Black Tom,* p. 165.

125 Finally, on September 3: "Cousin Pointed Out Black Tom Suspect."

126 Only one lawyer: Landau, *The Enemy Within,* p. 135.

126 He had left: Swaine, *The Cravath Firm,* p. xxii.

126 Peaslee was just: Interview with Dick Peaslee, August 13, 2002.

127 During World War I: Ibid.

127 Shortly after being: Peaslee, brief, August 15, 1924.

127 On May 24: Ibid.

128 During his conference: Ibid.

128 They had been: Ibid.

129 In one of: Ibid.

129 For the next: Ibid.

129 In the end: Ibid.

130 "The evidence is": Ibid.

130 He cabled: Van Wyk, "German-American Relations," p. 127.

130 Paying off: Ibid., p. 129.

130 He argued that: Ibid., p. 130.

131 Even Wilhelm Kiesselbach: Ibid., pp. 163–64.

131 He warned: Ibid., p. 129.

132 One afternoon: Reginald Hall and Amos J. Peaslee, *Three Wars with Germany* (New York: G. P. Putnam's Sons, 1944), p. 72.

132 The former ambassador: Van Wyk, "German-American Relations," pp. 136–37.

133 Boy-Ed backed up: Ibid., p. 139.

133 Although the German: Ibid., p. 148.

134 Now, in the spring: Hall and Peaslee, *Three Wars with Germany*, p. 72.

134 Back home, he: Interview with Dick Peaslee, August 13, 2002.

134 He saw a yellowed: Hall and Peaslee, *Three Wars with Germany*, p. 72.

135 On July 29: Ibid., p. 75.

135 On August 14: Ibid., p. 78.

135 Peaslee called on: Ibid., p. 81.

136 As Peaslee presented: Ibid.

136 Finally, Hall cut: Ibid.

136 Inside were ten thousand: Ibid.

136 After the United States: Frederick Herrmann Affidavit, October 11, 1933, NA (College Park).

137 On April 3: Hall and Peaslee, *Three Wars with Germany*, p. 84; Final Decisions and Opinions, 1939, p. 112.

137 Peaslee copied another: Hall and Peaslee, *Three Wars with Germany*, p. 83.

137 He already had: Ibid., p. 107.

138 On February 26: Van Wyk, "German-American Relations," p. 157.

138 "I have personally": Ibid., pp. 165–66; U.S. Department of State, memorandum, Settlement Talks, August 15, 1928, NA (College Park).

139 Finally, in early: Landau, *The Enemy Within,* p. 177.

139 In March, nearly: Memorial Submitted by American Agent, March 14, 1927, NA (College Park).

Chapter Ten

140 Alcie had fallen: Alcie Martin Death Certificate, September 15, 1928, Maine Dept. of Human Services.

140 Within twenty-four hours: *Professional Guide to Diseases* (Philadelphia: Springhouse, 2001), pp. 654–55; *Taber's Cyclopedic Medical Dictionary* (Philadelphia: F. A. Davis, 2001), p. 1343; *Stedman's Medical Dictionary* (Philadelphia: Lippincott, Williams and Wilkins, 2000), pp. 1169–70.

141 On September 29: U.S. Department of State, telegram, Martin's Trip, September 27, 1928, NA (College Park).

141 Armed with $200: Wire Transfer, September 28, 1928, NA (College Park).

141 On the second: Martin to Bonynge, October 9, 1928, NA (College Park).

141 She offered her: Francesca Martin to Harold Martin, undated, NA (College Park).

142 The Germans had: Martin to Bonynge, December 29, 1927, NA (College Park).

142 The Americans built: Memorial Submitted by American Agent, March 14, 1927.

143 In October 1928: Rudolf Nadolny Affidavit, October 16, 1928, NA (College Park).

143 Nadolny began by: Ibid.

144 Once considered royalty: Final Decisions and Opinions, 1939, p. 193.

144 A tire business: Carl Ahrendt Affidavit, March 20, 1929, NA (College Park).

144 Now Hilken worked: Final Decisions and Opinions, 1939, p. 193.

144 Sitting with Peaslee: Paul Hilken Affidavit, October 12, 1928, NA (College Park).

145 "Shortly after Black": Ibid.; Landau, *The Enemy Within,* p. 179.

145 He found Fred Herrmann's: Landau, *The Enemy Within,* p. 187.

146 On the last: Herrmann Affidavit, October 11, 1933.

146 For several days: Ibid.

146 In early January: Herrmann Affidavit, August 26, 1930.

146 Von Lewinski unveiled: Witcover, *Sabotage at Black Tom,* p. 272.

147 The captain, named: Ibid.

147 "To drive away": Ibid.

147 The *Santa Marie:* Herrmann Affidavit, August 26, 1930.

147 Herrmann arrived at: Ibid.

148 Herrmann told Lemberg: Herrmann Affidavit, October 11, 1933.

148 "What brings you": Herrmann Affidavit, August 26, 1930.

148 Herrmann said: Ibid.

148 Hilken thought he: Herrmann Affidavit, October 11, 1933.

148 Hilken then handed: Ibid.

149 "What kind of": Ibid.

149 Then Herrmann brought: Ibid.

149 If he signed: Ibid.

149 He told the German: Ibid.

149 The Germans had: Herrmann Affidavit, August 26, 1930.

149 "How can this": Ibid.

150 "Nadolny is": Herrmann Affidavit, October 11, 1933.

150 "I'm not going": Ibid.

150 "This testimony is": John Schroeder Affidavit, October 13, 1933, NA (College Park).

151 A month after: Herrmann Affidavit, October 11, 1933.

151 "I'm positive": Ibid.

151 Green politely dismissed: Ibid.

152 A week later: Ibid.

152 Back at the bank: Ibid.

152 In 1929, Ahrendt: Ahrendt Affidavit, March 20, 1929.

152 During a visit: Leonard Peto Affidavit, July 14, 1930, NA (College Park).

153 Two weeks before: Ahrendt Affidavit, March 20, 1929.

Chapter Eleven

155 "The duty that": Oral Arguments, April 3, 1929, NA (College Park).

156 Nadolny had already: Ibid.

156 Bonynge now told: Ibid.

157 "He acted as": Ibid.

157 "The present claims": Ibid.

158 "It was certainly": Ibid.

158 "It was not": Ibid.

158 Parker interjected: Ibid.

159 After nine days: Ibid.

159 "It was incumbent": Ibid.

160 Parker was skeptical: Hall and Peaslee, *Three Wars with Germany,* p. 119.

160 During World War I: "Judge E. B. Parker Dies at Home Here," obituary, *Washington Post,* October 31, 1929.

161 Von Lewinski claimed: Hall and Peaslee, *Three Wars with Germany,* p. 119; Martin to Bonynge, August 30, 1929, NA (College Park).

161 During their brief: Martin to Bonynge, August 30, 1929.

161 He told Parker: Ibid.

161 Parker did his: Ibid.

162 "I cannot help": Ibid.

162 "If there is": Ibid.

162 On October 30: "Judge E. B. Parker Dies at Home Here."

162 Martin represented: Martin to Bonynge, November 1, 1929.

162 Martin wrote that: Ibid.

162 Undersecretary of State: Van Wyk, "German-American Relations," p. 185.

163 Its choice for: "R. W. Boyden Dies in Church," obituary, *New Bedford Standard,* October 26, 1931.

163 Boyden wasn't overjoyed: Van Wyk, "German-American Relations," p. 184.

163 Boyden stressed that: Ibid., p. 185.

163 Although Herrmann had: Herrmann Affidavit, October 11, 1933.

163 The wreckage had been: Landau, *The Enemy Within,* p. 92.

163 Carl mentioned his: Herrmann Affidavit, October 11, 1933.

164 On January 30: Herrmann Affidavit, August 26, 1930.

164 Herrmann's stipend of: Ibid.

164 When Herrmann told: Ibid.

165 In 1918, shortly: Ibid.; Landau, *The Enemy Within,* p. 194.

165 On January 31: "Fight New Evidence in Black Tom Claim," *New York Times,* January 31, 1930.

165 Von Lewinski was: Martin to Bonynge, February 1, 1930, NA (College Park).

166 Sure enough, Martin: Martin to Bonynge, August 30, 1929.

166 "I agree that": Martin to Bonynge, February 1, 1930.

167 The brothers were: Herrmann Affidavit, October 11, 1933.

167 Several days later: Ibid.

167 Instead, he suggested: Ibid.

168 The U.S. contingent: Peaslee to Bonynge, April 3, 1930, NA (College Park).

168 Carl met his: Ibid.

168 "In our judgment": Ibid.

169 Peto joined them: Herrmann Affidavit, October 11, 1933.

169 When Peaslee rejoined: Ibid.; Hall and Peaslee, *Three Wars with Germany,* p. 112.

169 Before he'd left: Herrmann Affidavit, October 11, 1933.

169 "We're not interested": Peaslee to Bonynge, April 3, 1930.

169 The next day: Herrmann Affidavit, October 11, 1933.

170 Herrmann's train from: Ibid.

170 On the trip: Peaslee to Bonynge, April 3, 1930.

170 "Are you positive": Herrmann Affidavit, October 11, 1933.

171 Bonynge spent: Herrmann Affidavit, April 3, 1930.

171 "What conversation": Ibid.

173 Their testimony had: Peto Affidavit, July 14, 1930.

173 Hilken mentioned that: Ibid.

173 When Herrmann mentioned: Ibid.

173 Herrmann and Peto: Ibid.

174 The next call: memorandum, Examination of John Schroeder, October 15, 1933, NA (College Park).

174 When Peto returned: Peto Affidavit, July 14, 1930.

174 Herrmann couldn't resist: Ibid.

174 The lawyer made: Ibid.

175 Once, however, with: Ibid.

175 Returning to his: John McCloy, memorandum, The Collapse of Carl Ahrendt's Testimony, September 12, 1938, NA (College Park).

175 At four o'clock: Peto Affidavit, July 14, 1930.

176 Less than twenty-four: Carl Ahrendt Affidavit, April 10, 1930, NA (College Park).

176 "During the time": Ibid.

Chapter Twelve

179 Between September 1928: Carrie Supple, *From Prejudice to Genocide: Learning about the Holocaust* (London: Trentham Books, 1997), p. 74.

179 The anger toward: Ian Kershaw, *Hitler, 1889–1938: Hubris* (New York: W. W. Norton, 1998), p. 333.

180 In June, von Lewinski: Martin to Bonynge, June 18, 1930, NA (College Park); Landau, *The Enemy Within,* pp. 186–187.

180 When Marguerre was: Marguerre Affidavit, July 30, 1930.

181 Hinsch was deposed: Hinsch Affidavit, August 4, 1930.

181 "You had to": Ibid.

181 But shortly after: Ibid.

183 That same day: Bonynge to Martin, August 5, 1930, NA (College Park).

183 By early August: Ibid.; Oral Arguments, September 18, 1930, NA (College Park).

183 "Personally": Martin to Bonynge, August 18, 1930, NA (College Park).

183 He wrote to Bonynge: Ibid.

184 In early September: Hall and Peaslee, *Three Wars with Germany,* pp. 131–32.

184 Shortly before 10:00 a.m.: Oral Arguments, September 18, 1930.

184 Alone in the courtroom: "Reich Won't Submit Sabotage Evidence," *New York Times,* September 19, 1930.

185 At exactly 10:30: Oral Arguments, September 18, 1930.

185 And then Bonynge: Ibid.

187 When the hearings: Ibid.

187 Kristoff, a convicted: Witcover, *Sabotage at Black Tom,* p. 258.

187 "It is admitted": Oral Arguments, September 18, 1930.

188 The next morning: Ibid.

188 "American investigators came": "Identifies Suspect in Black Tom Blast," *New York Times,* September 20, 1930.

188 The next day: "Says Reich Ordered Black Tom Blast," *New York Times,* September 21, 1930.

188 The story landed: "Germans Used Disease Germs Here," *New York Times,* September 24, 1930.

189 "It is not": Oral Arguments, September 18, 1930.

189 After listening to: Bird, *The Chairman,* p. 80.

189 GERMANY ADMITS USE: "Germany Admits Use of Bombs and Germs Here in 1915 and 1916," *New York Times,* September 25, 1930.

189 Five minutes into: Oral Arguments, September 18, 1930.

190 He began by: Ibid.

Chapter Thirteen

192 Bonynge sailed back: "Robert Bonynge Back," *New York Times,* October 18, 1930.

192 Martin remained in: Martin to N. H. Loomis, November 22, 1930, NA (College Park).

192 When his ship: "Washington Loses Black Tom Claims," *New York Times,* November 14, 1930.

192 The judges had: Martin to Loomis, November 22, 1930.

193 The commission agreed: German-American Mixed Claims Commission Opinion, October 15, 1930, NA (College Park).

194 Two days after: "Black Tom Blast Laid to Mosquitoes," *New York Times,* November 17, 1930.

194 Shortly thereafter, Martin: Bonynge to Martin, December 1, 1930, NA (College Park).

194 When Bonynge met: Van Wyk, "German-American Relations," p. 192.

195 "He was desperate": Bird, *The Chairman,* p. 79.

195 The American commissioner: "C. P. Anderson Dies; Authority on Law," obituary, *New York Times,* August 3, 1936; Van Wyk, "German-American Relations," p. 93.

195 The American lawyers: Martin to Bonynge, November 20, 1930, NA (College Park).

195 "I suppose you're": Ibid.

196 On Christmas Eve: Final Decisions and Opinions, 1939, p. 192.

196 Rummaging through: Paul Hilken Affidavit, May 8, 1931, NA (College Park).

197 Gerdts was the gofer: Raoul Gerdts Affidavit, January 18, 1929, NA (College Park); Landau, *The Enemy Within,* p. 85.

197 Together, Herrmann and: Final Decisions and Opinions, 1939, p. 167.

197 Adam Siegel was: Statement of Lothar Witzke to Thomas Tunney, September 19, 1919, NA (College Park); Final Decisions and Opinions, 1939, pp. 168–69; Gerdts Affidavit, January 18, 1929.

198 On April 12: Supplemental Petition for Rehearing, July 1, 1931, NA (College Park).

198 Later that day: Ibid.

198 The Germans cabled: Ibid.

198 There he found: Final Decisions and Opinions, 1939, p. 183.

198 Upstairs, he and: Herrmann Affidavit, October 11, 1933.

199 He wrote the word: *Blue Book,* January 1917, NA (College Park).

199 They began the message: Ibid.

199 When he was: Herrmann Affidavit, October 11, 1933.

199 Upon arriving in: Final Decisions and Opinions, 1939, p. 182.

199 After dinner: Ibid.

199 The heel of: Landau, *The Enemy Within,* p. 245.

199 The sentences that: Paul Hilken Affidavit, May 9, 1931, NA (College Park).

200 "Have seen von Eckhardt": Ibid.

200 It was a verse: Ibid.

201 "Whatever you do": Interview with John McCloy II, April 15, 2002.

201 During another trip: Ibid.; Bird, *The Chairman,* pp. 83–84.

202 The advertisements: Van Wyk, "German-American Relations," p. 215.

203 One of his: Sidney Sutherland, "The Most Popular Story Ever Written,"
    Liberty, January 18, 1929.

203 In February 1931: Sidney Sutherland, "German Spies in America, Part I,"
    Liberty, February 21, 1931.

203 Shortly after the first: Final Decisions and Opinions, 1939, p. 192.

203 "I have bought": Ibid.

204 One night in: Ibid., p. 193; Landau, *The Enemy Within,* p. 244.

204 Once, in February: Final Decisions and Opinions, 1939, p. 195.

204 "I did not": Herrmann Affidavit, October 11, 1933.

204 The next day: Harold Martin, memorandum, April 24, 1931, NA (College
    Park).

204 Two days later: Herrmann Affidavit, October 11, 1933.

204 "This message looks": Martin to Bonynge, May 2, 1931, NA (College Park).

205 His first call: Harold Martin, memorandum, The Stein-Osborn Episode,
    undated, NA (College Park); Albert Osborn Affidavit, December 19, 1931, NA
    (College Park).

205 A few years: "New Jersey v. Hauptmann," *Time,* January 21, 1935.

205 Osborn recommended that: Martin, memorandum, The Stein-Osborn Episode.

205 On June 16: Henry Arnold Affidavit, September 23, 1933, NA (College Park).

205 "We felt that": Ibid.

206 On June 26: Eldridge Stein Report, June 26, 1931, NA (College Park).

206 The claimants shrugged: Arnold Affidavit, September 23, 1933.

206 Using a microscope: Aloysius J. McGrail Affidavit, June 28, 1931, NA (College
    Park).

207 First, Karl von Lewinski: "Lawyer for Germany in Big War Claims."

207 The American Embassy: Van Wyk, "German-American Relations," p. 232.

207 William Castle: Ibid., p. 209.

207 Tannenberg, naturally, questioned: Oral Arguments, July 30, 1931, NA
    (College Park).

208 The Germans were: Tannenberg to Osborn, September 19, 1931, NA (College
    Park).

208 Normally, he charged: Osborn to Tannenberg, September 16, 1931, NA
    (College Park).

208 Boyden decided that: Boyden to Bonynge and Tannenberg, October 14, 1931,
    NA (College Park).

209 On Sunday, October 25: "R. W. Boyden Dies in Church."

209 It would be: "Owen J. Roberts Named to Claims Commission," *New York
    Herald,* March 27, 1932.

209 Three days after: Arnold Affidavit, September 23, 1933.

209 That afternoon, Albert: Herman Meyers Affidavit, October 29, 1932, NA (College Park).

210 Two days later: Ibid.

210 A week later: Ibid.

210 The store was: Picture of Abraham's Book and Magazine Shop, undated, NA (College Park).

210 Osborn introduced Meyers: Meyers Affidavit, October 29, 1932.

211 The next morning: Ibid.

211 On the morning: Arnold Affidavit, September 23, 1933.

211 But first, after: Ibid.

211 "It was the general": Ibid.

212 Instead, Arnold and: Ibid.

Chapter Fourteen

213 The two took: Martin Affidavit, May 29, 1932.

213 Hilken stayed and: Ibid.

214 Over the next: Ibid.

214 "This newly discovered": "Lay Sabotage to Berlin," *New York Times,* January 5, 1932.

215 "If Mr. Osborn": Edward Heinrich to Bonynge, January 16, 1932, NA (College Park).

215 Bonynge turned to: Osborn Affidavit, December 19, 1931.

215 He said that certain: Ibid.

216 "I don't trust": Hilken Affidavit, May 9, 1931.

216 In early March: Examination of John Schroeder, October 15, 1933, NA (College Park); American Brief in Support of Petition for Rehearing, May 4, 1933, NA (College Park).

217 "I fear": Hall and Peaslee, *Three Wars with Germany,* p. 147.

217 In March 1932: Martin to Bonynge, March 23, 1932, NA (College Park).

217 The fifty-seven-year-old: Robert H. Jackson, *That Man: An Insider's Portrait of Franklin D. Roosevelt* (New York: Oxford University Press, 2003), p. 203.

217 After World War I: Arthur M. Schlesinger, *The Politics of Upheaval, 1935–1936* (New York: Houghton Mifflin, 2003), pp. 464–65.

218 In private practice: Decision of the Commission, June 3, 1936, NA (College Park).

218 In a brief: Robert Bonynge, brief, Herrmann Message, February 29, 1932, NA (College Park).

218 "There is a veiled": Osborn to Tannenberg, April 21, 1932, NA (College Park).

218 Tannenberg forwarded Osborn's: Final Decisions and Opinions, 1939, p. 252.

219 In June 1932: "Von Papen Forms Rightist Cabinet," *New York Evening Post,* June 2, 1932.

219 But Gerdts, when: Gerdts Affidavit, January 18, 1929.

219 Hinsch testified: Frederick Hinsch Affidavit, June 28, 1932, NA (College Park).

219 "Invisible writing fluids": Ibid.

220 Herrmann's other Mexican: Adam Siegel Affidavit, March 16, 1932, NA (College Park).

220 But Gerdts had: Gerdts Affidavit, January 18, 1929.

220 "I distinctly remember": Hinsch Affidavit, June 28, 1932.

220 The Americans countered: McGrail Affidavit, June 28, 1931; Edward Heinrich Affidavit, May 31, 1932, NA (College Park); William J. Hurst Affidavit, May 26, 1932, NA (College Park); Harold Hibbert and Jessie Minor Affidavit, May 28, 1932, NA (College Park); Gustavius Esselen Affidavit, May 28, 1932, NA (College Park).

220 During weekends at: Interview with John Zinsser, April 14, 2003.

221 "Not only is": Esselen Affidavit, May 28, 1932.

221 Shortly after Roberts: Final Decisions and Opinions, 1939, p. 48.

222 On Friday, November 4: Arnold Affidavit, September 23, 1933; Stein to Bonynge, November 4, 1932, NA (College Park).

222 Stein accused Arnold: Arnold Affidavit, September 23, 1933.

222 "so that some": Stein to Bonynge, November 4, 1932.

222 He called Stein: Arnold Affidavit, September 23, 1933.

222 At 10:00 a.m.: Ibid.; Bonynge to Martin, November 5, 1932, NA (College Park); Amos Peaslee, memorandum, November 5, 1932, NA (College Park).

223 He asked Stein: Ibid.

224 When Bonynge asked: Ibid.

225 That afternoon, back: Bonynge to Martin, November 5, 1932.

226 "I have not": Bonynge to Martin, November 7, 1932, NA (College Park).

226 Like Hoover: Van Wyk, "German-American Relations," p. 277.

226 The *Washington Star:* "German Sabotage Cases Revived," *Washington Star,* November 20, 1932.

227 "You will find": Oral Arguments, November 21, 1932, NA (College Park).

227 They had been: Final Decisions and Opinions, 1939, p. 264.

228 He became disoriented: Oral Arguments, November 21, 1932.

228 "I do not": Ibid.

228 "There is no": Ibid.

229 On December 3: Decision of the Commission, December 3, 1932, NA (College Park).

230 In an opinion: Chandler Anderson Dissent, December 3, 1932, NA (College Park).

Chapter Fifteen

231 Stimson thought so: Bird, *The Chairman,* p. 86.

232 He told McCloy: Isaacson and Thomas, *The Wise Men,* p. 182.

232 During Hull's first: Van Wyk, "German-American Relations," p. 261.

233 In letters he: Ibid., p. 264.

233 He wrote to: Ibid., p. 266.

233 Roosevelt sensed his: Ibid., p. 267.

233 As a result: Ibid., p. 268.

234 "Certain important witnesses": American Brief in Support of Petition for Rehearing, May 4, 1933.

234 The most incendiary: Witcover, *Sabotage at Black Tom,* p. 297.

234 The Germans, meanwhile: Decision of the Commission, December 15, 1933, NA (College Park).

234 On December 15: Ibid.

235 Days after Roberts's: Van Wyk, "German-American Relations," pp. 280–81.

235 Late one night: John McCloy Affidavit, February 8, 1934, NA (College Park); Interview with John McCloy II, November 8, 2003.

236 Another line on: McCloy Affidavit, February 8, 1934; C. P. Palmer Affidavit, October 26, 1935, NA (College Park).

236 The agent wrote: McCloy Affidavit, February 8, 1934.

236 Late in the morning: Ibid.

237 After the McCloys: Interview with John McCloy II, November 8, 2003; Interview with John Zinsser, April 14, 2003.

237 Ellen was committed: Interview with John McCloy II, November 8, 2003.

237 McCloy had become: Swaine, *The Cravath Firm,* p. 640.

237 "yellow padding": Isaacson and Thomas, *The Wise Men,* p. 184.

238 The dogged lawyer: Bird, *The Chairman,* p. 86.

238 Years later: Ibid.

238 He was still: Larkin, *Larkin,* p. 260.

238 McCloy arrived in: McCloy Affidavit, February 8, 1934.

240 As soon as: Ibid.

243 Both the *New York Times:* "Spy Story Revived in Black Tom Blast," *New York Times,* April 7, 1934; John McCloy Affidavit, August 15, 1935, NA (College Park).

243 When the *Times:* "Spy Story Revived in Black Tom Blast."

244 He considered: Gerhard Weinberg, "Hitler's Image of the United States," *American Historical Review* 69 (July 1964): 1010.

244 As one representative: Van Wyk, "German-American Relations," p. 302.

244 In May 1934: Ibid., p. 282.

244 His replacement was: Ibid., p. 284.

244 After Roberts ruled: Opinion of the Umpire, November 24, 1934, NA (College Park).

244 Roberts waited three: "New Data Offered in Black Tom Case," *New York Times,* March 1, 1936.

245 During the fall: Van Wyk, "German-American Relations," pp. 310–11.

245 Peaslee knew a man: Ibid., p. 312.

245 In the spring: Ferdinand Mayer to Cordell Hull, memorandum, May 6, 1936, Phillips Papers, Houghton Library, Harvard College.

245 Goering, a decorated: Louis Snyder, *Encyclopedia of the Third Reich* (Hertfordshire: Wordsworth, 1998), pp. 122–23.

246 On the afternoon: Mayer to Hull, memorandum, May 6, 1936.

247 At sixty-two, Mitchell: Doug Heidenreich, "William D. Mitchell," speech given at William Mitchell College of Law, July 28, 1998, William Mitchell College of Law; "Hometown Recalls Mitchell as a Boy," *New York Times,* March 1, 1929.

247 By mid-May: Weather, *Washington Post,* May 9–12, 1936.

248 Before arguments began: Oral Arguments, May 12, 1936, NA (College Park).

248 "There is one": Ibid.

248 "Before you go": Ibid.

250 On June 3: Decision of the Commission, June 3, 1936.

250 The day after: Landau, *The Enemy Within,* p. 290.

Chapter Sixteen

251 The American contingent: Bonynge and Martin to Cordell Hull, July 11, 1936, NA (College Park).

251 The McCloys checked: Bird, *The Chairman,* p. 89.

251 One evening, they: Interview with John McCloy II, April 15, 2002.

252 Goering had designated: Bonynge and Martin to Hull, July 11, 1936.

252 A former leader: Witcover, *Sabotage at Black Tom,* p. 300.

252 When the Americans: Bonynge and Martin to Hull, July 11, 1936.

252 "It was terrifying": Bird, *The Chairman,* p. 90.

252 Raising his voice: Interview with John McCloy II, April 15, 2002.

252 The Germans and: Bonynge to Hauptmann von Pfeffer, July 1, 1936, NA (College Park).

253 Von Pfeffer submitted: von Pfeffer to Bonynge, July 6, 1936, NA (College Park).

253 He offered the Americans: Ibid.

253 "I have the honor": Bonynge to von Pfeffer, July 6, 1936, NA (College Park).

254 "You will make": Final Report of the American Agent, 1941, p. 30.

254 As the meal: Bird, *The Chairman,* p. 90.

254 The next morning: Bonynge and Martin to Hull, July 11, 1936.

255 On July 17: "War Claims on Reich Settled by Bonynge," *New York Times,* July 18, 1936.

255 He said that he: "Black Tom Accord Likely," *New York Times,* July 19, 1936.

255 This group included: Bird, *The Chairman,* p. 91.

255 He carried a letter: Ibid.

256 The Nazis built: Jeffrey O. Segrave, "Hitler's Ambitious Plans for the 1936 Olympics" (August 23, 2004), History News Network, http://hnn.us/articles/6875.html.

256 Those who couldn't: "The 1936 Berlin Olympics," History Learning Site, http://historylearningsite.co.uk./1936_berlin_olympics.htm.

256 But as the games: Bird, *The Chairman,* p. 90.

256 Huge platters of: Interview with John McCloy II, April 15, 2002.

257 Germany had won: International Olympic Committee, "Berlin, 1936, Medal Table," http://www.olympic.org/uk/games/past/index_uk.asp? OLGT=1&OLGY=1936.

257 McCloy watched as: Bird, *The Chairman,* p. 90; "Military Spectacle in Olympic Stadium," *New York Times,* August 14, 1936.

258 The military band: "Military Spectacle in Olympic Stadium."

258 Shortly after the May: "Anderson Dies; Famed World Law Authority," obituary, *Washington Post,* August 3, 1936.

258 Meanwhile, Hitler's own: Van Wyk, "German-American Relations," pp. 328–29.

259 In late November: Ibid., p. 335.

259 Harold Martin's frustration: "Pre-Holiday Weddings Hold General Interest," *Washington Star,* December 3, 1936.

260 On January 4: Final Report of the American Agent, 1941, p. 37.

260 McCloy made a note: McCloy to Martin, May 13, 1937, NA (College Park).

260 In April 1937: Final Report of the American Agent, 1941, p. 35.

261 In July, the MCC: Hall and Peaslee, *Three Wars with Germany,* p. 170.

261 Roberts was still: Final Decisions and Opinions, 1939, pp. 243–44.

263 As the wife: Interview with Ellen McCloy Hall, May 14, 2003; Interview with John McCloy II, November 8, 2003.

263 Through her charity: Interview with John McCloy II, November 8, 2003.

263 By pumping oxygen: Isidor Rubin, "The Nonoperative Determination of Patency of Fallopian Tubes," *Journal of American Medicine* 75 (September 4, 1920): 661–67.

263 Ellen's were entirely: Interview with John McCloy II, November 8, 2003.

263 It was an invasive: Ibid.; Rubin, "Patency of Fallopian Tubes."

263 On the days: Interview with John McCloy II, November 8, 2003.

263 After every trip: Ibid.

264 She looked up: Ibid.

264 John J. McCloy II: Ibid.

264 In August 1938: Bird, *The Chairman,* p. 92.

264 While Ellen spent: Ibid., p. 93.

265 In June 1938: Witcover, *Sabotage at Black Tom,* p. 303; John McCloy, memorandum, The Collapse of Carl Ahrendt's Testimony.

265 Neatly typed and: Final Report of the American Agent, 1941, p. 57.

265 In 1930, the: Ahrendt Affidavit, April 10, 1930.

266 "We have no": John McCloy memorandum, The Collapse of Carl Ahrendt's Testimony.

Chapter Seventeen

267 Robert Bonynge sat: Oral Arguments, January 16, 1939, NA (College Park).

267 All day, a freezing: Weather, *Washington Post,* January 15, 1939.

267 The former attorney: Bird, *The Chairman,* p. 93.

268 Mitchell spent: Oral Arguments, January 16, 1939.

268 At times, Mitchell: Hall and Peaslee, *Three Wars with Germany,* p. 180.

268 "It was written": Oral Arguments, January 16, 1939.

268 Mitchell then read: Ibid.

269 Even Roberts couldn't: Hall and Peaslee, *Three Wars with Germany,* p. 180.

269 Years later, when: Announcement of the Death of Hon. Robert W. Bonynge, The American Agent, October 30, 1939, NA (College Park).

269 Yet on Friday: Oral Arguments, January 16, 1939.

269 He began by: Ibid.

270 Over the last: Final Decisions and Opinions, 1939, p. vii.

270 By March 1: Ibid., pp. i–iii.

270 That June, when: Ibid., pp. ix–x.

271 Bonynge and Martin: "Black Tom Disaster Laid to Germany," *Washington Evening Star,* June 15, 1939.

271 "The retirement of": "Black Tom Verdict Blames Germany; Fraud Is Charged," *New York Times,* January 16, 1939; Final Decisions and Opinions, 1939, p. 309.

271 "I concur with": Final Decisions and Opinions, 1939, pp. 310–12.

272 The Reich's official: "Black Tom Ruling Rejected by Reich," *New York Times,* January 16, 1939.

272 In early September: "Robert Bonynge, Lawyer 54 Years."

272 McCloy wrote to: Van Wyk, "German-American Relations," p. 376.

272 At a special: Announcement of the Death of Hon. Robert W. Bonynge.

273 Peaslee sent Martin: Peaslee to McCloy, August 15, 1939, NA (College Park).

273 At the hearing: "Black Tom Losses Put at $50,000,000 as Reich Protests," *New York Times,* October 31, 1939.

273 The remaining $29 million: "Black Tom Awards," *New York Times,* October 31, 1939.

273 "The procession of": Manchester, "The Black Tom Case."

273 Harold Martin retired: "It Took 18 Years to Complete War Claims Job," *Washington Times-Herald,* June 29, 1941.

274 When he died: "Harold Martin Services Set for Thursday," obituary, *Washington Post and Times-Herald,* March 30, 1955.

274 Amos Peaslee eventually: Bird, *The Chairman,* p. 94.

274 He bought a stately: Interview with Dick Peaslee, August 13, 2002; History and Genealogy, Township of East Greenwich, New Jersey.

274 Years later, he: Amos J. Peaslee Debate Society, Swarthmore College, "History," http://www.sccs.swarthmore.edu/org/debate.

274 He served as: Interview with Dick Peaslee, August 13, 2002; History and Genealogy, Township of East Greenwich, New Jersey.

275 His interest in: Amos J. Peaslee, *Constitutions of Nations* (Concord, N.H.: Rumford Press, 1950).

275 "When he'd go": Interview with Dick Peaslee, August 13, 2002.

275 In 1953, President: U.S. Department of State, "Chiefs of Mission by Country, 1778–2004: Australia," http://www.state.gov/r/pa/ho/po/com/10368.htm.

275 He had won: Bird, *The Chairman,* p. 122; Interview with John McCloy II, November 8, 2003; Carl de Gersdorff to John McCloy, October 15, 1941, John J. McCloy Papers, Amherst College Archives and Special Collections.

275 One afternoon, while: Isaacson and Thomas, *The Wise Men,* p. 182.

276 He thought: Bird, *The Chairman,* p. 113.

276 That spring, high-profile: Miller, *Spying for America,* p. 202.

276 After the explosion: Ibid., p. 203.

276 Meanwhile, his counterpart: Ibid., pp. 203–4.

277 Hoover quickly established: Ibid., p. 203.

277 But when May 1: Finnegan, *Military Intelligence,* p. 44.

277 A three-year-old: Leone and Anrig, *The War on Our Freedoms,* pp. 34–35.

278 It was called: *Spying for America,* p. 210.

278 Armed with: Ibid.

278 Living above his: Ibid., p. 211.

278 He deciphered messages: Ibid., pp. 211–12.

278 He was appalled: Finnegan, *Military Intelligence,* p. 47.

278 Yardley was given: Miller, *Spying for America,* p. 213.

278 The book became: Bird, *The Chairman,* p. 85.

279 Not much had: Ibid., pp. 113, 121–22.

279 Three years earlier: Miller, *Spying for America,* p. 209.

279 According to General: Finnegan, *Military Intelligence,* pp. 43–44.

279 Then, in 1936: FBI, "FBI History," http://www.fbi.gov/fbihistory.htm.

279 The head of: Bird, *The Chairman,* p. 118.

279 "Only a well": Ibid.

280 He called this: Ibid.

280 In January 1942: Isaacson and Thomas, *The Wise Men,* p. 197.

280 California congressman: Ibid.

280 Roosevelt made McCloy: Witcover, *Sabotage at Black Tom,* p. 311.

281 Stimson trusted him: Bird, *The Chairman,* p. 123.

281 That kind of: Isaacson and Thomas, *The Wise Men,* p. 183.

281 Even when he: Bird, *The Chairman,* p. 19.

281 When McCloy died: "John J. McCloy, Lawyer and Diplomat, Is Dead at 93," obituary, *New York Times,* March 12, 1989.

281 From the pulpit: Bird, *The Chairman,* p. 16.

281 Secretary of State: Ibid.

Selected Bibliography

Andrew, Christopher. *For the President's Eyes Only: Secret Intelligence and the American Presidency from Washington to Bush.* New York: HarperCollins, 1995.
————. *Her Majesty's Secret Service: The Making of the British Intelligence Community.* New York: Penguin Books, 1986.
Binder, Frederick M., and David M. Reimers. *All the Nations under Heaven: An Ethnic and Racial History of New York City.* New York: Columbia University Press, 1995.
Bird, Kai. *The Chairman: John J. McCloy — The Making of the American Establishment.* New York: Simon & Schuster, 1992.
Brands, H. W. *Woodrow Wilson.* New York: Henry Holt, 2003.
Brinkley, Alan. "Minister without Portfolio." *Harper's,* February 1983.
Brown, G. I. *The Big Bang: A History of Explosives.* Gloucestershire: Stroud, 1998.
Conrad, Joseph. *The Secret Agent.* New York: Signet Classic, 1983.
Davis, Belinda. *Home Fires Burning: Food, Politics, and Everyday Life in World War I Berlin.* Chapel Hill: University of North Carolina Press, 2000.
Diehl, Lorraine. *The Late Great Pennsylvania Station.* New York: American Heritage, 1985.
Doerries, Reinhard R. *Imperial Challenge: Ambassador Count Bernstorff and German-American Relations, 1908–1917.* Chapel Hill: University of North Carolina Press, 1989.
Finnegan, John Patrick. *Military Intelligence.* Washington, D.C.: Center for Military History, U.S. Army, 1998.
Gaddis, John Lewis. *Surprise, Security, and the American Experience.* Cambridge: Harvard University Press, 2004.
Gilbert, Martin. *The First World War: A Complete History.* New York: Henry Holt, 1994.
Hall, Reginald, and Amos J. Peaslee. *Three Wars with Germany.* New York: G. P. Putnam's Sons, 1944.

Holland, Max. "Citizen McCloy." *Wilson Quarterly,* Autumn 1991.

Homberger, Eric. *The Historical Atlas of New York.* New York: Henry Holt, 1994.

Isaacson, Walter, and Evan Thomas. *The Wise Men: Six Friends and the World They Made.* New York: Simon & Schuster, 1986.

Jackson, Kenneth T. *The Encyclopedia of New York City.* New Haven, Conn.: Yale University Press, 1995.

Jackson, Robert H. *That Man: An Insider's Portrait of Franklin D. Roosevelt.* New York: Oxford University Press, 2003.

Kershaw, Ian. *Hitler, 1889–1938: Hubris.* New York: W. W. Norton, 1998.

Landau, Henry. *The Enemy Within.* New York: G. P. Putnam's Sons, 1937.

Lankevich, George J. *American Metropolis: A History of New York City.* New York: NYU Press, 1998.

Lanning, Michael Lee. *Senseless Secrets: The Failures of U.S. Military Intelligence from George Washington to the Present.* Secaucus, N.J.: Carol Publishing Group, 1996.

Larkin, Emmet. *James Larkin: Irish Labour Leader, 1876–1947.* Great Britain: Routledge and Kegan Paul, 1965.

Leone, Richard C., and Greg Anrig Jr. *The War on Our Freedoms: Civil Liberties in an Age of Terrorism.* New York: PublicAffairs, 2003.

Lopate, Phillip. *Waterfront: A Journey around Manhattan.* New York: Crown Publishers, 2004.

Luebke, Frederick C. *Bonds of Loyalty: German-Americans and World War I.* De Kalb: Northern Illinois University Press, 1974.

Macmillan, Margaret. *Paris 1919: Six Months That Changed the World.* New York: Random House, 2001.

Manchester, Harland. "The Black Tom Case." *Harper's,* December 1939.

Melanson, Philip H., with Peter F. Stevens. *The Secret Service: The Hidden History of an Enigmatic Agency.* New York: Carroll & Graf Publishers, 2002.

Miller, Nathan. *Spying for America.* New York: Paragon House, 1989.

The 9/11 Commission Report: Final Report of the National Commission on Terrorist Attacks upon the United States. New York: W. W. Norton, 2004.

Peaslee, Amos J. *Constitutions of Nations.* Concord, N.H.: Rumford Press, 1950.

Reiling, Johannes. *Deutschland: Safe for Democracy.* Stuttgart: Franz Steiner Verlag, 1997.

Rosen, Jeffrey. *The Unwanted Gaze.* New York: Random House, 2004.

Roth, Joseph. *What I Saw: Reports from Berlin, 1920–1933.* New York: W. W. Norton, 1996.

Saunders, Kay, and Roger Daniels, eds. *Alien Justice: Wartime Internment in Australia and North America.* Queensland: University of Queensland Press, 2000.

Schlesinger, Arthur M. *The Politics of Upheaval, 1935–1936.* New York: Houghton Mifflin, 2003.

Snyder, Louis. *Encyclopedia of the Third Reich.* Hertfordshire: Wordsworth, 1998.

Supple, Carrie. *From Prejudice to Genocide: Learning about the Holocaust.* London: Trentham Books, 1997.

Swaine, Robert. *The Cravath Firm and Its Predecessors, 1819–1948.* Vol. 2. Privately published, 1948.

Tunney, Thomas J. *Throttled! The Detection of the German and Anarchist Bomb Plotters.* Boston: Small, Maynard, 1919.

Van Wyk, Russell. "German-American Relations in the Aftermath of the Great

War: Diplomacy, Law, and the Mixed Claims Commission, 1922–1939."
Dissertation, University of North Carolina, 1989.

von Rintelen, Franz. *The Dark Invader: War-Time Reminiscences of a German Naval Intelligence Officer.* New York: Penguin Books, 1939.

Weinberg, Gerhard. "Hitler's Image of the United States." *American Historical Review* 69 (July 1964).

Witcover, Jules. *Sabotage at Black Tom: Imperial Germany's Secret War in America, 1914–1917.* Chapel Hill, N.C.: Algonquin Books, 1989.

Index